MURDER AND SPIES, LOVERS AND LIES

MURDER AND SPIES, LOVERS AND LIES

SETTLING THE GREAT CONTROVERSIES OF AMERICAN HISTORY

MARC MAPPEN

AVON BOOKS ◆ NEW YORK

MURDER AND SPIES, LOVERS AND LIES is an original publication of Avon Books. This work has never before appeared in book form.

AVON BOOKS
A division of
The Hearst Corporation
1350 Avenue of the Americas
New York, New York 10019

Copyright © 1996 by Marc Mappen
Published by arrangement with the author
Library of Congress Catalog Card Number: 95-41401
ISBN: 0-380-77514-X

Library of Congress Cataloging in Publication Data:

Mappen, Marc.
Murder and spies, lovers and lies : settling the great controversies of American history / Marc Mappen.
    p.   cm.
Includes bibliographical references and index.
1. United States—History. 2. United States—Historiography.
I. Title.
E178.6.M27 1996   95-41401
973—dc20   CIP

First Avon Books Trade Printing: April 1996

AVON TRADEMARK REG. U.S. PAT. OFF. AND IN OTHER COUNTRIES, MARCA REGISTRADA, HECHO EN U.S.A.

Printed in the U.S.A.

OPM   10   9   8   7   6   5   4   3   2   1

To my children,
Benjamin and Rebecca

ACKNOWLEDGMENTS

Permission to quote from the following material is gratefully acknowledged:

Excerpt from *Code Name "Zorro": The Murder of Martin Luther King, Jr.* by Mark Lane and Dick Gregory. Prentice Hall, 1977. Reprinted by permission.

Excerpt from *He Slew the Dreamer: My Search for the Truth about James Earl Ray and the Murder of Martin Luther King* by William Bradford Huie. Delacorte Press, 1968. Reprinted by permission.

Excerpt from "Hiss Guilty as Charged," by Sam Tanenhaus, *Commentary*, April 1993, pp. 32–37. Reprinted by permission of *Commentary*.

Excerpt from *The Real Anita Hill: The Untold Story* by David Brock. Copyright © 1993 by David Brock. Reprinted by permission of the Free Press, an imprint of Simon & Schuster.

Excerpt from *The Wolf by the Ears: Thomas Jefferson and Slavery* by John Chester Miller. Macmillan Publishing Company, 1977.

CONTENTS

PREFACE

There are some great, overarching questions debated by students of American history: Was the Civil War inevitable? What was the effect of the frontier on American civilization? Why did socialism not flourish in the United States? These questions, sometimes derisively referred to as "thumbsuckers," are impossible to answer with any finality, and they have in fact pretty much fallen out of fashion.

This book deals with another variety of historical question, much more narrowly focused, that mostly requires a simple yes or no answer; for example, was Marilyn Monroe murdered? Was the USS *Maine* sabotaged? Was Alger Hiss a Communist spy? Some of these questions are of great significance to American history—for example, whether the Roosevelt administration plotted to bring the United States into the Second World War—others such as whether Lizzie Borden murdered her parents are less profound. What these puzzles have in common is the fact that they can be solved; not to everyone's satisfaction, but at least to the reasonable reader.

The method used here is to look for the commonsense answer that seems best supported by the evidence, rather than attempting to find an airtight solution. To borrow a concept from the legal world, there are two kinds of proof used in trials. The one used in criminal cases is proof beyond a reasonable doubt. The other, in civil suits, is the preponderance of evidence. The first type of proof calls for a reasonable certainty of a fact; the second for only a reasonable probability.

There is an anecdote told about Lincoln that illustrates the principle (although like many Lincoln anecdotes, its truth is open to question—see chapter 6). At a trial in rural Illinois the jury asked the court for an explanation of the preponderance of evidence rule. The presiding judge, followed by the attorney for one side, tried but failed to enlighten the jury. Then Lincoln rose to his feet. He asked the jurors to imagine a pair of ordinary scales, the kind seen in every general store, and to think of the evidence placed on the scales for weighing. Even if one side is only a small bit heavier, he said, it will tip that side of the scale down; that side bears the preponderance of evidence.

Each chapter of this book is an attempt to weigh the evidence of a controversial issue to see which side tips the balance. I attempt to distill the welter of books and articles on each issue into opposing arguments, and then present those arguments to the reader in as objective a fashion as I can muster. My purpose is to act as a reliable guide, leading the reader through the jungle of clashing interpretations. At the conclusion of each chapter, I drop the mask of objectivity and offer my own opinion on where the weight of the evidence rests.

The reader is, of course, welcome to disagree, and I have offered an annotated bibliography so that anyone who wishes to delve deeper into the subjects treated here can do so.

A word of thanks to the ace reference staff of the Rutgers University Library, especially Stan Nash and Linda Langschied, who tracked down obscure references and fetched distant sources; thanks also to Harriet Bloom, Lisa Considine, David Highfill, Carl and Ann Kessler, Gerard McCauley, and to the many others who read chapters, made suggestions, or otherwise helped bring this book into the world. Thanks especially to my wife, Ellen, and to my children, Benjamin and Rebecca, for their love and encouragement.

MURDER
AND SPIES,
LOVERS
AND LIES

1

WHAT HAPPENED TO THE LOST COLONY?

In August 1590, the ships *Hopewell* and *Moonlight*, five months out of Plymouth, England, approached the barrier islands off what is now North Carolina, the location of a tiny English colony that had been established on Roanoke Island.

On board the *Hopewell* was John White, who must have felt strong emotion as the ships neared the shore. He was returning to the colony after an absence of three years; during that time neither he nor anyone else in England had heard from the approximately 110 colonists who had remained behind.

It is hard to imagine just how precarious the situation was for those colonists. In that age before telephones and jet planes, they were utterly cut off from their countrymen on the other side of the Atlantic. The Roanoke Colony was the first toehold of the English on the vast North American continent: the establishment of the first permanent colony at Jamestown, Virginia, lay twenty years in the future; the landing of the Pilgrims in Plymouth was thirty years away.

There were other Europeans settled in the New World, but they were the Spanish who had colonized Florida and Latin America, and who would have liked nothing better than to exterminate the English outpost on their doorstep. A threat even closer to the colonists than the Spanish were the Algonquian natives of the Carolinas. Because the settlers had so little experience in raising or gathering food in their unfamiliar environment, and because they were so vastly outnumbered by the Indians, their survival depended on their fragile friendship with the tribes that surrounded them.

The Roanoke Colony originated in the year 1584, when the nobleman Sir Walter Raleigh received a patent from Queen Elizabeth I to establish a settlement in North America. An expedition funded by Raleigh deposited 107 men on Roanoke Island in the following year. The colony did not do well, in part because the settlers treated the Indians with contempt, and in part because the English were ignorant of how to survive in the New World. Unable to feed themselves adequately and faced with hostility from the Indians, the colonists thankfully departed in 1586 when an English fleet happened by.

Sir Walter decided to try once again, this time with a group of men, women, and children who were brought to Roanoke Island in 1587 to establish a new colony with the grandiose title "Cittie of Ralegh." Sir Walter appointed John White, one of the more experienced colonists, as governor. Shortly after the settlers' arrival, White's daughter Eleanor and her husband Ananias Dare gave birth to a girl, who was named Virginia in honor of their new home; Virginia was a general term for the land claimed by the English in North America. Virginia Dare is thought to be the first English child born in the territory that became the United States.

Governor White stayed only one month. At the insistence of the other settlers, and against his own judgment, he returned to England to arrange for more supplies. The outbreak of open war between England and Spain frustrated his plans to return to Virginia, and prevented any contact between the colony and the mother country for three long years.

Now White was returning with the *Hopewell* and the *Moonlight*, not knowing whether he would find his granddaughter or anyone else alive. He and a party of sailors landed cautiously on Roanoke Island. Coming up from the beach they encountered a large tree upon which the letters "C-R-O" had been carved. Farther inland, White and his party found an abandoned fort. The houses built near the fort had been dismantled, and the village was overgrown with grass and weeds. Carved five feet up on a tree that formed part of the fort was the word "CROATOAN," the name of an island a few miles to the south.

The Roanoke landing party also found five chests lying open

on the ground. The chests had been buried, but someone had dug them up and scattered the contents. Three of the chests belonged to White and had been left behind when he'd returned to England. Also strewn about were several large artillery pieces and cannonballs. All the boats belonging to the colony had vanished, along with smaller weapons. White and the sailors found not a single human being, alive or dead, on the island, although they did see what appeared to be the fresh footprints of an Indian on the beach.

John White was not disheartened by what he saw. Three years before, prior to leaving, he had arranged with the colonists that if they decided to leave Roanoke they would, in White's words, "write or carve on the trees or posts of the dores the name of the place where they should be seated." If there was any danger, they were also to inscribe a Maltese cross. The presence of the CROATOAN inscription and the absence of the cross were thus reassuring. The fact that the houses had been dismantled, the boats and lighter weapons were gone, and the chests had been carefully buried indicated that the colonists had made a planned departure.

The logical next step for White was to journey to Croatoan. But circumstances made that impossible. The weather was threatening, and the ships were low on food and fresh water. The *Hopewell* had lost two anchors, which made navigating close to shore highly dangerous. The *Moonlight* departed for England, but White and the captain of the *Hopewell* decided to head for the West Indies for the winter, where the ship could be repaired and stocked with food and water for a return to Croatoan in the spring.

As it happened, they never did return. The *Hopewell* encountered a storm that blew the ship off course, and the vessel limped back to England. John White was never able to go back to Roanoke to find out what had happened to his granddaughter and the others. In a letter he wrote a few years later describing his search for the lost colonists, White ended with a prayer beseeching the Lord to "helpe & comfort them, according to his most holy will & their good desire."

Later expeditions from England failed to find any trace of Virginia Dare and the other Roanoke settlers, and their fate has been one of the chief mysteries of American history ever since. Did they starve? Drown? Die at the hands of the Indians or the

Spanish? Or did they somehow survive and raise children whose descendants are among us today?

WHERE DID THEY GO?

Croatoan was a logical spot for the Roanoke colonists to relocate. White described the island as "the place where Manteo was borne, and the Savages of the lland our friends." The savages were the Croatoan Indians (later known as the Hatteras Indians), who had been friendly to the colonists. Manteo was a Croatoan encountered by the first English expedition to the Carolinas some years before. The explorers took him to England; once back in the Carolinas, he treated the English as allies. The grateful English, in turn, baptized him and gave him the title "Lord of Roanoke."

But there is an ambiguous reference that suggests that despite the carving on the tree, some or all of the colonists did not go to Croatoan. White wrote that at the time he departed Roanoke in 1587, the colonists "were prepared to remove from Roanok 50 miles into the maine." This is puzzling, since fifty miles would have taken them far beyond Croatoan into the mainland.

David Beers Quinn, an English historian regarded as the leading authority on the Roanoke Colony, believed it likely that the colonists' destination was somewhere to the north on Chesapeake Bay. The Chesapeake had long been recognized as a good location for settlement. It was far better than Roanoke, whose location on the treacherous Hatteras coast made it a dangerous place for ships to land, and whose soil was far from optimal. Indeed, White and the colonists who arrived in 1587 had originally wanted to settle on the Chesapeake, but an impatient ship captain forced them to disembark on Roanoke.

One problem with assuming that the colonists went to the Chesapeake, however, is that the distance from there to Roanoke is about 130 miles, far beyond the 50 miles mentioned by White. A possible destination on the mainland that lies within the 50-mile radius is the Chowan River, an area that had been explored by the English and thought to be suitable for settlement.

If they did not go to Croatoan, why did the colonists carve that location on the trees? Quinn thought that the colonists may have split into two groups. The larger group might have left Roanoke to settle elsewhere, perhaps along the Chowan River or Chesapeake Bay. A smaller group might have remained on Roanoke in order to tell White when he returned where the others had gone. But when White did not return, that second group, perhaps threatened by hostile Indians or running out of food, might have abandoned Roanoke for the protection of Manteo at Croatoan. If everything had worked as planned, White would have seen the carving on the tree, gone to Croatoan, and learned where the main settlement was located.

Other explanations have been advanced over the years. One Virginia writer in the 1920s, Conway Wittle Sams, was struck by the fact that on the first tree encountered by White, only the first three letters of the word Croatoan had been carved. Sams imagined a dramatic scene in which the colonists, threatened by hostile Indians, decide to abandon the island and go to Croatoan. As they are about to depart on their boats, they stop to leave one more sign on a large tree near the water. But before they can get beyond the letters "C-R-O," the Indians burst out of the woods and massacre them.

Another hypothesis, advanced in 1938 by North Carolina writer Robert E. Betts, was that the colonists were killed or captured by the Spanish. Certainly the Spanish were anxious to locate and destroy the intrusive enemy colony, and they sent out several expeditions for that purpose. But searches through the Spanish archives indicate that the Spaniards were never able to locate the Roanoke settlement.

Still another possibility is that the colonists starved to death, presumably at Roanoke or Croatoan. The Virginia writer David Stick objected that this theory ignores the fact that the barrier islands off the Carolina coast were fertile, with abundant game and sea life.

Could the colonists have attempted to sail back to England and been lost in the Atlantic? The colony had a pinnace—a small sailing vessel—and could have made such an attempt. But critics of this theory object that the pinnace would have been much too small to hold the more than 110 men, women, and children of the colony. A majority would have had to remain behind, which leaves us with the original problem of where they went.

What England Knew

Some historians believe that the lost colony was never lost at all, that people in England knew of the whereabouts of the colonists and kept some limited contact with them, at least at some point during the period between John White's 1590 voyage and the next attempt of the English to colonize the New World at Jamestown in 1607.

The evidence for this is tantalizing. In the play *Eastward Ho*, performed in London in 1605, one of the comic characters, Captain Seagull, describes the wonders of Virginia:

> A Whole Country of English is there, man, bred of those that were left there in '79; they have married with the Indians and make them bring forth as beautiful faces as any we have in England: and therefore the Indians are so in love with them, that all the treasure they have they lay at their feet.

Seagull goes on to say that the land abounds in riches, and that even the chamber pots are made of gold. (Note, though, that this passage contains an error; the colonists were left behind in 1587, not 1579.)

Another hint is in a fragmentary report that two or more "Virginians" rowed a canoe on the Thames River in London near the home of an English nobleman on a September day in 1603. Presumably these Virginians were Indians; presumably they had recently been brought from the New World.

Possible evidence of the continued existence of the colony can also be found in the writings of the Spanish, who jealously kept an eye on English in the New World. There are rumors reported in Spanish documents that an English colony still existed somewhere to the north of Spanish possessions. The strongest statement came in an account by a Spanish diplomat, Juan Fernández de Velasco, who was in England in 1604 to negotiate a peace treaty between his country and the British government. The diplomat recalled later that one stumbling block to excluding the English from Virginia was the fact that they had been in "peaceful possession" of that territory for thirty years.

If all this is true, by what means could England have maintained contact with the colonists? There is some indication that Englishmen continued to visit the North American coast. A brief passage in a book on English exploration in the New World, published in 1602, referred to Captain Samuel Mace, a seafarer employed by Sir Walter Raleigh, who had "been at Virginia twice before." Other English sea captains could conceivably have stopped in the Roanoke-Chesapeake area.

From this evidence, some historians have built a picture of the colonists living among the Indians, but continuing to practice the religion, customs, and farming methods of their homeland. They imagine Virginia Dare growing to womanhood in this environment. And they imagine that the existence of the colony was known in England all the way from dockside taverns to the royal court. Except for a few fragments such as the speech of Captain Seagull, however, they believe that that knowledge is lost to us.

But the evidence of this lost knowledge is shaky. The dialogue in *Eastward Ho* is certainly not definitive. The "Virginians" on the Thames were probably Indians brought over from the New World, but not necessarily from Roanoke, since "Virginia" in that era referred to almost the entire east coast of the present United States. The belief of the Spanish that the colony continued to exist was based on unreliable accounts provided by deserters and prisoners from English ships who fell into their hands, and who may have told their captors whatever they wanted to hear.

Some in England also had a personal motive for allowing a belief that the colony continued to exist. As the historian Karen Ordahl Kupperman noted, Sir Walter Raleigh's patent from the queen required that a settlement remain in existence, so it was not in Sir Walter's interest to declare that his colonists were dead and the colony lost. Similarly, the English government may have wanted to convince the rest of Europe that the colony was still alive in order to maintain English claims to North America.

WIPED OUT

There is some evidence that Roanoke colonists survived as a group until about 1607, at which time they were slaughtered. The main source is William Strachey, who was secretary of the fledgling Jamestown colony in 1610-1611. When he returned to England, Strachey wrote a manuscript entitled *The History of travell into Virginia Britania,* dated 1612. In this work, Strachey reported that the Roanoke colonists had gone to the Chesapeake Bay, where they "lyved and intermixed" with the Chesapeake (or Cheseppian) Indian tribe. But Powhatan, the chief of a rival tribe, attacked the Chesapeakes and wiped them out, along with the Whites in their midst. Strachey said the massacre was done at the urging of Powhatan's priests. He said further that King James I was informed of this event, and ordered that measures be taken to punish the Indian priests and bring Powhatan under the command of the king.

When did the massacre happen? Strachey said it occurred "when our Colony (under the conduct of Captain Newport) landed within the Chesapeak Bay." "Captain Newport" was the Christopher Newport who brought the first Jamestown settlers to the Chesapeake in April 1607. Strachey's words have led some historians to picture the survivors of the Roanoke Colony, including the grown-up Virginia Dare, peacefully tending their fields in April 1607, when suddenly Powhatan's Indians fall upon them with murderous intent—while at that very moment, a few miles away, their English countrymen are arriving on the shore of Virginia to establish a new colony.

Historian David Beers Quinn accepted the possibility that an attack on the colonists occurred, but argues that it may not have taken place at exactly the date specified by Strachey; that what Strachey may have meant was that Powhatan's attack on the Chesapeakes occurred before the arrival of Captain Newport and the Jamestown colonists. Strachey was also vague about where the massacre of the Roanoke settlers actually occurred. He identified Chesapeake Bay at one point, but at another he seemed to say it occurred on Roanoke Island.

What evidence exists to support Strachey's account? In 1609 the Royal Council of Virginia, the London-based governing body of the Jamestown Colony, issued orders referring to Powhatan's slaughter of the Roanoke colonists, which took place "uppon the first arrivall of our Colonie." The same orders warned the Jamestown colonists not to trust Powhatan or his murdering priests, and to take measures against them. This tends to confirm Strachey's statement that the king of England learned of the massacre and took steps to punish the Indians.

The celebrated Captain John Smith, hero of the Pocahontas story and military leader of the Jamestown Colony, met Powhatan on several occasions. In 1625, a history of exploration in the

New World written by the Englishman Samuel Purchas reported that at one of those meetings in 1608, Powhatan confessed to Smith that "he had been at the murder of that colony and showed to Captain Smith a musket barrel and a bronze mortar and certain pieces of iron which had been theirs." If this story is true, why did Smith not report this confession at the time in his many boastful accounts of his experiences? It has been suggested that King James's government was trying to placate Powhatan to make sure he remained at peace with the Jamestown Colony. It would thus have been impolitic for Smith to open up a source of discord.

SURVIVORS

Whether or not there was an attack by Powhatan on the lost colonists, did they or their descendants survive into the era when other Englishmen began to settle North America?

The first permanent English settlement was the Jamestown Colony, established in 1607. The Jamestown settlers were anxious to locate the lost colonists, not out of any abstract scholarly interest, but for reasons of survival. The knowledge that the Roanoke settlers possessed would be useful in planting crops, scouting out the land, and dealing with the natives in this strange, new land of Virginia. Thus, the early writings of the Jamestown colonists demonstrate that they were intensely interested in rumors reaching them of Whites living in the vicinity. John Smith reported that in 1607 an Indian chief told him "of certaine men cloathed at a place called Ocanahonon, clothed like me [i.e., dressed like Smith]." Powhatan told Smith of a land where the people lived in walled houses like the English and knew how to use brass. Smith sent out two expeditions to find surviving colonists, but both were unsuccessful.

Jamestown settler George Percy reported seeing in 1708 "a Savage Boy, about the age of ten yeares, which had a hair of a perfect yellow and a reasonable white skinne, which is a Miracle amongst all Savages." A map dating from the early settlement of Jamestown has a notation about one area: "Here remayn the 4 men clothed that came from roonock to okonohowan." A pamphlet published in England in 1609 said that "some of our Nation planted by Sir Walter Raleigh" lived fifty miles away from Jamestown, and that two men who set out to find them discovered "Crosses & Leters, the Characters & assured teste-monies of Christians newly cut in the barkes of trees." The reference to a group of English who carved messages in trees is obviously intriguing.

In his *History of Travell into Virginia Britania,* Strachey reported hearing that at a place called Ritanoe, seven English people—four men, two boys, and a girl—worked for an Indian chief producing copper. The seven were said to be survivors "who had fled up the River of Choanoke." Survivors of what? Possibly Powhatan's attack on the lost colonists.

The problem is that these accounts, most of which were sec-ondhand, may not be reliable. The colonists' understanding of the Indians' language was limited, and they may well have misinterpreted what they heard. Furthermore, the Jamestown colonists were told many tall stories by the Indians, such as the existence of apes and gold mines. Tales about Englishmen living nearby may have been some combination of English wishful thinking and Indian desire to please. Another problem is that there may well have been other groups of "lost" strangers in America besides the Roanoke settlers, due to shipwrecks, deser-tions, abortive attempts at colonization, and other hazards of exploration. In 1586, for example, Sir Francis Drake seems to have abandoned in the Carolinas a large group of Black slaves and South American Indians he had captured from the Spanish possessions. In the same year, a garrison of fifteen or so En-glishmen was lost on the Carolina coast.

GOING NATIVE

One popular theory about the fate of the lost colonists is that they and their descendants, cut off from other Europeans, inter-married with the surrounding native population and eventually took on all of their characteristics. Two nineteenth-century North Carolinians, Hamilton McMillan and Stephen B. Weeks, argued that the Lumbee Indians who dwelt in Robeson County, North Carolina, were the descendants of the Roanoke settlers.

McMillan and Weeks believed that the Roanoke colonists merged with the Indians on Croatoan, and eventually migrated westward to become the Lumbees. The Lumbees were said to use Elizabethan dialect and vocabulary, for example, pro-nouncing "father" as "fayther." They also bore surnames similar to those of the Roanoke colonists. Weeks calculated that of the ninety-five different surnames of the Roanoke settlers, forty-one were represented among the Lumbees. The Lumbees themselves told visitors that they were descended from the Roanoke colonists.

Critics of the Lumbee theory say that there is no proven link between the Lumbees and either the Hatteras Indians who inhabited Croatoan or the lost colonists. More likely, according to John R. Swanton, an ethnologist from the Smithsonian Institution, the Lumbees were descended from Sioux Indians who had inhabited the interior of North Carolina. In addition, some of the evidence used by supporters of the Lumbee theory is dubious. For example, none of the Lumbees had the surname Dare, but rather slightly similar names such as Darr, Durr, and Dorr.

A variant on the Lumbee theory is a report of the Reverend Morgan Jones that in 1660 he found near the Pamlico River a tribe that spoke Welsh. The writer David Stick replied that similar tales of Welsh-speaking Indians have been reported over the years about other tribes and that, moreover, very few of the colonists had surnames that could even remotely be considered Welsh.

A more conservative position on the descendants of the lost colonists is that they may have intermarried with the Hatteras Indians who lived in the vicinity of Roanoke Island. Early in the eighteenth century, the surveyor-general of the Carolina colony, John Lawson, observed:

> These [Hatteras Indians] tell us that several of their ancestors were white people who could talk in a book [i.e., read] as we do; the truth of which is confirmed by gray eyes being frequently found among these Indians and no others.

Lawson speculated that after they were abandoned, the Roanoke colonists went to live with the Indians, "and that in process of Time, they conform'd themselves to the Manners of their Indian Relations."

THE DARE STONES

One of the most freakish controversies about the lost colonists concerns a trail of stones that purports to show their fate.

In the late 1930s, forty-eight rock slabs were discovered in various out-of-the-way locations in North Carolina, South Carolina, and Georgia. They appeared to contain crude messages inscribed on them to John White from his daughter, Eleanor Dare, who, along with her daughter, Virginia, and her husband, Ananias, was among the lost colonists. Among the messages on the stones were the following:

➤ Ananias Dare & Virginia went hence unto heaven in 1591

➤ Father soone After you goe for Englande we cam hither/ onlie misarie & warre two yeare/ Above halfe DeaDe ere two yeere moor from sickenes

➤ Father wee dweelde in greate rock uppon river neere heyr Eleanor Dare 1598

➤ Father shew moche mercye tow grate salvage lodgement Ther King hab mee tow wyfe sithence 1593

➤ Father I hab dowter heyr al save salvage king angrie

➤ Father sithence 1593 wee hab manye salvage looke for you

➤ Father I beseeche you have mye dowter goe to englande

➤ Father some amange us putt manye message fo you Bye Trale

➤ Father I hab moche suddianne sickness

These stones came into the possession of Haywood Jefferson Pearce, the president of a private college in Georgia, and his son, Haywood Jr., an official of the college and professor of history at Emory University. Newspapers reported the sensational discoveries, and replicas of the stones were displayed at the Georgia exhibit at the 1939 New York World's Fair. A team of scholars, led by the distinguished Harvard historian Samuel Eliot Morison, came to Georgia to examine the evidence. The team declared that "the preponderance of evidence points to the authenticity of the stones."

The *Saturday Evening Post* sent a reporter, Boyden Sparkes, to investigate the story. Sparkes's article, "Writ on Rocke: Has America's First Murder Mystery Been Solved?" appeared in the

Post in 1941. After consulting experts on Elizabethan English and talking to the men who claimed to have found the stones, Sparkes concluded that the stones were forgeries. He said that words such as "primeval" and "reconnoitre," which were found on the stones, would not have been used by English people in the Elizabethan age, and that the stones were also written in a script not in common use in England in that age. Sparkes quoted a geologist to the effect that at least one of the stones had been recently carved. Sparkes reported further that the younger Pearce had attempted to sell the story of the Dare stones to Hollywood, and that some of those who purported to have found the stones were men of dubious character. Sparkes declared that by reading the inscriptions as acrostics, he could make out words like "Emory," "Atlanta," "Pearce," and even "Fake."

This was not the last word from Eleanor Dare. A diary she was alleged to have written surfaced in the 1940s. It too is now regarded as a hoax.

Weighing the Evidence

One enormous problem in trying to determine what happened to the lost colonists four hundred years ago is the paucity of documents from that era and the difficulty of interpreting the few that have survived. When Governor White said that the colonists had gone "50 miles into the maine," what did he mean? When the orders of the Council of Virginia referred to "the slaughter of Powhatan of Roanocke" did they mean that Powhatan killed the English on Roanoke Island, or rather that he attacked those who had come from Roanoke?

Indeed, our basic knowledge of the events in this story is woven from very slender thread: the entire account of John White's 1590 voyage comes from a 1593 letter of his, written from Ireland, which appeared in a book published in England in 1600. There is no other source to confirm his story of the carving on the trees or the other details of his return to the island. No records indicate what happened to John White after he wrote that 1593 letter; he has vanished from history as utterly as the Roanoke colonists. There is even some debate about the number of colonists on Roanoke Island. Depending on how one reads the sources, the number could be anywhere from 110 to 119.

Historians of the Roanoke saga admit the stark limitations of tracing the lost colonists. The interpretation of where the English settlers went and what happened to them can only be based on a string of possibilities, maybes, and perhapses. But possibly, maybe, and perhaps there is one theory that does have the weight of evidence behind it: the attack by Powhatan on the colonists around the year 1607. That event is mentioned in Strachey's 1612 *History* and in the 1609 orders from the Royal Council of Virginia. There is corroboration in the secondhand account of Powhatan's confession to John Smith.

If this story is true, it means that the colonists did not starve, nor were they attacked by the Spanish. It means further that if some did attempt to sail to England, the majority remained behind. That majority evidently managed to survive as a group for as long as two decades. Where? The Chowan River or Chesapeake Bay are the best guesses.

Some of the colonists may well have survived after Powhatan's attack, particularly since it was not the custom of the Indians to kill women and children. The survivors would most likely have lived out their days among the Indians in the coastal areas of Virginia and North Carolina. While it is highly improbable that they migrated as a block to the interior and became the modern day Lumbee Indians, it is possible that they did contribute to the gene pool of the Native American population, demonstrated perhaps by the gray-eyed Indians observed by Lawson.

The above scenario about the fate of the lost colonists echoes the consensus of three historians—David Beers Quinn, William S. Powell, and C. Christopher Crittenden—who discussed the mystery in a 1959 panel discussion held, appropriately enough, on Roanoke Island during the intermission of *The Lost Colony*, a musical drama.

Will we ever know anything more? It is still possible that there may be an archaeological breakthrough—some hard evidence of sixteenth-century English men and women cohabiting with Native Americans. But failing that, our knowledge about the fate of the lost colonists will be as tenuous as that of Governor John White when he wandered through the abandoned and silent Cittie of Ralegh in the summer of 1590, searching in vain for his granddaughter.

2

WAS GENERAL CHARLES LEE A COWARD?

George Washington was angry. With his aides riding beside him, he galloped onto the battlefield at Monmouth Court House around noon on Sunday, June 28, 1778. From what he could see, a disaster was unfolding: American soldiers appeared to be in retreat in the face of the British. Washington accosted the officer in charge of the American force, Major General Charles Lee.

"What is the meaning of this, sir?" Washington demanded of Lee. "Sir? Sir?" Lee stammered back in confusion.

This dramatic moment is the centerpiece of one of the thorniest puzzles of the Revolutionary War. Was Charles Lee a brilliant strategist who at that moment was maneuvering his troops into position to defeat the enemy, or was he a coward who had lost control of his army? Or even worse, was he a traitor to the American cause who was deliberately seeking a British victory?

THE CURIOUS CHARLES LEE

General Lee was an ungainly figure of a man—thin and slovenly, with an enormous nose. He was born in England in 1731, and entered the British army in his seventeenth year. Lee served as an officer on the North American frontier and in Portugal,

15

Poland, the Balkans, and Turkey. While stationed in the American colonies, he was adopted into an Indian tribe, marrying (more or less) the daughter of a chief. He left her and his two children when the army moved on.

Lee was retired as a colonel on half-pay from the British army at the end of the Seven Years' War in 1763. He had strong liberal sentiments, and just before the Revolution he journeyed to America with the purpose of helping the American cause. (He was no relation, incidentally, to the Lee family of Virginia.) When war erupted he lobbied the Continental Congress to be appointed one of the commanders of the newly created American army; because of his military experience, Congress named him a major general. Within a short period of time he became second in command to Washington.

Lee performed well on campaigns in Massachusetts and South Carolina. But in December 1776, he was captured at a New Jersey inn by a detachment of British cavalry. It has been observed that if Lee had died resisting capture at this moment, he would have been remembered as one of the great heroes of the Revolution. Alas for his reputation in history, there were a few more chapters to be written.

Lee was held prisoner by the British in New York for a year and a half before being exchanged. He rejoined Washington's army in the spring of 1778. It was a hopeful moment for the American cause. The Continental army had emerged from the ordeal at Valley Forge well-trained and well-equipped, with its numbers increased by new recruits. The alliance with France had just been announced, which gave promise of an American victory. Washington learned that Sir Henry Clinton and his army of ten thousand British and Hessians had evacuated Philadelphia and were marching through New Jersey on the way to British-occupied New York. With them went a long, vulnerable line of supply wagons.

Washington realized that for once he held the upper hand. He gave Lee command of an advance force of approximately 4,240 Continental soldiers and 1,200 New Jersey militia, who were to catch up to the British and Hessians. Washington, with the remaining 7,500 or so Continentals, followed behind.

On the morning of June 28, 1778, Lee clashed with the enemy at Monmouth Court House in New Jersey. As Washington rode up later that day, he saw soldiers from Lee's command streaming to the rear in apparent disorder. It was at this point that

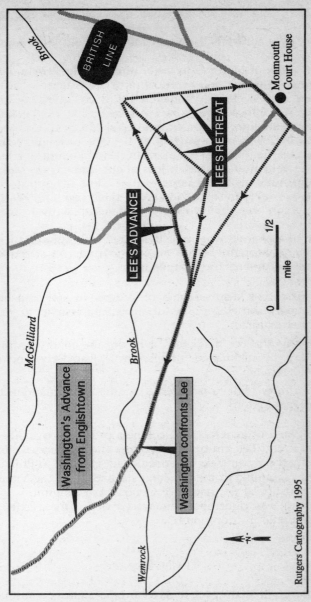

Lee's Advance and Retreat
Battle of Monmouth, June 28, 1778

Washington confronted Lee on the battlefield and berated him for his retreat.

The battle of Monmouth lasted through the remainder of the day, with Washington in command of the American side. There is some debate about whether it could be called an American victory. Washington remained in possession of the field, and American soldiers demonstrated that they could hold their own against the British in a pitched battle. One estimate of the casualties puts the number of American dead at about one hundred, and the British and Hessian loss about three times higher. But Clinton, with his army largely intact and his supply wagons secure, was able to reach New York safely. So both Washington and Clinton were able to leave Monmouth with a measure of credit.

But Charles Lee was a clear loser. Washington had him arrested and brought before a court-martial. As stated on that original document, the charges were:

- ➤ *First:* For disobedience of orders, in not attacking the enemy on the 28th of June, agreeable to repeated instructions.
- ➤ *Secondly:* For misbehavior before the enemy on the same day, by making an unnecessary, disorderly, and shameful retreat.
- ➤ *Thirdly:* For disrespect to the Commander-in-Chief [Washington].

The panel of generals and colonels presiding over the court-martial found Lee guilty on all counts and suspended him from the army for a year. Lee never returned. He died in Philadelphia in 1782, claiming to the last that he had been the victim of a great injustice at the hands of General Washington.

So who was right and who wrong about the events on the field of battle in Monmouth?

"TINSEL DIGNITY"

The charge of disrespect to Washington stemmed from an exchange of letters between Lee and Washington beginning two days after the battle. On June 30, Lee wrote to Washington complaining about their encounter on the battlefield. Your words, said Lee, "imply'd that I was guilty of either disobedience of orders, of want of conduct, or want of courage." Lee went on in the same letter to question Washington's judgment:

> Your Excellency must give me leave to observe, that neither yourself, nor those about your person, could from your situation, be in the least judges of the merits or demerits of our manoeuvers; and, to speak with a becoming pride, I can assert, that to these manoeuvers the success of the day was entirely owing. ... I ever had (and I hope ever shall have), the greatest respect and veneration for General Washington; I think him endow'd with many great and good qualities; but in this instance, I must pronounce, that he has been guilty of an act of cruel injustice towards a man who certainly has some pretensions to the regard of ev'ry servant of this country; and I think, Sir, I have a right to demand some reparation for the injury committed.

Washington wrote back that he found this letter "highly improper," and that he believed Lee guilty of "misbehaviour before the enemy . . . in not attacking them as you had been directed, and in making an unnecessary, disorderly, and shameful retreat." Lee then wrote in reply to Washington, asking for a court-martial and saying hotly that the commander in chief was being led by "the temporary power of office, and the tinsel dignity attending it" to obscure the truth.

Lee's defenders believe that by speaking so bluntly he brought the court-martial on his head. Had Lee not pressed the issue, Washington might have come to recognize that his second in command had acted properly at Monmouth. Lee might also have been better off speaking to Washington in person, rather than putting his words on paper. Until he received the letter from Lee, Washington may have been willing to either let the matter drop or even reconsider his judgment: as proof, Lee's defenders cite the fact that after the battle and before the exchange of letters, Washington assigned Lee the normal administrative duties in rotation.

Lee's champions believe that although he erred in writing so harshly to Washington, Lee was entitled to be angry for the way in which he had been publicly censured on the battlefield by the commander in chief. If Lee's stiff-necked pride got in the way of his good sense, they say, so did Washington's. After receiving the first letter, Washington should have understood his subordinate's injured feelings and tried to settle the matter amicably.

DISOBEDIENCE?

The question of whether Lee disobeyed his orders at Monmouth depends on what those orders were. Was he specifically instructed by Washington to engage the enemy in battle, or did his orders give him freedom to decide whether or not to attack? In military parlance, the first type of orders are described as "positive," the second as "discretionary."

As Lee saw the matter, and as those historians who have defended him ever since have seen it, his orders from Washington were clearly discretionary. Lee's supporters believe that from the beginning of the campaign, when word first reached the Continental army that the British were leaving Philadelphia, Washington's plan was not to take the risk of a full-scale attack. Rather he wanted to harass the enemy, and perhaps to strike a swift blow, such as cutting off the rear guard or capturing the wagon train, if the opportunity presented itself. This was the consensus, say Lee's partisans, of the councils of war that Washington held with his officers on June 17 and 24.

Lee testified that this was his understanding of his orders, and that he received no contrary commands from Washington:

> No letter I received, no conversation I ever held with him, indicated an intention or wish to court a general engagement; if he had, I protest solemnly, that, whatever I might have thought of the wisdom of the plan, I should have turned my thoughts solely to the execution.

But Lee's critics say that the orders were positive, not discretionary. They believe that whatever Washington might have previously thought about the need for caution, on the eve of battle he decided that the enemy should be struck hard. They say that at a meeting with Lee and his other generals on June 27, Washington made his intent plain. Brigadier General Charles Scott testified at the court-martial that at this meeting:

[I] heard General Washington say in presence of General Lee, the Marquis de La Fayette, General Maxwell, and myself, that he intended to have the enemy attacked the next morning, or words to that effect, under the command of General Lee.

Lieutenant Colonel Richard Meade testified that at the request of Washington he rode out on the morning of the battle to convey orders to Lee. Said Meade:

I then told him [Lee] that General Washington had ordered the troops under his command to be put in motion immediately, and that General Washington desired he would bring on an engagement, or attack the enemy as soon as possible, unless some very powerful circumstances forbid it, and that General Washington would soon be up to his aid.

Meade emphasized that Washington "seemed exceedingly anxious to bring on an attack, and desired me to tell General Lee to bring on an attack."

General Anthony Wayne testified that at one point in the battle, Lee had asked him why he was not joining the retreat. "I told him," said Wayne, "that General Washington's positive order [was] to make a stand there, and defend that post as long as possible, till he could form the troops." Alexander Hamilton, who was a lieutenant colonel on Washington's staff, summed it up in a letter: "From everything I know of the affair, General Washington's intention was fully to have the enemy attacked on their march."

At the trial, Lee tried to shake this interpretation of his orders. General Scott was asked whether he "positively" heard Washington order Lee to attack the next morning. Scott equivocated: "I cannot say that it was a positive order, but it did not admit of a doubt with me, but that he meant that General Lee should attack the enemy the next morning."

Hamilton bent a bit on the stand also. When asked whether Washington's orders were for Lee to attack the enemy no matter what the circumstances, Hamilton replied, "I can't conceive that General Washington could mean to give orders so extremely positive, but that circumstances, which had been unforeseen, might arise, to leave the officer, who had the execution of them, liberty to deviate." Hamilton added, however, that such circumstances would have to be "very extraordinary and unforeseen."

Douglas Southall Freeman, a biographer of Washington, summed up the argument of Lee's critics this way:

> Although many words subsequently were wasted in argument over the limits [Washington] did or did not set to this undertaking, no doubt of Washington's purpose can exist: he wanted to strike the rear of the British on the march, and he intended that nothing less than some major, unforeseen obstacle should keep him from delivering such an attack and from exploiting if an opportunity offered.

The "Unnecessary, Disorderly, and Shameful" Retreat

Lee's version of the battle, and the one echoed by his defenders, proceeds as follows. On the morning of June 28, he marched his army to Monmouth, where he intended to harass the British. He faced several obstacles, however. First, it was blisteringly hot—close to one hundred degrees. His troops were tired from the march to the battlefield, whereas the British were well rested. And unlike the British who had passed through the area, he did not have reliable information about the terrain. He soon discovered that the ground was unfavorable. It consisted of deep ravines with narrow passages over them, which put him at a grave disadvantage in facing the enemy.

Lee sent a portion of his troops forward to scout the British position and begin the engagement. His original idea was to cut off and surround the enemy rear guard. But as the battle opened and Continental troops traded musketry and artillery fire with the enemy, Lee discovered that he was up against not a small British detachment far from the main force but rather the much larger main force itself, which was moving to attack him.

Events beyond his control began to unfold. His artillery ran out of ammunition and had to withdraw. Two of the senior officers under his command, Scott and Lafayette, found themselves in an exposed position and retreated without his consent. Lee had no idea of where Washington was or when he would arrive with the rest of the army.

Under these unfavorable circumstances, Lee decided to move

his troops to the rear. This was not a retreat, say his defenders, but rather a "retrograde movement," designed to establish the army on a better, more defensible position. As he moved backward he first considered making a halt in the village of Monmouth, but found that it was too open and exposed. He then considered a position pointed out to him by General du Portail, a French engineer serving with the American army. But this too was flawed; a nearby knoll, if captured by the British, would enable enemy artillery to rain down on his position. Lee then conferred with a captain in the New Jersey militia, Peter Wikoff, who was familiar with the ground at Monmouth. Wikoff told Lee about a hill position further to the rear with a ravine in front and woods on either side—an ideal location from which to meet the British. Lee was establishing his position on this line when Washington finally arrived on the battlefield. The rearward movement had covered about three miles and had occurred over a span of about three hours.

As Lee saw it, then, he had performed with great ability. Despite the unauthorized retreat by generals under his command, despite being attacked by the best units of the British army, and finding himself on unfavorable, unreconoittered ground with exhausted troops, he had managed to maneuver his army into a position where victory could be won. And as Lee and his supporters point out, it was precisely from that position that Washington successfully fought the rest of the battle. Lee felt he had accomplished all this in a calm, professional manner, taking care to support his artillery with infantry and to protect his flanks.

Thus, he said, he was astonished when Washington rode up and berated him:

> So far was I from conceiving ourselves as beaten or disgraced, that I really thought the troops entitled to the highest honor; and that I myself, instead of the thundering charges brought against me, had merited some degree of applause from the General and from the public.

Lee's champions believe that his retrograde movement saved the Continental army from crushing defeat and made possible a victory for Washington. Witnesses friendly to Lee testified at the court-martial that the move was fully justified by events, and that it had been well organized, with a minimum of confusion and disorder, and with Lee firmly in command. If there was disarray, it was a minor and normal part of such a difficult battlefield maneuver, and only affected troops on the fringes. Lee's defenders cite the opinion of the British commander, General Clinton, who said later that it would have been a disaster for the Americans to remain on the ground originally occupied by Lee. Mark Lender, a historian of the battle of Monmouth, believed that Lee's retrograde movement was "one of the best-conducted and most important operations of the war."

But Lee's critics paint a dramatically different picture. They say that Lee exaggerated the difficulty of his position and the size of the enemy force he faced. They believe he could have held the British until Washington arrived with the rest of the army. A nineteenth-century historian, John Fiske, thought that Lee needlessly threw away an unparalleled chance for victory:

> Lee's force was ample, in quantity and quality, for the task assigned it, and there was fair ground for hope that the flower of the British army might thus be cut off and captured or destroyed. Since the war began there had hardly been such a golden opportunity.

Lee's critics believe that far from being the master of the situation, Lee did not adequately control his troops. Men were scattering to the rear; officers were without orders. One witness at the court-martial, General David Foreman, said that "the body of the troops seemed to be confused and in disorder." Alexander Hamilton said the troops were retreating in a rout, "without order or design, as chance should direct."

TREASON

A curious episode occurred when Lee returned from his British captivity to rejoin Washington at Valley Forge, two months before Monmouth. The Continental Congress had passed a law requiring every officer in the American army to take an oath acknowledging the independence of the United States and forswearing allegiance to King George. According to Lafayette, who was present at the time, Lee twice took his hand off the Bible while Washington was administering the oath to him. When asked by Washington why he had done so, Lee replied to the amusement of onlookers that he was willing to renounce allegiance to King George, "but I have some scruples about the Prince of Wales."

Was this simply a joke, or was there something deeper in Lee's mind that caused him to hesitate? Some of his critics believe that his errors at Monmouth were more than poor generalship; he may have deliberately intended to put the American cause in peril.

In the mid–nineteenth century, the historian George H. Moore came across what appeared to be an incriminating document. It was an eight-page manuscript written in Lee's handwriting and dated March 29, 1777. On the back, in the handwriting of the secretary to British general Sir William Howe, was the notation "Plan of Mr. Lee, 1777." The document was a proposal for how the British army could win the Revolutionary War. It called for cutting off the southern states and New England from the Middle Atlantic states. The author of the document predicted that such a move would end the rebellion in a mere three months.

Lee's critics believe the plan was written by Lee when he was a prisoner of the British. They reason that when his capture brought him into the company of his brother officers from his days in the King's army, his pro-British sentiments surfaced, and he decided to help his friends crush the rebellion. He drafted the plan for Sir William Howe, the commander of King George's forces in America.

According to this interpretation, Lee was thus a traitor to the American cause. Lee's more extreme critics believe that when he returned to the American side his purpose was to bring about Washington's defeat on the battlefield. Lee would then take command of the army and negotiate peace with Britain. An 1860 account of the Revolution claimed that an army physician and chaplain, Dr. David Griffith, came to see Washington the night before the battle of Monmouth to warn him of Lee's treachery.

Lee's defenders do concede that the "Plan" was written by their man and given to the British high command, but they put it in a less sinister light. They believe that Lee felt an attachment to England, as well as to America, and sincerely hoped for an honorable reconciliation between the two—a reconciliation that Lee had supported publicly. His plan did not constitute a betrayal of the American cause in the manner of Benedict Arnold, but was simply part of his concern for a quick and relatively bloodless end to the war, which would serve the best interests of Americans and Britons. His defenders say that no matter what he wrote while a captive in Manhattan, he was firmly committed to the American cause when he fought at Monmouth. They regard the story of Dr. Griffith's visit to Washington as an unconfirmed legend.

The historian John Alden, Lee's strongest supporter, suggested that the plan may actually have been a ruse; that Lee was trying to get the British to waste their resources in a futile attempt to divide the regions of the country.

Another accusation about Lee is that he was part of the so-called Conway Cabal, a clique of disgruntled army officers and members of Congress who regarded George Washington as a failure. This faction, some historians believe, sought to unseat Washington as commander in chief and replace him with General Horatio Gates, the American victor of the Battle of Saratoga. During a period of defeat for the Continental army in 1776, Lee wrote a letter to General Gates in which he criticized Washington: "Entre nous [between us], a certain great man is damnably deficient."

But Lee's defenders say that there was no organized conspiracy. They believe that the cabal existed mostly in the minds of Washington and his loyal aides, like Alexander Hamilton, who magnified minor criticism of the commander in chief into a full-blown plot. Lee may have come to disrespect Washington, say his supporters, but he was not a player in any conspiracy.

WASHINGTON VS. LEE

Those who criticize Charles Lee believe that he had deep flaws of character that emerged at Monmouth. Historian John Fiske expressed his loathing of the man:

> Lee was nothing but a selfish adventurer. He had no faith in the principles for which the Americans were fighting, or indeed in any principles. He came here to advance his own fortunes, and hoped to be made commander-in-chief. Disappointed in this, he began at once to look with hatred and envy upon Washington, and sought to thwart his purposes, while at the same time he intrigued with the enemy.

Even more moderate historians find little to love. They believe Lee was an egotistical man who habitually thought himself superior to those under whom he served. As a young captain in the British army, Lee referred to his commanding general as a "damn'd beastly poltroon" and "our booby in chief." Lee's critics say that he had little experience to justify his arrogant view of others; that until Monmouth he had never actually commanded an army in battle.

The critics say that Lee also had a British officer's arrogant scorn of the ability of Colonial troops and regarded Washington's Continentals as hopelessly inferior to Clinton's regulars. In the councils of war leading up to Monmouth, Lee argued against an attack on Clinton, saying that the British evacuation of Philadelphia was enough of a victory. He felt it would be folly to risk the American cause in a full-scale attack, particularly since America now had an alliance with France that could lead to a successful end to the war. For that reason Lee expressed the hope for a "golden bridge" that would take the British from Philadelphia to New York. At Monmouth, Lee is reported to have remarked to Lafayette, "You do not know British soldiers. We cannot stand against them."

When Washington offered Lee the command of the advance force to be sent after Clinton's army, Lee declined. Washington then gave the assignment to Lafayette. But Lee soon changed his mind, and asked Washington to appoint him to lead the advance corps. Washington complied, which was how Lee found himself facing the British on the fateful Sunday of the battle. "Under the circumstances," observed the historian James Thomas Flexner, "Lee should never have accepted the command of the advance force."

In sum, Lee's critics find him vacillating, arrogant, and insubordinate.

But Lee's defenders say that it was Washington whose character was flawed. The commander in chief, they point out, had never defeated a British army on the battlefield, and had been outmaneuvered and outfought by the enemy during the previous three years of war. He was hypersensitive to criticism of his generalship, they say, and he magnified threats to his command out of proportion. Thus, say Lee's defenders, Washington overreacted when he arrived on the Monmouth battlefield and saw what he thought was Lee throwing away the chance for a long-sought victory.

Lee's defenders believe that because of Washington's influence, the outcome of the court-martial was predetermined. The officers who presided over the trial were Washington's lieutenants, who knew that to acquit Lee would be to embarrass the commander in chief. Many of the witnesses who testified against Lee were Washington's personal aides, who, in the opinion of Lee's partisans, sought to curry favor with their master.

Lee's defenders believe that in the verdict of the court-martial, there are hints that the officers who sat in judgment of Lee realized that the charges were unjust. The sentence of a one-year suspension from the army was absurdly light, say Lee's supporters, given the seriousness of the allegations. And it is revealing that although the original accusation was that Lee had been responsible for an "unnecessary, disorderly, and shameful retreat," the final verdict changed the wording to "an unnecessary, and in some few instances, a disorderly retreat."

In accordance with the law, the court-martial verdict went to Congress for review. There was much sympathy for Lee among the members but, say the critics, the body could not afford to divide the American cause by offering a rebuke to Washington, and the final vote upheld the original decision.

In short, Lee's defenders say that their man was not guilty of cowardice, but rather of crossing swords with the jealous god Washington; Lee was sacrificed to Washington's ego and to the larger cause of maintaining the war effort.

Weighing the Evidence

How do the charges against Lee stand up? Of the third charge, disrespect to the commander in chief, Lee was most certainly guilty. Even Lee's firmest modern supporters believe that his angry letters written after the battle overstepped the proper boundary between a subordinate and his commanding officer.

Of the charge that Lee disobeyed his orders, the weight of the evidence is that Lee was not guilty. It has simply not been established that Washington ordered Lee to attack the enemy at all costs, even at the risk of being overwhelmed. Even Alexander Hamilton, one of Lee's harshest critics, conceded as much when he testified at the court-martial. Besides which, there is some merit to the argument of Lee's supporters that he had not abandoned Washington's desire to engage the enemy but was simply seeking a better position from which to do so.

All of which leads us to the most serious accusation against Lee, that of an "unnecessary, disorderly, and shameful" retreat. Whether Lee was justified in moving away from the enemy is an enormously subjective question. Lee clearly thought he was in a dangerous situation that required him to place his troops in a safer position. Another, more aggressive soldier might have seen the same situation in a different light and stood his ground. A battle, of course, is not a laboratory experiment. We cannot run the event over again to see what might have happened if Lee had not retreated, or what Lee might have accomplished on his new defensive line if Washington's arrival had been delayed. But it does seem fair to say that Lee's interpretation of his situation was not unreasonable, and that a rearward movement to a stronger position was a plausible and sensible response to a difficult set of circumstances.

It can be conceded that Lee was a poor leader of men on the battlefield and an insubordinate second-in-command, and that the flaws of vanity, instability, and arrogance that his critics have identified were amply present in his personality. But the weight of the evidence is that at the battle of Monmouth on June 28, 1778, Charles Lee was no coward.

What of the accusation that came out against Lee decades after his death—that the plan he submitted to the British proved he was a traitor? His actions certainly approached the line of treason. If an American general had been captured by the Germans during the Second World War and he had prepared for Hitler some helpful suggestions about how to defeat the Allies, his actions would be deemed traitorous. But the situation in 1778 was different. The English-born Lee made no secret of his desire for a negotiated peace, and his plan betrayed no more information than any educated observer of the war would possess. Writing the plan was undoubtedly a stupid act, but it did not mean that Lee was a traitor at Monmouth.

3

DID THOMAS JEFFERSON
HAVE A SLAVE MISTRESS?

Thomas Jefferson, "the Sage of Monticello," was the most brilliant of the Founding Fathers: a philosopher, scientist, architect, writer, and political leader. He was the author of the Declaration of Independence and the Virginia Statute of Religious Liberty; the founder of the University of Virginia; the third president of the United States; and the progenitor of the Democratic Party—the oldest political party in the world. And dogging his memory for two hundred years has been the allegation that he carried on a long-term sexual relationship with one of his slaves.

The allegation first appeared in print in 1802 in an article by one James Callender in the *Richmond Recorder*, an anti-Jefferson, Federalist newspaper:

> It is well known that the man, *whom it delighteth the people to honor*, keeps and for many years has kept as his concubine, one of his slaves. Her name is SALLY. The name of her eldest son is Tom. His features are said to bear a striking though sable resemblance to those of the president himself. The boy is ten or twelve years of age.

Callender's exposé went on to describe how Jefferson flaunted his relationship with Sally, and how he had fathered several more illegitimate children by her. The attack on the president was denounced by newspapers loyal to Jefferson, but it was gleefully taken up by other Federalist papers and embellished with ribald details and smutty rhymes, like this from the Philadelphia *Port Folio:*

> *Resume thy shells and butterflies,*
> *Thy beetle's heads and lizard's thighs,*
> *The state no more controul:*
> *Thy tricks, with* sooty Sal *give o'er:*
> *Indulge thy body, Tom, no more;*
> *But try to save thy* soul.

The rumors about "sooty Sal" did not end with the death of Jefferson twenty-four years later. Abolitionists used the story to depict the malignant effects of slavery. More lurid details were added, such as the accusation that one or more of Jefferson's illegitimate children had been sold at a New Orleans slave market.

Most historians, from the nineteenth century to the present, have resolutely denied the allegation that Jefferson had a slave mistress. Jefferson's most distinguished modern biographers— Dumas Malone, Julian Boyd, and Merrill Peterson—all took pains to investigate the charge and refute it. Yet a few historians were less confident. Winthrop Jordan, in his Pulitzer Prize– winning 1968 book *White Over Black,* cautiously ventured the opinion that a liaison with a slave woman might not be entirely out of keeping with the character of Jefferson.

In 1974, the allegations received new attention when Fawn Brodie, a professor of history at the University of California Los Angeles, published *Thomas Jefferson: An Intimate History.* In this 594-page book, with scholarly apparatus of footnotes and appendices, Brodie boldly stated that the story of Jefferson's liaison with Sally Hemings was completely true. Brodie's book received wide attention, and her account of the love affair between Jefferson and one of his slaves was accepted as fact in articles in publications such as *Parade,* the *New York Times,* the *Chicago Tribune,* and *Newsweek.* The 1972 novel *Sally Hemings* by Barbara Chase-Riboud and the 1995 movie *Jefferson in Paris* echoed the same theme.

Academic historians were generally cool to the book. Some praised Brodie's writing skills, but most remained unconvinced by her evidence. Some were utterly hostile, like Clifford Egan of the University of Houston, who used Brodie's book as the subject of an essay entitled "How Not to Write a Biography," published in *Social Science Journal*. The journalist and historian Virginius Dabney devoted an entire 1981 book—*The Jefferson Scandals: A Rebuttal*—to attacking Brodie. "In the grave at Monticello," intoned Dabney, "lie the bones of one whose fame is secure, no matter what slanderous falsehoods were spread against him long ago."

THE ACCUSATION

All parties to the debate acknowledge that Jefferson did own a slave named Sally Hemings. She was born in 1773 on the Virginia estate of John Wayles, Thomas Jefferson's father-in-law. When Wayles died, Sally, along with her mother, her brothers, and her sisters, became the property of Thomas Jefferson. For almost fifty years she was Jefferson's slave. She resided on the Monticello estate, except for the years 1787 to 1789, when she was sent overseas to Paris to work in the household of Jefferson, who was then serving as American minister to France. Sally was said to have been light-skinned and remarkably attractive. According to the plantation records, she had five children. She was still a slave when Jefferson died in 1826. She was given her freedom some time later by Jefferson's daughter, and went to live with two of her children. She died in 1835.

The following points are at the center of the debate; Jefferson's accusers say they happened, while his supporters say they never did:

Jefferson fell in love with young Sally when she was in his Paris household. Sally became pregnant. She wanted to remain in France where, she knew, she and her child would be free, but Jefferson persuaded her to return with him to Virginia, promising her that he would eventually free her and any children she might have. For the next thirty-nine years Jefferson and Sally were lovers. When he was president, Jefferson would frequently journey back from Washington to Monticello to be with her. They produced perhaps as many as seven children— the number is uncertain—and the liaison ended only with Jefferson's death.

JEFFERSON'S LOVE LIFE

Those who believe in the Jefferson-Hemings affair say that while Jefferson was a great man, he was still a man. Brodie pointed out that he was passionately in love with his wife, Martha, and that when she died after ten years of marriage, Jefferson was desolated. He was widowed at age thirty-nine, and as Brodie said, "Passion does not usually disappear in a man's life unless his capacity for passion is constricted and warped from the beginning."

There are two episodes in Jefferson's life that indicate he was capable of passion with someone other than his wife. In an 1805 letter, Jefferson admitted that thirty-seven years before, "when young and single I offered love to a handsome lady." Jefferson was referring to his unsuccessful attempt to seduce Betsy Walker, the wife of a friend. Evidently Jefferson made advances to her, she rebuffed him, and that was the end of the episode.

The second episode was Jefferson's affair (if that is what it was) with Maria Cosway. In 1786, four years after his wife's death, the forty-three-year-old Jefferson met the beautiful twenty-seven-year-old Maria Cosway in Paris. The Englishwoman Cosway was a talented musician and artist, locked in an unhappy marriage with a British painter. Jefferson and Maria Cosway developed a close relationship. When Cosway left Paris, Jefferson wrote her a remarkable letter that has come to be known as "My Head and my Heart," which depicts his cool, rational head arguing with his romantic, impulsive heart over the issue of proper behavior. Brodie is convinced that Jefferson and Cosway had an affair, and that the head and heart letter reveals Jefferson's lifelong struggle between his sensualism and his rationalism. Other biographers doubt that this was anything more than a flirtation, although Merrill Peterson, a twentieth-century Jefferson defender, said of the possibility that the two made love: "If he [Jefferson] as a widower ever engaged in it, this was the time."

The defenders of Jefferson minimize the Walker and Cosway episodes, and speak instead of Jefferson's character. His family and friends were unwavering in their belief in his personal integrity. In the 1850s, one granddaughter recalled, "I have never known anywhere, under any circumstances, so good a domestic character as my grandfather Jefferson. I have the testimony of his sisters and his daughter that he was, in all the relations of his private life, at all times, just what he was when I knew him."

The historian John Chester Miller, in his 1977 book, *The Wolf by the Ears: Thomas Jefferson and Slavery*, argued that the "sooty Sal" story violates everything we know of Jefferson's character:

> To give credence to the Sally Hemings story is, in effect, to question the authenticity of Jefferson's faith in freedom, the rights of man, and the innate controlling faculty of reason and the sense of right and wrong. It is to infer that there were no principles to which he was inviolably committed, that what he acclaimed as morality was no more than a rhetorical facade for self-indulgence, and that he was always prepared to make exceptions in his own case when it suited his purpose. In short, beneath his sanctimonious and sententious exterior lay a thoroughly adaptive and amoral public figure—like so many others of the present day. Even conceding that Jefferson was deeply in love with Sally Hemings does not essentially alter the case: love does not sanctify such an egregious violation of his own principles and preachments and the shifts and dodges, the paltry artifices, to which he was compelled to resort in order to fool the American people.

Dumas Malone, in his 1970 biography of Jefferson, could not imagine that the Sage of Monticello could flout public opinion, jeopardize his presidency, and shame his daughters. "To charge him with that degree of imprudence and insensitivity requires extraordinary credulity."

Brodie accuses Jefferson's defenders of hero worship. "They glorify and protect by nuance, by omission, by subtle repudiation, without being in the least aware of the strength of their internal commitment to canonization." As for Jefferson's descendants, she says, they practiced a "family denial" because they could not bear to have their illustrious ancestor depicted as a fornicator.

SLEEPING WITH SLAVES

Miscegenation between masters and slaves was not uncommon in the Old South. The classic statement was expressed by Southern diarist Mary Chestnut at the time of the Civil War:

God forgive us but ours is a monstrous system, a wrong and an iniquity! Like the patriarchs of old, our men live all in one house with their wives and concubines; and the mulattoes one sees in every family partly resemble the white children. Any lady is ready to tell you who is the father of all the mulatto children in every household but her own. Those, she seems to think, drop from the clouds.

A Massachusetts clergyman visiting in Charleston in 1773 wrote in his diary, "The enjoyment of a negro or mulatto woman is spoken of as quite a common thing: no reluctance, delicacy or shame is made about the matter."

Brodie argued that this widespread miscegenation makes the relationship between Jefferson and Hemings quite plausible. She cited the case of John Wayles, Thomas Jefferson's father-in-law. The plantation owner Wayles was married and widowed three times, and had four daughters from these unions. One of those daughters, Martha, became the wife of Thomas Jefferson. After the death of his third wife, Wayles was said to have embarked on a long-term sexual relationship with one of his light-skinned slaves, Betty, and to have had six children by her. The youngest of those children was in fact Sally Hemings. Brodie says that Sally Hemings was thus the half sister of Jefferson's wife.

Jefferson himself had a deep abhorrence of miscegenation. He believed that Blacks should eventually be freed, and then deported from the United States; perhaps to Africa or to western North America. To allow the races to intermingle, Jefferson thought, would bring ruin to everything the White race had created. He wrote that "the amalgamation of whites with blacks produces a degradation to which no lover of his country, no lover of excellence in the human character, can innocently consent." Jefferson's defenders offer this as proof that he could never have had an affair with a Black woman. Brodie replied that Jefferson could have hated miscegenation at the same time he was practicing it:

Jefferson had been responsible for miscegenation—but innocently—with love and without debauchery of the slave woman. But his octoroon children had been subjected by Virginia society to the same degradation as the blackest African, and he had been pilloried for siring them. Amalgamation for Jefferson truly did not raise the black; it only degraded the white.

Truth or Lies?

The two main sources of the Jefferson-Hemings story come from newspaper accounts seventy-one years apart: The 1802 articles by James Callender in the *Richmond Recorder* and 1873 memoirs in the *Pike County (Ohio) Republican* by Madison Hemings and Israel Jefferson.

James Thomson Callender was a Scotsman by birth and a journalist by trade. In the 1790s he fled from England to America to avoid being punished for his attacks on the Crown. His diatribes against England came to the attention of the Anglophobe Jefferson, who began to discreetly supply Callender with cash. In return, the Scotsman used his writing talents on behalf of Jefferson's Democratic Party, producing stinging attacks on Federalist leaders like John Adams and Alexander Hamilton.

Callender was arrested under the Alien and Sedition Acts for defaming the government and sentenced by a Federalist judge to nine months in jail and a two hundred dollar fine. When he became president in 1801, Jefferson pardoned all those who had been imprisoned under the law, including Callender. But Callender emerged from jail filled with bitterness. When his two hundred dollar fine was not refunded promptly, he blamed Jefferson—despite the fact that Jefferson dipped into his own pocket to return part of the fine. And Callender was furious when the administration refused to give him a job as a local postmaster.

Instead he went to work for the Federalist *Richmond Recorder,* where he attacked Jefferson and the Democrats with the same fervor he had used against Adams and the Federalists. At first his revelations concerned the fiscal and political wrongdoings of Jefferson. Then he turned to the president's private life, and on September 1, 1802, he unleashed his accusations about the slave concubine of Monticello. Callender continued to publish denunciations of Jefferson and the Republicans, sinking deeper into fury. He drank, talked of suicide, and quarrelled with his friends. On July 17, 1803, he was found drowned in the James River; it was quite possibly suicide.

To the modern defenders of Jefferson, Callender was a scoundrel who fabricated the accusation. Said historian John Chester Miller:

> Callender made his charges against Jefferson without fear and without research. He had never visited Monticello; he had never spoken to Sally Hemings; and he never made the slightest effort to verify the "facts" he so stridently proclaimed. It was "journalism" at its most reckless, wildly irresponsible, and scurrilous. Callender was not an investigative journalist; he never bothered to investigate anything. For him, the story, especially if it reeked of scandal, was everything; truth, if it stood in his way, was summarily mowed down.

Brodie agreed that Callender was a venomous scandalmonger, but she believed that "while Callender repeated and exaggerated scandal, he did not invent it." She pointed out that another of his accusations—that Jefferson had tried to seduce Betsy Walker—was later admitted by Jefferson. And Callender had also been correct when, in one of his earlier exposés, he had uncovered an affair between Alexander Hamilton and the wife of another man.

So a key question is how the story originated. Did Callender make it up, or did it come from some other source? The very fact that he named a particular slave woman and knew that she had been in Paris with Jefferson would suggest that he had done some research. Callender claimed that the rumor was widespread in the vicinity of Monticello: "There is not an individual in the neighbourhood of Charlottesville who does not believe the story, and not a few who know it." Brodie cited an 1856 statement by a biographer of Jefferson that Callender was "helped by some of Mr. Jefferson's neighbors," which Brodie used as evidence that Callender had done research in Charlottesville. All of this does not prove that Callender's accusation was true, but it does suggest that it was a neighborhood rumor, and not entirely the creation of Callender's own imagination.

Although books, poems, and articles about Jefferson and Hemings appeared for years after Callender's death, no new information of any substance supporting the charge was published until 1873. On March 13 of that year, the *Pike County Republican* of Ohio carried an article entitled "Life Among the Lowly, No. 1," which purported to be an interview with Madison Hemings, an elderly Black resident of the county. Madison Hemings stated that he was the son of Sally Hemings, and he provided important new details to the story about the family background of Sally, about life at Monticello, about his brothers and sisters, and about his mother's relationship with Jefferson, who he claimed was his father. Madison Heming's statement was corroborated in another "Life Among the Lowly" article published nine months later in the same paper. This one purported to be the reminiscences of Israel Jefferson, who had been a house slave at Monticello. He confirmed that Sally Hemings was Jefferson's concubine. The testimony of Madison Hemings and Israel Jefferson is obviously of great importance to Brodie's argument. If genuine, their statements provide verification of Callender's old accusations by two witnesses who were alive when Jefferson and Sally Hemings were living at Monticello.

The defenders of Jefferson concede that Madison Hemings and Israel Jefferson were living in Ohio at the time the articles appeared, but they contend that the testimony of these two men is flawed. First, it seems unlikely that ex-slaves, who by their own admission were poorly educated and who spent their lives as laborers, would write or speak in the high-toned language attributed to them in the newspaper. Hemings, for example, used words such as "concubine," "consequently," "womanhood," and "enciente" (the latter a misspelling of the French word for pregnant). Jefferson's defenders say this vocabulary demonstrates that the article was written by an experienced journalist—probably S. F. Wetmore, the editor of the paper.

Jefferson's defenders also point to the political climate of Ohio in 1873. This was the era of Reconstruction, when Northerners and Republicans were trying to discredit the old slave regime of the South and counter the resurgent Democratic Party. The reminiscences of Madison Hemings could thus be used as yet one more revelation of the horrors of slavery and an attack on the founder of the Democratic Party, Thomas Jefferson. The *Waverly Watchman,* a Democratic rival to the *Pike County Republican,* dismissed Madison Heming's reminiscences: "The fact that Hemings claims to be the natural son of Jefferson does not convince the world of its truthfulness."

Those who defend Jefferson say that although Madison Hemings and Israel Jefferson did live at Monticello, they came upon the scene rather late and so are not reliable witnesses. Madison was born in 1805, eighteen years after the start of the supposed relationship between his mother and Jefferson. Presumably, what he knew of his parentage was told to him by his mother. Jefferson's defenders argue that his mother may have simply been lying to her children about who their father was—perhaps out of vanity or to gain status in their eyes.

The Hemings Clan

An important piece of evidence is the fact that Jefferson was at Monticello roughly nine months before the birth of each of Sally Hemings's children. Said historian Winthrop Jordan:

> She bore five, from 1795 to 1808; and though he was away from Monticello a total of roughly two-thirds of this period, Jefferson was at home nine months prior to each birth. Her first child was conceived following Jefferson's retirement as Secretary of State with nerves raw from political battling with Hamilton. Three others were conceived during Jefferson's summer vacations and the remaining child was born nine months after his very brief return to Monticello for the funeral of his daughter.

The defenders of Jefferson concede that he was in residence at Monticello at the time necessary for him to have fathered Sally's children, but they describe this as negative evidence that does not prove the case.

Another significant point for Jefferson's accusers is the fact that Sally Hemings, her siblings, and her children received favored treatment at Monticello. Sally's brother, Robert, was trained as a barber and given his freedom in 1794; brother James was a trusted personal servant who, at Jefferson's direction, was trained in Paris as a master chef and who was freed in 1796; brother John became a skilled carpenter and was freed in Jefferson's will. Sally herself was a house maid. Her son, Madison, recalled that her duties were "to take care of his [Jefferson's] chamber and wardrobe, look after us children and do such light work as sewing, &c." Madison Hemings also described how he and his siblings were treated:

My brothers, sister Harriet and myself, were used alike.
They were put to some mechanical trade at age fourteen.
Till then we were permitted to stay about the "great
house," and only required to do such light work as going
on errands. Harriet learned to spin and to weave in a little
factory on the home plantation. We were free from the
dread of having to be slaves all our lives long, and were
measurably happy. We were always permitted to be with
our mother, who was well used.

The children of Sally Hemings were of very light complexion.
According to Madison Hemings's testimony, Harriet and Beverly married White spouses and moved into White society. The
overseer at Monticello, Edmund Bacon, described Harriet as
"nearly as White as anybody and very beautiful."

Those children of Sally's who survived infancy did not long
remain in slavery. Sally's son Beverly (b. 1798) and her daughter
Harriet (b. 1801) were listed as runaways in Jefferson's farm
book when they were twenty-four and twenty-one, respectively.
Her other sons, Madison (b. 1805) and Eston (b. 1808), were
freed in Jefferson's will. There is strong evidence that the "running away" was done with Jefferson's connivance. The overseer,
Bacon, said years later of Harriet: "When she was nearly grown,
by Mr. Jefferson's direction I paid her stage fare to Philadelphia
and gave her fifty dollars."

The fact that Sally Hemings's family was treated so well has
been used as evidence of her special relationship with Jefferson.
Indeed, all five slaves freed in Jefferson's will were members of
the Hemings family. But why was Sally herself not given her
freedom in Jefferson's will? Brodie suggested that Jefferson's
freeing the woman rumored to be his lover would result in
painful publicity for his family. Thus, said Brodie, he made
arrangements for Sally to be freed at a later time by his
daughter.

The defenders of Jefferson admit that the Hemings family
received special treatment. But they contend that this was
largely because the clan carried the blood of Jefferson's father-
in-law, John Wayles.

There is one other controversy regarding the children of Sally
Hemings: the reality of "Yellow Tom." Callender stated em-
phatically that Jefferson and Sally's eldest son was named Tom,
that he was about ten or twelve years old, and that he bore a

striking resemblance to the president. This "President Tom" or "Yellow Tom" has been an important part of the accusation. But there is no Tom or Thomas listed among the slave children of Sally Hemings in Jefferson's plantation records, and Jefferson's defenders point to his absence as evidence that Callender's accusation was a complete fabrication.

But Brodie used the absence of Tom in the plantation records as evidence to support her argument: she said that Jefferson may have regarded Tom as free from the time of his birth. Brodie's critics say if that was the case, why did Jefferson list the other children of Sally, and why did Madison Hemings not mention a grown brother named Tom in his memoir? What Madison did say was that his mother gave birth to a child after returning from Paris, but that "it lived but a short time."

PSYCHOLOGICAL CLUES

The most controversial aspect of Brodie's *Intimate History* is her use of psychological evidence. She painted a Freudian picture of Jefferson as a man constantly at war with himself, hiding secret shame and guilt over his passions; she searched for proof of this analysis in his writing. The following are some examples Brodie used from the time Jefferson supposedly first fell in love with Sally Hemings in Paris.

➤ In an account of a trip through Europe, he repeatedly described the soil as "mulatto." Brodie ascribed this to his growing unease about the mulatto Sally Hemings.

➤ In a letter about the cold weather in Paris, Jefferson described himself humorously as "an animal of a warm climate, a mere Oran-ootan." Brodie said that at the time, orangutans were thought to be sexually attracted to Black women, just as Black women were thought to be attracted to White men, and that Jefferson's reference to himself as an orangutan reflected the fact that he had just begun his relationship with Hemings.

➤ In another letter, Jefferson made a joking reference to the large nose of a character in the novel *Tristram Shandy*. Said Brodie, "If Sally Hemings . . . retained a suggestion of her grandmother's physical heritage in the shape of her nose, it could be that Jefferson, caught up in a new passion, was cursing the world's insistence on caring about such matters."

➤ Jefferson wrote to Maria Cosway that he greatly admired a painting he had seen in Dusseldorf that depicted the biblical figure Abraham with his young, partially unclothed concubine. Brodie said that by so doing he was "betraying, inadvertently as a man often does to an old love, that he had been captured by a new one."

Jefferson's defenders dismiss this psychological evidence as claptrap. Yellowish-brown soil was commonly referred to as mulatto, they say, and Jefferson, an avid farmer, would naturally have commented on it. They similarly argue that the references to orangutans, noses, and oil paintings are just what they appear to be—not desperate expressions of inner torment and guilt. When Jefferson made an offhand reference to the "infidelities in the post office" in a letter to Maria Cosway, Brodie interpreted this as indicating that Jefferson was concerned that gossip about their affair was spreading. But the historian Gary Wills, in a slashing attack on Brodie's method, said that Jefferson was simply making "a natural eighteenth century expression of exasperation with the mail's untrustworthiness." Wills mockingly declared:

Ms. Brodie's easy method for uncovering scandal would, if followed logically, reveal not only Jefferson's affair with Mrs. Cosway, but a more shocking one with Ralph Izard, to whom Jefferson wrote: "The infidelity of the post offices, of both England and of France, are not unknown to you."

Wills said of Brodie's method:

She has managed to write a long and complex study of Jefferson without displaying any acquaintance with eighteenth-century plantation conditions, political thought, literary conventions, or scientific categories—all of which greatly concerned Jefferson.

THE RASCAL CARR BROTHERS

If Jefferson did not father the children of Sally Hemings, who did? Jefferson's defenders allege that the culprit was one of Jefferson's nephews, Peter or Samuel Carr.

Peter and Samuel were the sons of Jefferson's widowed sister, Martha. Jefferson cared deeply for the boys, and they were frequent visitors to Monticello. A key element linking the Carr brothers to Sally Hemings is an 1868 letter written by a Jefferson biographer, Henry S. Randall, reporting a conversation he had with a grandson of Jefferson, Thomas J. Randolph, at Monticello. Randolph told Randall that Sally had been the mistress of Peter Carr, and Sally's sister Betsy had been the mistress of Samuel Carr. The fact that the brothers slept with slaves was "perfectly notorious" at Monticello, said Randolph.

An 1858 letter from a granddaughter of Jefferson alleged that Samuel was "the most notorious good-natured Turk that ever was a master of a black seraglio kept at other men's expense," and that all of Sally Hemings's children were fathered by Samuel. In 1862, Jefferson's former overseer, Edmund Bacon, said of Sally's daughter Harriet: "She was not his [Jefferson's] daughter; she was _____'s daughter. I know that. I have seen him come out of her mother's room many a morning when I went up to Monticello very early." Defenders of Jefferson assert that the deleted name was Samuel Carr's.

The involvement of the Carr brothers would explain such troubling facts as why the Hemings children received favorable treatment, why Jefferson did not fight back at his accusers by naming the actual father of the Hemings children, and why those children were said to bear a family resemblance.

Brodie dismissed the accusation against Peter and Samuel Carr as another example of the "family denial"—an alibi created by the descendants of Jefferson to shield the Sage of Monticello. She said that neither of these young men could have been the father of Sally Hemings's children because much of the time they lived away from Monticello and had lives of their own. This is true for Peter, who moved to Baltimore. But Samuel lived in the vicinity of Charlottesville, which was close enough to enable him to visit easily.

Weighing the Evidence

There is no smoking gun in this story of Jefferson and Hemings;
no irrefutable proof one way or the other to determine whether
the Sage of Monticello had a slave mistress. The best we can
do is to look at both sides of the argument to see which is
most convincing.

The best evidence on the prosecution side can be summed
up as follows:

➤ Miscegenation between masters and slaves was not
uncommon.

➤ Rumors that Jefferson cohabited with a slave seem to have
been current in the neighborhood of Monticello and pre-
dated the article by Callender.

➤ Jefferson was at Monticello about nine months before each
of Sally Hemings's children was born.

➤ The Hemings family received lenient treatment at
Monticello.

➤ Jefferson was not an ascetic. He tried to seduce a friend's
wife when he was a young man, and as a middle-aged
man he seems to have had an affair, or at least a flirtation,
with a younger woman. He was also not above a bit of
prevarication, as when he slipped money to Callender.

Those who defend Jefferson have the difficult task of trying to
prove a negative—to demonstrate that the alleged affair never
happened. The following is the best evidence on their side of
the argument:

➤ Most historians who have studied Jefferson's character in
depth conclude that it is unlikely that he would have kept
a slave mistress.

➤ No scrap of genuine evidence of the liaison appears in the
thousands of letters Jefferson wrote and received in his
life; no visitor to Monticello ever mentioned such an
affair.

➤ The "psychological evidence" offered by Brodie to prove Jefferson's obsession with Sally Hemings is largely unconvincing.

➤ There is little evidence for the first-born love child, "Yellow Tom."

➤ There is a reasonable possibility that if a White man was intimate with Sally Hemings, it was one of Jefferson's nephews.

On balance, the weight of the evidence rests with the defenders of Jefferson. It is unlikely that Jefferson had the passionate, loving, thirty-nine-year affair with Sally Hemings that Brodie describes.

But there is one other alternative to consider. Most of those who have written on this subject, both the critics and the defenders of Jefferson, seem to assume that the story must be entirely true or entirely false. Either Jefferson had an intense, passionate, and anxiety-ridden relationship from 1787 to 1826 with Sally Hemings, or else he had absolutely nothing to do with her. But what if it was not undying love but something more casual and more carnal? If we strip aside the talk of a love affair and red herrings like "Yellow Tom," then what is left is a case of a plantation owner who occasionally had intercourse with one of his attractive slaves, from which may or may not have resulted some illegitimate children. Gary Wills suggested that this was in fact the case. He stated that Sally was like a "healthy and obliging prostitute, who could be suitably rewarded but would make no importunate demands. Her lot was improved, not harmed, by the liaison." This approach somewhat increases the plausibility of the accusation. But it still remains unproved, and the balance of probability remains on the side of Jefferson's defenders.

Perhaps more interesting than the guilt or innocence of Jefferson is the larger issue of why this 1802 accusation has continued to preoccupy Americans for two centuries. The fact that the Sage of Monticello may have had an affair with Maria Cosway, for which there is tantalizing evidence, seems to be a subject only for Jefferson specialists. The more remote possibility, however, that Jefferson had a relationship that crossed the color line is the subject of an endless debate carried over in books and articles (this one not excepted). The answer is that race, not sex, is our national obsession, and the separation of the White and Black races by prejudice and hostility continues to confound us. This is the real tragedy at the heart of the story.

4

WAS AARON BURR
A TRAITOR?

The patriots who won the Revolution and built a new nation constituted an amazing generation of Americans. Benjamin Franklin, Alexander Hamilton, James Madison, John Adams, and Thomas Jefferson (with or without Sally Hemings) deserve their reputations as men of deep thought and high principle. And then there was Aaron Burr. Even those who admire Burr admit that he had an element of instability and impulsiveness, a fondness for intrigue, a philandering nature, and a restless desire for power.

Burr was born in New Jersey in 1756, the son and grandson of distinguished Protestant ministers. In the Revolutionary War he rose to the rank of lieutenant colonel in the Continental army. After the war he entered politics and became the leader of a powerful political faction in New York State. In the presidential election of 1800, he lost to Thomas Jefferson by one vote in the House of Representatives.

Burr became vice president under Jefferson. But he had earned the enmity of both the Democratic and Federalist parties, and his political career was on the skids. Then, in a duel at Weehawken, New Jersey, in 1804, Burr shot and killed his political enemy, Alexander Hamilton. With this hotheaded act, Burr destroyed his last chance to become a major force in national politics—at least through any conventional means.

Over the course of the next three years—1804 to 1807—Burr embarked on a curious odyssey that has come to be known as the "Burr Conspiracy." Before his term as vice president ended, he held private conversations with influential people in Philadelphia, Washington, and New York: military men, foreign ambassadors, and adventurers. When his term expired in March 1805, he journeyed to the American West, where he traveled along the Ohio and Mississippi Rivers, from Pittsburgh to New Orleans, raising money and volunteers for a project that remains mysterious to this day.

The West in that era was filled with possibilities for a clever, ambitious man like Burr. The states of Ohio, Kentucky, and Tennessee had only recently entered the union. New territories were waiting to be settled, including the enormous, unchartered Louisiana Purchase west of the Mississippi. There was tension between the expansionist West and the established East. There was also deep hostility toward Spain, whose colonies of Mexico, East Florida, and West Florida seemed to hem in the West. Sentiment for war with Spain was strong.

What was Burr up to? There was talk that he planned to run for political office, to make money in a canal scheme, or to speculate in land. Rumors eventually circulated that Burr's real aim was less innocent; that he wanted to invade the Spanish colonies to set up a new empire, or perhaps even to induce the western states out of the Union.

Word that Burr was planning treasonous activities reached President Thomas Jefferson in Washington. On November 27, 1806, Jefferson issued a proclamation warning citizens that a conspiracy was underway in the West by men who were "deceiving and seducing honest and well-meaning citizens, under various pretenses, to engage in their criminal enterprises." The proclamation did not cite Burr by name and was vague about the intent of the conspiracy, but it is clear that Jefferson thought Burr was up to no good and wanted him stopped.

Jefferson's proclamation called on federal and state officials to arrest the conspirators. Three months later, in February 1807, Burr was seized by a U.S. Army detachment in the Mississippi territory. He was brought back East under guard and put on trial in Richmond, Virginia, on a charge of treason against the United States—a crime punishable by hanging. Burr was found not guilty; but he was plagued by creditors and hostile public opinion, and he left the United States for a four-year, self-

imposed exile in Europe. He returned to practice law in New
York. Ever the intriguer, he was divorced on the grounds of
adultery by his second wife shortly before his death in 1836 at
age 80.

Burr consistently denied that he was a traitor. At the time of
the conspiracy he wrote to a friend:

> If there exists any design to separate the western from the
> eastern states, I am totally ignorant of it—I never harbored
> or expressed any such intention to any one, nor did any
> person ever intimate such a design to me. Indeed I have
> no conception of any mode in which such a measure could
> be promoted, except by operating on the minds of the
> people, and demonstrating it to their interests.

Was Burr as innocent of treason as he claimed?

"An Offer from Mr. Burr"

Anthony Merry was the British minister to the United States
from 1803 to 1806. Aaron Burr approached him on several occasions to obtain help from the British government for a plan of
conquest. On August 6, 1804, Merry wrote to his superiors in
London with details of Burr's project:

> I have just received an offer from Mr. Burr, the actual Vice
> President of the United States (which Situation he is about
> to resign), to lend assistance to his Majesty's Government
> in any Manner in which they may think fit to employ him,
> particularly in endeavoring to effect a Separation of the
> Western Part of the United States.

In later letters to London, Merry added more detail. He said
that Burr told him that the inhabitants of the western lands
would declare their independence of the United States once
they obtained "an assurance of protection and assistance from
some foreign power," preferably Great Britain. To make this
possible, said Merry, Burr wanted the British government to
supply him with one hundred thousand pounds and, at the
appropriate moment, a small fleet of ships at the mouth of the
Mississippi. The money would have to be provided secretly to

Burr so as not to create suspicion on the part of the American government. Nothing came of these overtures from Burr to Britain, but those who believe that Burr was guilty of treason regard Merry's letters as clear proof.

Those who defend Burr from the charge of treason paint a different picture. They believe that Burr was hoodwinking the British. He knew that London was hostile to the new American nation, and would go to great lengths to clip the wings of the American eagle. By falsely proposing to Merry that he could weaken the power of the new United States by separating the West, Burr thought he could obtain some of the cash he badly needed for his real purpose: to invade the Spanish territories of Mexico and Florida.

Burr made similar overtures to the Spanish minister from Spain to the United States, the Marqués de Casa Yrujo. A canny politician, Yrujo was continually on the alert to protect the Spanish colonies in the New World from invasion by American adventurers. From 1805 to 1806 he reported back to Spain on several occasions that Burr was planning a separation of the western states, which would have consequences for Spanish possessions in North America.

Some of Yrujo's information came from talking to Burr, and some came from Burr's associate, former New Jersey congressman Jonathan Dayton. The essence of what Yrujo reported back to Spain was that Burr sought to take Kentucky, Louisiana, Tennessee, and other parts of the West out of the Union, for which service he sought the financial assistance of Spain. On one occasion, Dayton told Yrujo that Burr planned to begin the revolt in Washington, D.C., itself, where he and his supporters would seize money and arms, kidnap Jefferson and other top officials, and then negotiate for power. If the scheme failed, Burr and his followers would burn the U.S. Navy's ships, except for those he needed to sail to New Orleans, where he would proclaim an independent nation.

To the accusers of Burr, this intelligence is yet more evidence that Burr was a traitor. But the defenders of Burr argue that Burr was hoodwinking the Spanish minister, Yrujo, the same way he had hoodwinked the British minister, Merry. Indeed, this was an even bolder hoodwink, they say, since Burr was trying to trick Yrujo into providing support not for dismembering the Union but for dismembering the Spanish colonies of North America.

So in his dealings with British and Spanish ministers, say his defenders, Burr may have been guilty of lying, but not of treason.

One of the witnesses against Burr at the treason trial was William Eaton, a former American consul in Tunis who had earned some fame for his military exploits during the war against Tripoli. At Burr's Richmond trial, Eaton testified that Burr had sought to enlist him as an officer in a military force that the former vice president was creating. According to Eaton, Burr told him that he planned to form a revolutionary government, headquartered in New Orleans, that would carve out a new country from Spanish Mexico and from American land west of the Appalachian Mountains.

Burr also told Eaton that he intended to overthrow the government of the United States and would "turn Congress neck and heels out of doors, assassinate the President, seize the treasury and Navy, and declare himself the protector of an energetic government."

Burr's champions describe Eaton as a completely unreliable character. He was said to be a heavy drinker and an eccentric— he could frequently be found in taverns, wearing a Turkish hat and sash in memory of his days in North Africa. He believed he was owed money by the government for his service in the Tripolitan war, and, say Burr's defenders, he may have thought that by testifying against Burr he would win his claim. The defenders also say that Eaton had not met Burr previously, and that it is unlikely that Burr would expose his secrets so easily to a stranger, particularly such an erratic one.

On his trip through the West, Burr visited Colonel George Morgan, an acquaintance from his college days at Princeton. Morgan lived with his two sons on a seven thousand-acre estate known as Morganza. The Morgans testified at the trial that Burr had told them that within the next five years the western states would pull out of the Union. According to one of Morgan's sons, Burr boasted that "with two hundred men, he could drive the president and congress into the Potowmac; and with four or five hundred he could take possession of the city of New-York."

Burr's defenders say that Morgan was a rather shady speculator who had unsavory dealings with the Spanish, and that he was also a Jefferson ally whose accusations against Burr were politically motivated. If Burr spoke loosely to the Morgans, he may have been indulging in a sort of tongue-in-cheek, half-jesting, extravagant talk that, according to his biographers, he sometimes used. Morgan's son, in fact, said that Burr appeared to be speaking in a frivolous manner.

Another accusation about Burr's plans came from Joseph Hamilton Daveiss, the United States Attorney for the District of Kentucky. Daveiss became alarmed at Burr's activities, and conducted an investigation. He concluded that the former vice president's aim was "to cause a revolt of the Spanish provinces, and a severance of all those Western States and Territories from the union to coalesce & form one government."

The defenders of Burr say that Daveiss was a hard-core Federalist who was trying to embarrass the Democratic Party of Burr and Jefferson, and that Daveiss was upset at never having been solicited by Burr to join the secret project. And when Daveiss presented his evidence against Burr to a Kentucky grand jury in 1806, the jurymen refused to return an indictment.

The Devious General Wilkinson

A key figure in the story of Burr's conspiracy is General James Wilkinson. The general was the commander of the American army in the West and governor of the Louisiana Territory. Burr knew Wilkinson well from their days as officers in the Revolutionary army. During the "conspiracy" period, Burr and Wilkinson met together privately on several occasions and exchanged frequent letters. Whatever Burr may have been up to, Wilkinson was clearly a party to it.

But then, as accusations began to circulate that Burr was planning treasonous acts, Wilkinson turned against his old friend. The general warned the government that Burr intended to attack New Orleans, capital of the American territory of Louisiana, where the former vice president and his followers intended to seize money from banks, incite the residents of the territory to revolt against the United States, and invade Mexico. Wilkinson prepared to repel this invasion, and he arrested associates of Burr in New Orleans. After Burr was arrested and brought to Richmond for trial, Wilkinson testified against him.

Wilkinson was thus the chief accuser against Burr, and the man who provided the most detailed and damaging testimony of a conspiracy. The defenders of Burr attack Wilkinson as com-

pletely untrustworthy. They point to his long history of subter-
fuge. As a soldier in the American Revolution he had plotted
against General Washington and skimmed money from the
American cause. Once in the West, he eagerly sold his services
to the Spanish, who secretly paid him thousands of dollars in
loans and outright bribes in exchange for his loyalty—this while
he was one of the highest officers in the United States Army.
In testifying against Burr, he repeatedly changed his story and
tampered with letters he had received from Burr in order to
exonerate himself.

The accusers of Burr admit that Wilkinson was a thoroughly
wicked man, up to his epaulets in intrigue. But they argue that
the very fact that Burr associated with him demonstrates that
the former vice president was up to no good and that the general knew what he was talking about when he denounced Burr
as a traitor.

THE CIPHER LETTER

Among the evidence presented by Wilkinson against Burr was
the so-called cipher letter, which was supposedly written by
Burr in Philadelphia to Wilkinson in New Orleans in July 1806,
when the two were still in league together. The letter was written in a secret code that Burr and Wilkinson shared. The decoded message is difficult to read—some of the sentences are
disjointed, and in some places Burr is referred to in the first
person as "I" and at other places in the third person as "Burr."
The following is an abridgment:

> Your letter postmarked 13th May is received. I have at
> length obtained funds, and have actually commenced. The
> Eastern detachments, from different points and under dif-
> ferent pretense, will rendezvous on Ohio [River] on 1
> November.
> Everything internal and external favors our view. Naval
> protection of England is secured. Truxton [a U.S. Navy
> commodore and friend of Burr's] is going to Jamaica to
> arrange with the [British] admiral there and will meet us
> at Mississippi. England [and] a navy of the United States
> [are] ready to join and final orders are given to my friends
> and followers. It will be a host of choice spirits. Wilkinson

shall be second to Burr only and Wilkinson shall dictate
the rank and promotion of his officers.

Burr will proceed westward 1 August—never to return.
With him go his daughter and grandson.

Our project my dear friend is brought to the point so
long desired. I guarantee the result with my life and
honor, with the lives, honor and the fortune of hundreds,
the best blood of our country.

Burr's plan of operation is to move down rapidly from
the Falls on fifteenth November, with the first 500 or 1000
men in light boats now constructing for that purpose; to
be at Natchez between the 5 and 15 December, there to
meet you; then to determine whether it will be expedient
in the first instance to seize on or pass by B.R. [Baton
Rouge, part of the Spanish colonies] On receipt of this
send me an answer. Draw on me for all expenses.

The people of the country to which we are going are
prepared to receive us—their agents, now with me, say
that if we will protect their religion and will not subject
them to a foreign power, that in three weeks all will be
settled.

The gods invite us to glory and fortune. It remains to
be seen whether we deserve the boons.

This letter is clearly a plan for a secret invasion by an armed
force of men traveling down the Ohio and Mississippi Rivers.
But what was the target of the invasion—the cryptic "country
to which we are going"? Burr's accusers say it was New Orleans, the capital of the American-held Louisiana Territory. The
people of that country whose religion must be protected, say
the accusers, were the Catholic Creoles of New Orleans. To the
accusers of Burr, then, the cipher letter is proof of treason.

The champions of Burr read the letter differently. They say
the "country to which we are going" was Spanish territory, as
evidenced by the mention of seizing the Spanish town of Baton
Rouge. But even beyond this, Burr's defenders say the letter is
worthless as evidence because it is a forgery that did not come
from Burr's pen. They argue that it was written in a bombastic,
boastful style that was unlike Burr's other writing. The letter
states that Burr planned to travel on the expedition with his
daughter and grandson; Burr's defenders say that he would
never have subjected his four-year-old grandson, whom he

deeply loved and who was gravely ill at the time, to a dangerous military campaign into foreign territory. The defenders also point to the curious shift from the first person to the third person by the author of the letter.

Further, Burr would not have written that a fleet of British and American ships would be located at the mouth of the Mississippi. His request for ships had already been turned down by the British government and by his friend, Commodore Truxton, so why would he tell Wilkinson a false story?

If Burr did not write the cipher letter, who did? At his trial, Burr would only say it was a forgery, without naming an author. Some of Burr's modern-day defenders say that on the basis of the handwriting and other evidence, it may have been written by Jonathan Dayton, Burr's associate. Dayton was with Burr in Philadelphia at the time the letter was written, and, say the defenders, he may have taken it upon himself to communicate with Wilkinson, going far beyond what Burr would have said.

THE BLENNERHASSET ISLAND INCIDENT

It is one thing to write code letters and talk about invasions. But was there an actual treasonous act perpetrated by Burr against the United States? The accusers of Burr say that such an act did in fact take place. The date was December 1806; the location was an island in the Ohio River.

The island belonged to Harmon Blennerhasset, a wealthy Irish immigrant who dwelt there with his wife and children. In the course of his travels in the West, Burr visited Blennerhasset's elegant island home, and evidently drew its owner into his schemes. With Blennerhasset's approval, Burr used the island as a staging area for his recruits. In early December 1806, about one hundred of Burr's supporters were gathered there, along with provisions and flatboats.

The local authorities became alarmed at the activities occurring on the island. According to an account by Jacob Allbright, a hired hand on the island, a militia general tried to arrest Blennerhasset on the night of December 10. He was prevented by Burr's followers, who leveled their muskets at the general. When the local militia invaded the island the next day, they found that Burr's men had fled downstream in the flatboats.

Burr's accusers seek to use this curious episode as hard evidence of an armed insurrection against the government of the United States. They say that Burr's followers had assembled on the island in order to launch the attack on New Orleans hinted at in the cipher letter. They cite the testimony of Peter Taylor, a gardener who worked for Blennerhasset, and Jacob Dunbaugh, a sergeant in the American army who later traveled with Burr, that the expedition that left the island was armed for war.

Burr's defenders dismiss these charges as ludicrous. They believe that the events on the island constituted nothing resembling an insurrection. They say that Allbright's charges were false; that the militia general who was on the island was there as a guest of his friend Blennerhasset. Dunbaugh and Taylor, they add, were completely unreliable. And if Burr's men did carry weapons, it was a common practice in the West.

What were the men doing on the island? Burr's defenders say that they were preparing to travel to a 400,000-acre tract of land along the Washita River in the Louisiana Territory, near the border with Mexico. Burr had purchased this tract some time before, and he now intended to settle it with his volunteers, perhaps as a jumping-off place for an invasion of Mexico. And finally, say his defenders, Burr could not have been the instigator of the insurrection at Blennerhasset Island, since at the time he was far away in Frankfurt, Kentucky.

MEN BEHIND THE SCENES:
THOMAS JEFFERSON AND JOHN MARSHALL

If Burr was not guilty of treason, why was he put on trial? His defenders lay much of the blame at the feet of President Thomas Jefferson. They say that at first, Jefferson supported, perhaps even secretly encouraged, Burr's plan to attack the colonies of His Catholic Majesty in North America. There was a great deal of antagonism between Spain and the United States, which for a time threatened to break into war. If that happened, Burr's expedition would help the American cause. But, say Burr's defenders, Jefferson backed down from conflict with Spain and began to negotiate a peaceful settlement. At that point Burr's activities constituted a threat to Jefferson's foreign policy. It was against this background that Jefferson issued his proclamation against his former vice president.

Besides these strategic considerations, say Burr's defenders, Jefferson despised Burr ever since the New Yorker had challenged the Virginian for the presidency and for the leadership of the Democratic Party. The conspiracy gave Jefferson new reason to hate Burr, since in Jefferson's view the opposition Federalists were using the episode to embarrass his administration.

Burr's defenders say that Jefferson exerted all his influence to have Burr convicted at the Richmond trial, and the president personally saw to it that witnesses were brought from around the country to Richmond to testify against his former vice president. Many of the witnesses were supporters of Jefferson, such as Morgan, the estate owner who testified that Burr boasted of how easy it would be to overthrow the government; or they were seeking money from Jefferson's government, such as Eaton, the former American consul in Tunis who believed he was owed for his service in the Tripolitan War. Jefferson offered a pardon to one of Burr's confederates if he would testify for the government's side. He also kept up a stream of advice to the prosecutor at the trial, George Hay, United States Attorney for the Virginia District. When Burr was acquitted, Jefferson wrote bitterly that "The criminal is preserved to become the rallying point of all the disaffected and the worthless of the United States."

Burr's accusers accept the fact that Jefferson worked behind the scenes, but they point to the fact that the presiding judge at the trial, Chief Justice John Marshall, was leaning in the other direction. The Federalist Marshall was a staunch political opponent of Jefferson, and the accusers say that as a result he interpreted the law to ensure that Burr was acquitted, and even took the improper step of attending a dinner with Burr in Richmond before the trial opened.

Burr, incidentally, did not testify at the trial, and no witnesses were called on his behalf. He and his lawyers based their defense on the grounds that the prosecution had failed to muster sufficient proof of treason as required by the law.

Weighing the Evidence

There is no question that Aaron Burr was up to something in the West. Both his defenders and accusers agree that he wanted to invade Spanish territory in North America and set up some sort of government. To do so would have been a violation of American law and treaty obligations. But where the accusers and defenders part company is whether Burr intended to take another step: to pull the western states and territories out of the Union. To have attempted that would have made Burr guilty of the much more serious crime of treason.

Treason is the only crime specifically defined in the United States Constitution. Article III, section 3 describes the act and sets exacting standards for conviction:

> Treason against the United States shall consist only in levying war against them, or in adhering to their Enemies, giving them Aid and Comfort. No Person shall be convicted of Treason unless on the Testimony of two witnesses to the same overt Act, or on Confession in open Court.

The Founding Fathers wanted to make sure that the charge of treason would not be used to crush dissent, as it had in despotic countries. After all, they themselves had been accused of treason against Great Britain.

At Burr's trial in Richmond, Chief Justice John Marshall adhered closely to the constitutional standard for a conviction of treason. He ruled that to prove Burr's guilt there had to be more than just words; there had to be an act of military force against the government attested to, by two witnesses, as the Constitution required. He concluded that the evidence presented by the prosecution did not meet that standard. The jury followed his interpretation of the law and found Burr innocent. Looking at the case two centuries later, this seems like a proper verdict. The cipher letter appears to concern an invasion of Spanish, not American, territory. And the comic opera on Blennerhasset Island can hardly be called an insurrection against the United States. In short, all the hard evidence suggests that Burr's purpose was solely to invade Mexico.

But in reaching its verdict, the jury used unusual wording. In place of the standard "not guilty," the jury foreman said: "We of the jury say that Aaron Burr is not proved to be guilty under this indictment by any evidence submitted to us. We therefore find him not guilty." The jurors seemed to be saying that while the case against Burr had not been proved in the constitutional sense, he might still bear some degree of guilt.

That seems like a fair assumption. One can imagine Burr as his vice presidency came to a close, with his political hopes collapsing around him, considering the options of a military adventure in Mexico. And it is hard to imagine that his restless, unrestrained mind would have stopped there, without contemplating the larger game of uniting territory won from Spain with the American West to form a mighty new nation.

This is especially likely, since in his time the United States was not the inviolable, indissoluble entity we think it today. Many Americans in that era believed that the Union, because of its vast size, might someday divide into separate nations. It was only later, after the ordeal of the Civil War, that the United States became a singular, rather than a plural, noun—when the idea of severing the nation became unthinkable.

There is ample evidence that Burr did think and speak about disunion, at least in the early stages of the conspiracy. He certainly talked about it to the Briton Merry and to the Spaniard Yrujo, and may have talked about it to the Morgan family and to William Eaton. The defenders try to explain this away by saying that Eaton was lying, that the Morgans misinterpreted a loose jest, and that Merry and Yrujo had been hoodwinked by Burr. But it is revealing that Eaton, Yrujo, and the Morgans independently reported hearing the same fantasy about invading Washington, D.C. Yrujo's secret report of this conversation was not discovered until the end of the nineteenth century in Spanish diplomatic archives, so it is highly improbable that the story could have been cooked up to frame Burr.

In the strict legal and constitutional sense, then, Burr was not guilty of treason. There is no firm evidence that he undertook the overt act of aggression against his own nation. But if we depart from the law (and from the concept of freedom of speech) to define treason more loosely to include the contemplation of such an act, then Aaron Burr was surely a traitor.

5

HOW DID MERIWETHER LEWIS DIE?

Grinder's Stand. A cold and grating name for a tragic place. The Stand (a local name for an inn) consisted of a couple of small cabins and outbuildings owned by a Mr. Robert Grinder and his wife in the backwoods of Tennessee. The Natchez Trace, a wilderness road leading from the Mississippi River to Nashville, ran past the establishment, and the Grinders offered accommodation to travelers seeking a place to stay the night. No picture survives of the Grinder property, but one imagines it a scraggly place with a muddy yard and stunted trees, under gray and threatening skies. For it was here in October 1809 that the great explorer Meriwether Lewis died violently at age thirty-five.

Meriwether Lewis was the Lewis of the Lewis and Clark expedition that traversed the continent from the Mississippi to the Pacific Ocean and back again in the years 1804–1806. It was an heroic feat of exploration that opened the far West to settlement and gave the United States a claim to the Pacific. As a result of this triumph, Lewis was appointed governor of the Louisiana Territory, with headquarters in St. Louis. He was making a trip from the territorial capital to Washington when he made his fatal visit to Grinder's Stand.

What happened there that snuffed out the life of so promising a young man?

SUICIDE?

Meriwether Lewis was a friend of Thomas Jefferson's, who had known Lewis's family in Virginia. When Jefferson became president, he hired the young Lewis, then a lieutenant in the American army, as his personal secretary. It was Jefferson who selected Lewis to head the expedition to the Pacific, and it was Jefferson who later appointed him to the governorship of the Louisiana Territory.

Jefferson was convinced that Lewis committed suicide at Grinder's Stand. In 1813, four years after the tragedy, the Sage of Monticello wrote an introduction to a history of the Lewis and Clark expedition. In it, he described how Lewis, suffering from "depressions of mind," had stopped at the inn, where "he did the deed which plunged his friends into affliction and deprived his country of one of her most valued citizens."

Other writers from the same period tended to support the opinion that Lewis committed suicide. The following are the principal sources:

➤ James Neelly, a government Indian agent, accompanied Lewis on his last trip along the Natchez Trace. About a week after Lewis's death, Neelly wrote a letter to Thomas Jefferson describing what he knew of the circumstances. Neelly's letter to Jefferson remains the most important narrative of the event, and the most direct evidence of Lewis's suicide.

➤ John Brahan, an army captain and friend of Lewis's, wrote letters at about the same time as Neelly to government officers describing the event. Brahan evidently learned much of his information from Neelly.

➤ Gilbert Russell was the commander of Fort Pickering, an army post in Tennessee where Lewis stopped on the way to Grinder's Stand. In 1811, Russell wrote a letter describing what he knew of the demise of Lewis.

➤ Alexander Wilson was the best known of this group. A scientist and writer, Wilson was traveling in Tennessee in 1811 when he stopped at Grinder's Stand to discover the facts of the Lewis tragedy. He wrote a letter about his investigation, which was published in a Philadelphia magazine.

From these sources, it is possible to piece together an account of the alleged suicide. In the late summer of 1809, Lewis left his territorial capital of St. Louis to journey to Washington on official business. He traveled by boat down the Mississippi to Fort Pickering at Chickasaw Bluffs (now Memphis). His original intent was to go on to New Orleans to take a ship to Washington, but because of rumors that war with Britain was about to break out, Lewis decided it would be safer to travel overland, taking the Natchez Trace to Nashville and from there on to Washington.

At Fort Pickering, he met James Neelly, the Indian agent, who was also planning to travel east along the Trace. They decided to ride together, each man accompanied by his servant. In Lewis's baggage were the original journals of his expedition to the West, along with the financial documents he needed for his business in Washington. He carried two pistols, a rifle, a dirk, and a tomahawk.

While camped along the trail, the group lost two of their packhorses. It was agreed that Neelly would remain behind to look for the horses while Lewis rode ahead. It was also agreed, in Neelly's words, that Lewis would stop "at the first house he Came to that was inhabited by white people," and that Neelly would join him there.

At around sunset on October 10, Lewis arrived at Grinder's Stand, where he was met by Mrs. Grinder; her husband was away at the time. Mrs. Grinder served dinner to Lewis. Then, because the governor seemed to be acting in an erratic fashion, she gave him the main cabin to sleep in, while she spent the night in the kitchen, an outbuilding not far from the cabin. The servants, who had arrived after Lewis, were sent to sleep in the barn.

Here are the grotesque events that happened next under the Tennessee moonlight, according to the account by Alexander Wilson:

The kitchen is only a few paces from the room where Lewis was, and the woman Mrs. Grinder being considerably alarmed by the behavior of her guest, could not sleep, but listened to him walking backwards and forwards, she thinks, for several hours, and talking aloud, as she said, "like a lawyer." She then heard the report of a pistol, and something fall heavily to the floor, and the words "O

Lord!'' Immediately afterward she heard another pistol, and in a few minutes she heard him at the door calling out, ''O madam! Give me some water and heal my wounds!''

The logs being open, and unplastered, she saw him stagger back and fall against a stump that stands between the kitchen and the room. He crawled for some distance, and raised himself by the side of a tree, where he sat about a minute. He once more got to the room; afterwards he came to the kitchen door, but did not speak; she then heard him scraping in the bucket with a gourd for water; but it appears that this cooling element was denied the dying man.

The terrified Mrs. Grinder remained locked in the kitchen during this whole time. Only when morning came did she summon the servants from the barn. When they entered the cabin they found that Lewis, still alive, had shot himself with his two pistols. One ball had struck his head; the other had entered his chest, below the breast. The wounded man died shortly thereafter. When Neelly arrived on the scene he arranged for Lewis to be buried nearby.

This, then, is the basic story of Lewis's suicide. Those who believe that Lewis was actually murdered point out that this account is entirely secondhand. None of those who wrote about the incident were present at the time; even Neelly, who was accompanying Lewis on the trip, did not arrive at Grinder's Stand until after Lewis died. Mrs. Grinder was presumably the main source of information for Neelly, Brahan, Russell, and Wilson about what happened at her tavern that night. Those who believe Lewis was murdered believe that she was lying.

THE CASE FOR MURDER

The opinion of Jefferson, Wilson, and the others that Lewis committed suicide was generally accepted in the half century after the event. But there were doubts. It is said that Lewis's mother and other members of the family believed from the start that he had been murdered. There is some evidence that residents who lived in the vicinity of Grinder's Stand (now Lewis County, Tennessee) shared the same opinion. An 1891 article in a Nashville newspaper said:

It has always been the firm belief of the people of this region that Governor Lewis was murdered and robbed. The oldest citizens now living remember the rumor current at the time as to the murder, and it seems that no thought of suicide ever obtained footing here.

The first published statement to the effect that Lewis was murdered appeared in a committee report to the Tennessee legislature during the 1849–1850 session. The committee had been charged with erecting a monument on the site of Lewis's grave, and in the course of its report to the legislature on the progress of the memorial, the committee ventured an opinion on the circumstances of Lewis's death:

> The impression has long prevailed that under the influence of disease of body and mind . . . Gov. Lewis perished by his own hand. It seems to be more probable that he died by the hands of an assassin.

Since then, the view that Lewis met with foul play at Grinder's Stand has gained adherents, to the extent that in the authoritative *Dictionary of American Biography* the entry on Lewis states that he was most likely murdered.

What grounds are there to conclude that it was murder? In large part the evidence comes from newspaper and magazine stories that appeared, mostly in Tennessee, during the late nineteenth and early twentieth century, along with unpublished notes compiled by local Tennessee historians. These accounts describe the reminiscences of elderly men and women about the circumstances of Lewis's death, and they contradict the earlier versions by Jefferson, Lewis, Russell, Brahan, and Wilson. The following are the principal points that emerged from these reminiscences:

➤ It was said that when Lewis's body was found, items were missing, including clothing, money, a watch, and a rifle.

➤ It was said that moccasin tracks and wadding from a firearm were found outside the cabin, proving that the shot came from outside.

➤ It was said that inspection of the remains showed that he had been shot from behind.

➤ It was said that the body was found not in the cabin but by the side of the road, indicating that he was out walking when he was shot.

How reliable are these accounts? Those who believe Lewis was murdered defend them; those who believe Lewis committed suicide dismiss them as folktales, as fluff from Sunday supplements, and as the flawed reminiscences of old folks about stories told them by their grandfathers.

For example, there has been debate over the story claiming that Lewis's body was found at the side of the road. According to local legend, the person who made the discovery was Robert O. Smith, a post rider on the Natchez Trace. Smith told this story in 1875 to a Tennessee attorney, who recounted it in a newspaper article. But skeptics claim that Smith had been born in 1809, the year of Lewis's death.

Another hotly debated piece of local tradition is whether there was a coroner's jury that investigated Lewis's death. If such a jury had actually been convened, it would have been an indication that foul play was suspected at the time. Local traditions are quite strong that such a jury did exist, even down to mentioning the names of some of the jurors. Skeptics point out that no contemporary record of any such jury exists.

Beyond these local traditions, what evidence is there that Lewis was murdered? Those who believe it was murder point to the inconsistencies in the various early accounts of the case. For example, who was present at Grinder's Stand? Neelly's account says when Lewis arrived at the inn, "no person [was] there but a woman," that is, Mrs. Grinder. In the versions by Russell and Wilson, however, Mrs. Grinder has children with her. Census records unearthed by historian Vardis Fisher show that a Robert Grinder, Sr. of Hickman County had some six children living with him in the year 1820. If this was the same Grinder who owned the Stand, it is possible that some of those children were present in 1809.

Similarly, Russell's description of the event says that in addition to shooting himself, Lewis slashed himself with his razors. But the other early accounts by Neelly, Brahan, and Wilson do not mention razor wounds. The words of the dying Lewis also change from version to version. In Neelly's account, the last words of Lewis to his servant are "I have done the business, my good Servant, give me some water." In the Russell version, "he lay down and died with the declaration to the Boy that he had killed himself to deprive his enemies of the pleasure and honor of doing it." In the Wilson version, he says, "I am no coward; but I am so strong, so hard to die."

There is also confusion about the degree of damage to Lewis's forehead. According to Russell, the shot only made a "furrow." But according to Wilson, "a piece of his forehead was blown off, and had exposed the brains."

Those who believe Lewis was murdered say that these different versions show that Mrs. Grinder made up her story and then kept changing it. The confusion about what Mrs. Grinder said is complicated by a late bit of testimony. In 1845 an article appeared in a New York newspaper reporting an interview with Mrs. Grinder conducted by a person described only as "a teacher in the Cherokee Nation." This interview introduced yet more conflicting details into the story. For example, Mrs. Grinder told the schoolteacher that when Lewis was at the inn he threatened to kill a group of travelers who tried to stop there.

MALINDA AND POLLY

Many years after Lewis's death, reports came out of Tennessee of two witnesses who claimed to have been at Grinder's Stand on the fatal night.

The first of these accounts appeared in 1891. James D. Park, an attorney from Franklin, Tennessee, wrote an article for the Nashville *Daily American,* in which he related the reminiscences of a Mrs. Christina B. Anthony, age seventy-seven, who lived two miles away from where Grinder's Stand once stood. Mrs. Anthony told Park that many years before she had known one Polly Spencer, a White woman, who, according to Mrs. Anthony, had been a fifteen-year-old hired girl at Grinder's on the night Lewis died. According to Polly (via Mrs. Anthony), she had been washing dishes in the kitchen when she heard a shot fired in Lewis's room. Rushing into the room, Polly and members of the Grinder family found Lewis dead; all of his money had been taken except for twenty-five cents. Polly said further that the owner of the inn, Robert Grinder, was suspected of having committed the crime.

Malinda's name appeared in a 1904 article in the *American Historical Magazine* by another Tennessee attorney, J. H. Moore.

Moore claimed that some years before he had interviewed an aged Black woman, Malinda, who as a twelve- or thirteen-year-old girl, had been a slave at Grinder's Stand. Malinda told Moore a story that paralleled the original accounts of suicide: Governor Lewis came to the inn, two shots were fired in the middle of the night, Lewis begged for water, Mrs. Grinder and the servants entered the room and found that the governor had shot himself, and Lewis died soon after.

What evidence is there to support the existence of Polly Spencer or Malinda? Vardis Fisher, after examining early records, found that there was in fact a slave named Malinda who was later sold by Robert Grinder, Sr. Again, this may well be the same Robert Grinder who owned the Stand. But there is no proof that Malinda was present at the Stand on the night of the murder.

There is no evidence at all for Polly Spencer. Fisher doubted that the Grinders would have been able to afford a White domestic servant, particularly if they had the slave girl Malinda. One writer, Elliott Coues, criticized Polly's story as "second hand, indirect, and circumstantial;" the recollection of a woman nearly eighty years old.

THE MIND OF MERIWETHER LEWIS

Thomas Jefferson was convinced that Lewis shot himself in a fit of depression. In his introduction to the account of the Lewis and Clark expedition, he described Lewis's mental history:

> Governor Lewis had, from early life, been subject to hypo-chondriac affections. It was a constitutional disposition in all the nearer branches of the family of his name, and was more immediately inherited by him from his father. They had not, however, been so strong as to give uneasiness to his family. While he lived with me in Washington I observed at times sensible depressions of mind; but knowing their constitutional source, I estimated their course by what I had seen in the family. During his Western Expedition, the constant exertion which that required of all the faculties of body and mind, suspended these distressing affections; but after his establishment at St. Louis in seden-

tary occupations, they returned upon him with redoubled vigour, and began seriously to alarm his friends.

Major Russell added more detail. The officer wrote in 1811 that when Lewis arrived at Fort Pickering, he was in a state of derangement, and that crew members on the boat that brought the governor to the fort said that their passenger had twice tried to kill himself. Russell said further that he confined Lewis to the fort until, after six days, he seemed to have recovered. Lewis then proceeded along the Natchez Trace accompanied by Neely. But according to Russell, after three or four days on the trail, Lewis "was again affected with the same mental disease."

More information on Lewis's mental condition comes from Neely's 1809 letter. While traveling together, Neely found Lewis to be "in very bad health," and at times "deranged in mind." Neely reported that when Lewis arrived at Grinder's Stand, the frightened Mrs. Grinder found the governor "deranged."

A confirmation of Lewis's mental illness comes from a September 28, 1809 letter from a Captain James House to a friend in the Louisiana Territory. House reported that he had learned that Lewis had arrived at Fort Pickering in a "state of mental derangement—that he had made several attempts to put an end to his own existence." The letter continues that the commander of the post, Russell, had put Lewis under watch "to prevent his committing violence on himself."

Those who think Lewis committed suicide believe that his personal circumstances aggravated his mental illness. As governor of the Louisiana Territory he faced serious political squabbles from other territorial officials and from rival groups of settlers. He was also caught up in a dispute with federal officials in Washington over his financial accounts. Because the government had refused to reimburse him for certain expenses he had incurred as governor, Lewis was now personally liable for these debts. His creditors, learning of his difficulty, were hounding him for money. His problem was compounded by failed efforts at land speculation. Lewis estimated that he owed some four thousand dollars, an astronomically high amount in that era. Indeed, his purpose in traveling to Washington was to settle his dispute with the government bookkeepers.

Those who believe Lewis did not die by suicide admit that he was having a difficult time, but they express doubt that his troubles were enough to drive him to madness. They note that his notebooks and letters from that period seem logical and well organized and that such disputes between territorial governors and the bureaucracy in Washington were not uncommon. As one murder theorist put it, if financial trouble with the federal government drove men to suicide, "the streets of Washington would be littered with corpses."

The murder theorists agree that Lewis does appear to have been ill on his trip to Washington, but they attribute it to malaria or some other physical ailment. They say that almost all accounts of Lewis's madness and self-destructive urge date from after his death, and therefore may have been greatly exaggerated in order to provide some justification for what appeared to be suicide.

One novel theory advanced in 1994 supported the idea of suicide. An epidemiologist, Reimert Thorolf Ravenholt, speculated that Lewis contracted syphilis through intercourse with an Indian woman on his expedition to the West. By the time of his suicide, said Ravenholt, the disease had damaged Lewis's nervous system and produced the mental disorder that caused him to take his own life.

SUSPECTS

If Meriwether Lewis was murdered at Grinder's Stand, who did it? Those who support the murder theory identify the following suspects:

➤ *Robert Grinder.* The adherents of the murder school believe that Mrs. Grinder, contrary to the story she gave out, may not have been alone at the inn when Lewis arrived. Her husband, they say, may have been there, and may have killed and robbed the apparently well-to-do stranger. There was a local legend in Tennessee that Grinder was brought to trial and acquitted. According to Polly Spencer, "Old Grinder, who was of Indian blood, was at once suspected of the murder, ran away, was captured on Cane Creek, brought back and tried, but the proof not being positive he was released." Other local rumors hold that after the death of Lewis, Grinder began to display great wealth.

➤ *Pernier.* The personal servant who accompanied Lewis from St. Louis is a shadowy figure; his name is variously given as Pernier, Pernia, Pierney, Purney, or Pyrna, and he is sometimes described as a Spaniard, sometimes as a Frenchman. Those who believe in Pernier's guilt say that he was bitter because he was owed back wages by his master. In the schoolteacher's interview with Mrs. Grinder, she makes the remarkable statement that on the morning after the shooting she found Pernier wearing Lewis's clothes and carrying his watch. When asked what he was doing with this property, he allegedly told Mrs. Grinder that his master had given it to him. There is a story handed down in the Lewis family that Pernier was seen later in a Mississippi town with Lewis's property. Yet another family legend holds that he visited Lewis's mother, who accused him of murdering her son, and that he subsequently committed suicide out of remorse for what he had done.

It is sometimes charged that Pernier disappeared right after his master's death. But this is incorrect. We know that he was loaned money by Neelly, and made his way back East. Jefferson met with Pernier less than two months after Lewis's death, and presumably spoke with him about the events at Grinder's Stand.

➤ *James Neelly.* Was Neelly something less than a friend to Lewis as the two rode together on the Natchez Trace? Critics have asked why, if he was concerned about his friend's health, he remained behind to search for the pack-horses while he let Lewis ride on ahead. It was said that Neelly was a heavy drinker and that he encouraged Lewis to imbibe alcohol while they were on the trail. After Lewis's death, Neelly asked to be reimbursed for money he claimed he had loaned the governor, and he was accused of taking illegal possession of Lewis's pistols and other property.

➤ *General James Wilkinson.* One writer, David Leon Chandler, theorized that when Lewis became governor of the Louisiana Territory, he uncovered double-dealing and fraud by his predecessor in that post, General James Wilkinson (the same Wilkinson whose role in the Burr conspiracy is described in the previous chapter). Chandler

believed that Wilkinson had Lewis assassinated in order
to prevent him from revealing these secrets.

➤ *An anonymous robber.* Those who believe it was murder
say that the Natchez Trace in that era was a dangerous
place, where robbery and murder were common. One
writer speaks of "those nameless horrors, inflicted by
noted bandits, continually harassing, pillaging, and murdering those traversing the 'Trace.' " Lewis, a territorial
governor traveling with a servant and packhorse, would
have been a tempting target. But those who believe Lewis
committed suicide argue that the Trace was not dangerous
by the year 1809.

Dawson A. Phelps, a National Park Service historian, described the Trace:

The mail passed over it regularly. No robbery had been
reported for years. At least seven inns, and probably more,
had sprung up to accommodate the numerous wayfarers
at fairly regular intervals. It was the only overland route
between two territorial capitals and the national capital,
and many men of prominence traveled that way.

Weighing the Evidence

The arguments used to support the theory that Lewis was murdered rest on two main supports; first, the weaknesses in the
early accounts of his death, and second, the strong local Tennessee tradition that he was murdered.

It is true that the letters that comprise the foundation of the
suicide theory—from Neelly, Wilson, and others written within
two years of Lewis's death—have shortcomings. None of the
writers were present at Grinder's Stand when Lewis died, and
comparing one writer to another does reveal contradictions.
Moreover, they are based to a large extent on the statements of
Mrs. Grinder—although not exclusively so, since the servants
were also on the scene that night, and Neelly may have spoken
to them as well as to the proprietress.

But the contradictions among the letters are not really vital. While there is disagreement about the number of persons present at the Stand; the nature of the gunshot wounds; Lewis's exact words; the chronology of events; and whether Lewis slashed himself with razors, the main thrust remains the same: Lewis arrived at the inn displaying signs of madness and in the course of the night shot himself with his own pistols.

What about the later Tennessee legends? Most of these did not appear in print until the 1890s, well over four-fifths of a century after Lewis's death. The vast majority are based not on direct testimony but on the reminiscences of what was learned secondhand from aged storytellers. A historian who supported the suicide theory, Dawson A. Phelps, dismissed these accounts as part of a "My Grandpa Told Me" tradition that, in Phelps's words, displayed "a total lack of evidential value." While Phelps was willing to accept as plausible the story that a coroner's jury was formed, he rejected the remainder of the handed-down tales.

The testimony of Polly Spencer and Malinda falls into this category of local tradition. The Malinda account, which supports the suicide theory, is actually more credible than the Polly account, since there is evidence that a slave named Malinda was owned by the Grinder family.

Perhaps the strongest argument for suicide is the abundant evidence that Lewis was deranged. This is a thread that runs through many different sources, and therefore seems highly probable. Jefferson, Neelly, Russell, Brahan, Wilson, the unnamed schoolteacher, and the elusive Malinda all mention it.

One important clue is the letter from Captain House that reported Lewis's arrival at Fort Pickering. The gossipy House conveyed the news that Lewis had attempted to kill himself on the journey by boat to the fort, and that the commander of the fort had confined Lewis to prevent him from harming himself. What makes this letter significant is the date: September 28, 1809—almost two weeks prior to Lewis's arrival at Grinder's Stand. Of all the sources that deal with Lewis's mental affliction, this is the only one that dates from *before* his death. It offers irrefutable proof that Lewis's suicidal urge was not something invented or exaggerated following his demise.

So in sum, the weight of the evidence is that Meriwether Lewis committed suicide. He had a history of mental illness, which was exacerbated by the prospect of crushing debt and failure. He had attempted to take his own life before, and at Grinder's Stand he was finally successful.

Most of Lewis's admirers in the nineteenth century found this hard to accept. The Tennessean James D. Park refused to believe that Lewis would take his own life:

> He was too brave and conscientious in the discharge of every duty, public and private; too conspicuous a person in the eyes of his country, and crowned with too many laurels, to cowardly sneak out of the world by the back way, a self-murderer.

William Clark, who accompanied Lewis on the great expedition to the West, named his eldest son Meriwether Lewis Clark in honor of his friend. In later life, the young Clark wrote that the allegation of suicide was a "stigma upon the fair name I have the honor to bear."

Many of those who argue that Lewis was murdered seem to be motivated by the same sentiment—that suicide was a dishonorable act that irreparably damaged one's reputation. They seem anxious to expunge this blot on the name of Lewis by denying that he took his own life.

Thomas Jefferson, too, was a friend and admirer of Lewis. To Jefferson's credit, he was able to accept the idea that the great explorer committed suicide without regarding it as a stain on the man's honor. To Jefferson, it was a tragic end to a promising life. By leading an expedition to the great West, said Jefferson, Lewis had extended to the American people a vast new country, "which their sons are destined to fill with arts, with science, with freedom and happiness." Despite the manner in which Meriwether Lewis ended his life, said Jefferson, he was a man "whom posterity will declare not to have lived in vain."

6

DID ABRAHAM LINCOLN
LOVE ANN RUTLEDGE?

From age twenty-two to twenty-eight, Abraham Lincoln lived in New Salem, Illinois, a frontier village on the Sangamon River. During his six years in New Salem, 1831 to 1837, the lanky young man worked as store clerk, surveyor, postmaster, and militia captain. He studied for the law, and he was elected to the state legislature by his fellow citizens. Lincoln's biographers say that by the time he left New Salem to take up a law practice in Springfield, he had changed from an aimless youth to a man with ambitions for greater things, and with a sense that he might achieve a place in history.

Was part of that change in personality due to his doomed relationship with a young woman of New Salem named Ann Rutledge? Many of those who have written about Lincoln believe so. This tragic love story has many variations, but the following are the key elements:

Ann Rutledge, born on January 17, 1813, was the third child of ten born to James and Mary Rutledge. Her father had been one of the founders of the New Salem settlement, and he owned a tavern where Lincoln sometimes boarded. Ann was an attractive and intelligent young woman, much sought after by the young men of the village. She and Lincoln fell in love. When the Rutledge family moved to a farm six miles away, Lincoln visited frequently to court her.

But there was a complication. Ann had earlier promised to marry John McNamar, a well-to-do local man. McNamar had gone back east to take care of family business. No one knew when he would return, and his letters to Ann became infrequent. Ann was torn by her love for Lincoln and her duty to McNamar. She agreed to marry Lincoln, but decided that she could not announce her engagement until McNamar returned and she could inform him of her change of heart.

Before this could be resolved, Ann died in August 1835 at age twenty-two. The cause is sometimes attributed to her mental confusion, to "brain fever," to malaria, or to typhoid fever. Ann's death affected Lincoln deeply—perhaps even driving him to the edge of suicide. He was finally consoled by his New Salem friends, but the death of his beloved Ann haunted him for the rest of his life, giving him an edge of melancholy. He was never able to experience true love with another woman again, and he turned away from domestic concerns toward public life.

Such is the story that appears in American history and biography, as well as in novels, plays, and movies. An epitaph written by the poet Edgar Lee Masters expresses the popular view of Ann Rutledge:

> *Out of me unworthy and unknown*
> *The vibrations of deathless music,*
> *"With malice toward none, with charity for all."*
> *Out of me the forgiveness of millions toward millions,*
> *And the beneficent fact of a nation*
> *Shining with justice and truth.*
> *I am Ann Rutledge who sleep beneath these weeds.*
> *Beloved in life of Abraham Lincoln,*
> *Wedded to him, not through union,*
> *But through separation.*
> *Bloom forever, O Republic,*
> *From the dust of my bosom!*

Some elements of this saga are true. There was an Ann Rutledge who lived and died in New Salem, and she undoubtedly knew Lincoln in that little community. But did they love each other, did she promise to marry him, and did her death so profoundly affect him that it changed the course of his life?

WILLIAM HERNDON AND THE ANN RUTLEDGE LEGEND

William Herndon was Lincoln's friend and, for seventeen years, his law partner. After Lincoln's assassination in 1865, Herndon set himself the goal of writing the definitive biography of his friend—a task that took him another twenty-four years. He corresponded with and interviewed dozens of men and women who had known Lincoln, and compiled lengthy notes on the details of Lincoln's life.

It was Herndon who gave the story of Ann Rutledge to the world. He first described her relationship to Lincoln in a lecture he delivered in Springfield, Illinois, in November 1866, and it appeared again in his three-volume biography of Lincoln published in 1889. The critics of Herndon say that although he presented the story as fact, it was in large part his own creation. Herndon had a deep romantic streak, say his critics, that caused him to magnify the rumor of Lincoln's relationship with Rutledge into a Victorian-style sentimental melodrama. Here is how Herndon described Lincoln's supposed anguish after the death of Rutledge:

> He slept not, he ate not, joyed not. This he did until his body became emaciated and weak, and gave way. His mind wandered from its throne. In his imagination he muttered words to her he loved. His mind, his reason, somewhat dethroned, walked out of itself along the uncolumned air, and kissed and embraced the shadows and illusions of the heated brain.

The critics say that Herndon sought to deify Lincoln; to create a portrait of the martyred president that would withstand attack from his enemies. He also had a particular dislike for Lincoln's widow, Mary Todd Lincoln. His statement that Lincoln never truly loved another woman after Ann's death infuriated Mrs. Lincoln, who called Herndon "a dirty dog." One mid–twentieth century critic, historian David Donald, said Herndon's account of Ann Rutledge may have been "an unconscious rationalization of his dislike for Mary Lincoln."

The defenders of Herndon say these charges are unfair. They believe that he was committed to searching out the truth about Lincoln and that he used his training as a lawyer to sift out the falsehood.

THE NEW SALEM WITNESSES

The voluminous records kept by Herndon of his research are the basis for the Rutledge story. Included in those records are letters he received from former residents of New Salem and notes of his interviews with them, mostly obtained in the years 1865–67.

The critics argue that these witness accounts are unreliable; that the New Salemites were remembering events that had occurred thirty years before, about a town that had since been abandoned, and concerning two people—Lincoln and Rutledge—who had since died. They say that this testimony was woven from flawed memories and wishful thinking, unsupported by any hard evidence from the time the romance supposedly occurred. Lincoln biographer James Randall, the sharpest critic of the Rutledge legend, described much of the testimony as "second- or third-hand, consisting of inference or supposition as to what 'must have been' true." Another critic, Paul Angle, suggested that the former residents of New Salem sought to fasten "all possible glamour to that forgotten village."

The critics say further that the story grew with each telling. According to David Donald:

> The more often old men and women repeated their tales the surer they became of the whole story. The hundreds of papers, letters, and interviews on the Ann Rutledge theme preserved in [Herndon's notes] show that the legend grew in color and in detail and that over the years the story crystallized from a floating rumor into a fixed romance.

Those who believe the story of Rutledge and Lincoln defend the New Salem witnesses as reliable sources, even though Herndon took their testimony decades after the fact. Said one defender, John Walsh, in his 1993 book *The Shadows Rise*:

> Thirty years is not really too long a period in which to hold, clear and undiminished, the memory of colorful and critical events. Where witnesses have remained close to the original site, have kept in touch with each other, and have passed the intervening years talking over how things

were "back then," an astonishing amount of factual truth
may be preserved.

One modern-day supporter of the Rutledge story, Douglas
Wilson, a professor of English at Knox College, read through
Herndon's notes and identified twenty-four witnesses who had
lived in New Salem and who had testified about the relationship between Lincoln and Rutledge. Wilson examined the account of each of these witnesses with three questions in mind,
and found remarkable unanimity of opinion:

	Yes	No	No Opinion
Did Lincoln love or court Ann Rutledge?	22	0	2
Did Lincoln grieve excessively at Ann's death?	17	0	7
Did they have an understanding about marriage?	15	2	7

But critics of the Rutledge story attack the credibility of these
witnesses. Mentor Graham, for example, had been the only
schoolteacher in New Salem and had instructed both Lincoln
and Rutledge. According to Herndon's rough notes, Graham
recalled in 1866 that "Lincoln and she was engaged—Lincoln
told me so—she intimated to me the same: He Lincoln told me
that he felt like committing suicide often, but I told him God
had a higher purpose." The defenders of the Rutledge legend
regard Graham's testimony as important, since by his account
he learned the story from both Lincoln and Ann.

But the skeptics say that Graham's memory may have been
flawed. He told Herndon on another occasion that in the years
1819 to 1820 he had been in Kentucky and had often seen the
young Lincoln. This could not have been the case, since Lincoln
moved from Kentucky in 1816. In his interview notes, Herndon
said of Graham that he was "cranky—flighty—at times nearly
non compos mentis [mentally unstable]—but good & honest."

The critics point out other shortcomings in the testimony of
the New Salem witnesses. James Short, for example, said, "I
did not know of any engagement or tender passages between
Mr L and Miss R at the time," but Short assumed that they
must have been engaged simply because Lincoln was "so much
affected and grieved so hardly" after she died. Another witness,

Henry McHenry, agreed that Lincoln seemed depressed, but
thought it was due to the pressure of his study of the law.

THE RUTLEDGE KIN

The members of the Rutledge family constitute an important
group among Herndon's twenty-four New Salem witnesses.
Robert B. Rutledge was Ann's younger brother. In response to
an 1866 letter from Herndon, Robert interviewed relatives and
furnished Herndon with a lengthy written statement containing
the family's reminiscences of Lincoln. Part of this statement af-
firmed the love between Lincoln and Ann.

The critics of the Rutledge story charge that this family testimony is deeply flawed. They say that the surviving Rutledges
wanted to magnify the family's connection with the martyred
president, so they exaggerated the relationship between Lincoln
and Ann far out of proportion. In his statement Robert said
he had received a letter from another relative, James McGrady
Rutledge, interpreting a statement Ann had made to him. Historian James G. Randall said sarcastically of this passage: "Here
is one person reporting what another person had written him
concerning what that person recollected that he had inferred
from something Ann had causally said to him more than thirty-
one years before!"

Randall also pointed out that in a letter to Herndon, Robert
Rutledge expressed doubts about the validity of his recollections:

> Many of my statements [Robert Rutledge wrote] are made
> from memory with the aid of association of events; and
> should you discover that the date, location and circum-
> stances, of the events here named should be contradictory
> to those named from other sources, I beg of you to con-
> sider well the testimony in each case, and make up your
> history from those statements, which may appear to you
> best fitted to remove all doubt as to their correctness.

The defenders of the Rutledge legend reply that the criticism
by Randall and other skeptics is not warranted; that the living
relatives of Ann were at first reluctant to talk to Herndon, and
that when they finally did, their statements were carefully made
and well researched.

THE *MENARD AXIS* ARTICLE

On February 15, 1862, an article appeared in an obscure Illinois newspaper, the *Menard Axis*. The article was a brief biography of Lincoln, and how he had risen from early hardship. Among other topics, it touched on the relationship with Ann Rutledge, without mentioning her name:

> He [Lincoln] chanced to meet with a lady who to him seemed lovely, angelic, and the height of perfection. Forgetful of all things else, he could think or dream of naught but her. His feelings he soon made her acquainted with, and was delighted with a reciprocation. This to him was perfect happiness, and with uneasy anxiety he waited the arrival of the day when the twain should be one flesh. But that day was doomed never to arrive. Disease came upon this lovely beauty, and she sickened and died. The youth had wrapped his heart with hers, and this was more than he could bear. He saw her to her grave, and as the cold clods fell upon the coffin, he sincerely wished that he too had been enclosed within it. Melancholy came upon him; he was changed and sad. His friends detected strange conduct and a flighty imagination. New circumstances changed his thoughts and at length he partially forgot that which for a time had consumed his mind.

The defenders of the Rutledge legend attach great importance to this account, which predates by four years Herndon's unveiling of the love story. The author of the article and editor of the paper, John Hill, was the son of a resident of New Salem who knew both Lincoln and Ann Rutledge. The defenders say that this article provides an independent confirmation of Herndon, and proves that the story of Lincoln's love for Rutledge was a long-standing tradition among those who had lived in New Salem. Hill later said of this article, "Every item in it I believe to have been true . . . I made good inquiry before writing & think I arrived at the truth."

But the critics find fault with Hill's newspaper story, regarding it as an unfriendly attack on Lincoln; moreover, it contained inaccuracies elsewhere and was published decades after the event.

ISAAC COGDAL'S CHAT WITH LINCOLN

For the Rutledge legend to have credibility, it would help to have some confirmation from Lincoln's own lips. But by Randall's account, there appears to be "no thoroughly verified utterance by Lincoln, written or oral, in which Ann Rutledge is even mentioned."

But those who believe the Rutledge story say that there is such a statement. The source is Isaac Cogdal, a Springfield, Illinois, lawyer. Cogdal, like Lincoln, had begun his life as a poor laborer, and he and Lincoln's friendship dated back to their younger days in New Salem. At some unknown point in the months between Lincoln's election to the presidency in November 1860 and his departure from Springfield for Washington in February 1861, the president-elect invited Cogdal for a friendly talk about old times. According to what Cogdal later told Herndon, the conversation turned to Ann Rutledge. Cogdal asked Lincoln point-blank: "Is it true that you fell in love with and courted Ann Rutledge?"

According to Cogdal, Lincoln replied "It is true—true indeed. I did. I have loved the name of Rutledge to this day. I have kept my mind on their movements ever since, and love them dearly."

Cogdal then asked, "Abe, is it true that you ran a little wild about the matter?" To which Lincoln replied: "I did really. I ran off the track. It was my first. I loved the woman dearly. She was a handsome girl; would have made a good, loving wife; was natural and quite intellectual, though not highly educated. I did honestly and truly love the girl, and think often, often, of her now."

The critics of the Rutledge legend attempt to poke holes in Cogdal's startling account of Lincoln's confession. First, they note that like all the reminiscences of the affair, Cogdal was recalling the conversation to Herndon many years after the fact, and whatever Lincoln may have actually said may have been embellished by Cogdal, and embellished still further by Herndon. Second, they argue that nobody referred to Lincoln to his face as "Abe." He was instead addressed by his last name, even by his Springfield friends. Third, the critics believe the whole tenor of the conversation is uncharacteristic of Lincoln. He was not a man who revealed his deepest feelings to others, and he would have been particularly unlikely to have said anything like this at the moment he was about to assume the presidency in a nation torn by the worst crisis in its history. To have confessed that he once went "off the track" would have been a politically damaging statement.

But the defenders of the Rutledge legend believe that Cogdal's account is true. They argue that Lincoln was indeed called "Abe" by some of his oldest friends. Another possibility is that in the notes of his conversation with Cogdal, Herndon was using "Abe" as a shorthand abbreviation for Abraham Lincoln, and that in the final version it came out as Abe. And if the nature of the conversation seemed atypical, it was an atypical time for Lincoln. Precisely because he was about to leave his familiar Springfield for the cauldron of national politics, he might have been in a nostalgic, contemplative mood. It was in this same period after the presidential election that he made a point of saying good-bye to old friends and of thinking about old times. As he said in his farewell address to his Springfield neighbors, "the strange, chequered past seems to crowd now upon my mind."

Missing Evidence

Those who criticize the Rutledge story have the difficult task of trying to prove the negative argument—that is, that nothing happened between Lincoln and Rutledge. To support their case, they argue that if the story were true, it would appear somewhere else besides the reminiscences of the New Salem witnesses. For example, Ann Rutledge's name does not appear in any surviving writing of Abraham Lincoln, and except for the reminiscences of Isaac Cogdal, there is no record that he mentioned her name to any of his friends in later life. Yet Lincoln did write about other women he had known. One of these women was Mary Owens, whom he courted in the fall of 1836, about a year after the death of Ann Rutledge. They had talked of marrying, but Lincoln eventually backed out. Several letters from Lincoln to Mary Owens survive, along with a humorous letter he wrote to a friend about his close scrape with marriage.

Critics of the Rutledge story question why, if Ann was the love of Lincoln's life, he so quickly began a courtship of another woman. Asked historian Paul Angle, "Does a man give evidence of having been grief-stricken to the point of insanity by the death of his fiancee when within a year he proposes to another woman?" And why does Mary Owens, a passing fancy, enter his correspondence, but not Ann Rutledge? The defenders reply that the relationship with Mary Owens only shows that Lincoln's grieving for Ann had finally come to an end. Why, ask the critics, did Lincoln never mention the story to Joshua Speed, perhaps his closest friend, to whom he confided many of his private thoughts? After Herndon first made public the Rutledge story in 1866, Speed wrote a letter to Herndon about the account of Lincoln's love for Ann in which he said, "It is all new to me." But the defenders of the legend note that in the same letter to Herndon, Speed expressed a willingness to believe the story.

The critics also point to the testimony of one of the key figures in the Rutledge-Lincoln story, John McNamar. McNamar was Lincoln's rival, the New Salem man who was engaged to Ann Rutledge but who left the settlement to go east and who returned to New Salem after Ann's death. McNamar wrote to Herndon, "I never heard any person say that Mr. Lincoln addressed Miss Ann Rutledge in terms of courtship, neither her own family nor my acquaintances otherwise." Surely, say the critics, McNamar would have heard such gossip if any existed.

Another bit of negative evidence is a letter that Matthew Marsh, a resident of New Salem, sent to his parents in New Hampshire in September 1835. Marsh thanked his parents for sending him one hundred dollars, and noted casually that the previous day he had walked into the post office and picked up the money. "The Post Master Mr. Lincoln is very careless about leaving his office open & unlocked during the day—half the time I go in and get my papers etc. without anyone being there as was the case yesterday." Marsh went on to say that Lincoln was "a clever fellow and a particular friend of mine," who would arrange to have Marsh's reply sent to his parents free of charge, a small violation of postal laws. Lincoln did so, "franking" the letter by signing his name on the upper right corner on September 22. Two days later, Lincoln surveyed a tract of land that Marsh had purchased, and signed the survey.

Marsh's visit to the post office occurred only three weeks after Ann's death; a time when, according to the legend, Lincoln was still stricken by grief for his lost love. The critics ask, If

Lincoln was so overcome, how was it that he was able to attend his usual business as postmaster and surveyor?

The defenders of the Rutledge tradition say that this episode in fact provides a small clue that Lincoln was not functioning normally. The fact that he had left the post office unattended and that he carelessly violated the postal laws by franking a friend's letter, said John Walsh, "unerringly reveal the operation of those subtle distortions of character often incident to spells of clinical melancholia."

Hints of Love

Because the Lincoln-Rutledge relationship is so shrouded in doubt, the defenders of the story emphasize small clues that help to make their case.

One of these clues is a postscript to a July 27, 1835 letter from Ann's brother, David, to their father. David Rutledge was away at school in Jacksonville, Illinois, and he was writing home to report on how he was faring. He added a note to the letter addressed to sister Ann: "I am glad to hear that you have a notion of comeing [sic] to school, and I earnestly recommend to you that you would spare no time from improving your education and mind." According to local legend, Ann had planned to further her education at a women's school in order to make herself a fit wife for the aspiring lawyer, Lincoln. David's postscript to Ann lends credence to that legend.

Another clue is provided by Lincoln's love of the poem "Mortality" by William Knox. Lincoln committed the fifty-six-line poem to memory, recited it to friends, and twice wrote it out. This lugubrious poem concerns the fleeting nature of life, and how soon death and the grave overcome us. One verse runs:

> The maid on whose cheek, on whose brow, in whose eye
> Shone beauty and pleasure, her triumphs are by;
> And the memory of those who loved her and praised,
> Are alike from the minds of the living erased.

Lincoln himself wrote poems, one of which was published in an Illinois newspaper in 1847:

> *O Memory! thou midway world*
> *'Twixt earth and Paradise,*
> *Where things decayed and loved ones lost*
> *In dreamy shadows rise,*
> *And freed from all that's earthly vile,*
> *Seem hallowed, pure, and bright,*
> *Like scenes in some enchanted isle*
> *All bathed in liquid light.*

Those who believe in the Rutledge story say that these poems demonstrate the enduring impact of Ann's death on Lincoln.

A more concrete link between Lincoln and Rutledge is a copy of a grammar textbook originally in the possession of the Rutledge family and now in the rare book room of the Library of Congress. The book is an 1828 edition of *Kirkham's Grammar*, which seems to have passed from hand to hand in New Salem. One of those believed to have owned the book was Lincoln; a receipt he signed is pasted in the book. According to tradition, Lincoln walked eight miles to obtain the grammar. A half-dozen other names, mostly New Salem residents, are written in it as well. One of these is Ann's: on the title page is the handwritten inscription "Ann M. Rutledge is now learning Grammar."

John Walsh, a modern supporter of the Rutledge story, admitted that this book does not prove a romance between Ann and Abe, but, said Walsh, it is the closest that any document from the 1830s comes to linking the names of the village girl and the future president. It also seems to demonstrate that Ann was pursuing her education, as she had supposedly promised Lincoln.

LOVE LETTERS FOUND?

In the late 1920s, the prestigious *Atlantic Monthly* provided an apparent solution to the Ann Rutledge controversy. In a series of three articles published from December 1928 to February 1929, the magazine printed excerpts from a collection of newly unearthed nineteenth-century documents, which included love letters exchanged between Rutledge and Lincoln.

"At last," trumpeted the *Atlantic*, "after nearly a century during which their existence was always suspected and hoped for, appear the priceless documents which lift the veil shrouding

the love affair between Abraham Lincoln and the young Ann
Rutledge."

The collection was the property of Miss Wilma Frances Minor
of San Diego, who said the documents had been handed down
in her family. The *Atlantic* had been contacted by Miss Minor,
who wanted to tell the world about the Lincoln-Rutledge romance. The magazine responded enthusiastically, promising
Miss Minor thousands of dollars for the rights to publish articles
and a book about the collection.

The editors of the magazine were convinced of the authenticity of the documents, as were some prominent experts on Lincoln, including popular writer and poet Carl Sandburg. Part of
the allure of the papers was Miss Minor herself, a young, attractive woman who had a talent for captivating male editors and
historians. But there was other proof: a chemical analysis
showed that the documents were written on nineteenth-
century paper.

There were doubters, however, among whom was Lincoln
expert Paul M. Angle, who was the first to publicly question
the authenticity of the Minor collection. One item in the collection was an 1834 letter, supposedly from Lincoln to a friend,
which reported that some neighbors were leaving for a "place
in Kansas." But, said Angle, that territory was not open to settlement at that time, and the word "Kansas" did not come into
common use until years later. In the same letter Lincoln referred
to land in an Illinois township as "Section 40," but the township
sections in the western United States were numbered only from
1 to 36; there could be no such thing as a section numbered 40.
In a letter supposedly from Ann, the schoolteacher Mentor Graham was referred to incorrectly as "Newton Graham." In another passage, Ann, who died in 1835, refered to a penmanship
book that was not published until 1848.

Angle also found that the handwriting and style in the Minor
collection did not match Lincoln's authenticated letters from the
same period.

Angle's conclusions won out, and the contrite *Atlantic* published an article he wrote exposing the fraud. Confronted by
the evidence, Miss Minor confessed that she had written the
material herself on paper ripped from old books, although she
said in her defense that Abraham Lincoln and Ann Rutledge
had sent her messages from beyond the grave through a spiritu-
alist. The Rutledge-Lincoln case has produced other forgeries,

such as a stone from New Salem supposedly inscribed with Lincoln's and Rutledge's names and the date of their engagement.

Weighing the Evidence

Unlike some other questions asked in this book—for example, whether or not Meriwether Lewis committed suicide—the question of whether or not Lincoln loved Ann Rutledge does not require a stark yes or no answer. The defenders and the critics of the Lincoln-Rutledge legend are not separated by an unbridgeable chasm. Paul Angle cast grave doubt on the evidence of the story, but conceded that it could have happened; that Lincoln and Ann may have formed a mutual attachment and possibly were in love.

Even the severest critic, James G. Randall, did not dismiss the story as impossible, but only as unsupported by the evidence. Observed Randall: "Whatever may have been the true situation as to Lincoln and Ann, that situation seems now well nigh unrecoverable. As to a romantic attachment, it has not been *dis*proved. It is more correct to characterize it as *un*proved." Because the story is based on tradition, said Randall, "it does not belong in a recital of those Lincoln episodes which one presents as unquestioned reality."

The modern defenders of the Rutledge legend, such as Douglas Wilson and John Simon, do not claim that the story is unquestionable reality, but only that it carries the same weight as other episodes in Lincoln's life that have become generally accepted by Lincoln scholars. One of those generally accepted episodes is the wrestling match that took place between Lincoln and Jack Armstrong, the leader of a group of New Salem young men. The episode is often mentioned in biographies of Lincoln as a pivotal step in Lincoln's rise; by battling Armstrong he earned the respect of New Salemites. The documentation for the wrestling story is every bit as belated and contradictory as the Rutledge story; indeed, both have been constructed from the accounts collected by Herndon.

Wilson argued that much else we believe about Lincoln's life is equally shaky:

Virtually everything we know about Lincoln as a child and as a young man—his incessant reading and self-education, his storytelling, his honesty, his interest in politics, and so forth—comes exclusively from the recollections of the people who knew him. Non-contemporary, subjective, often unable to be confirmed even by the recollections of others, to say nothing of contemporary documents, this evidence is sheer reminiscence.

Wilson's argument was that those who attack the Rutledge legend are using impossibly high standards for establishing the truth of this historical episode, standards that are not applied to other elements of Lincoln's biography.

In sum, the critics of the Rutledge legend are not saying that the episode never happened, and the defenders of the legend are not saying that it is proved beyond doubt. The debate is more a question of shading.

The problem seems to rest with Herndon. We owe a debt to Herndon for collecting the evidence, but he deserves some blame for taking the simple memories of Lincoln's neighbors and weighing down those memories with elements of undying love, unbearable grief, and mighty significance for American history. If we strip away Herndon's Victorian embellishments, we are left with a much more plausible story.

Even the critics of the legend grant that Herndon did not create the story out of whole cloth. The 1862 *Menard Axis* article is strong evidence that before Herndon gave his 1866 lecture unveiling the story to the world, there was a tradition among New Salem residents that Lincoln and Rutledge had an attachment and that Lincoln grieved at her death. And the fact that a majority of the two dozen New Salemites queried by Herndon agreed on essential elements of the relationship is strong indication that the story had at least some basis in truth.

On the other hand, the fact that Lincoln never mentioned or wrote about Ann Rutledge to any of his close friends (with the questionable exception of Isaac Cogdal) suggests that his relationship with Ann was not the melodramatic, epochal experience that Herndon painted.

Putting all this together, it is possible to construct a version of events that might prove acceptable to both the partisans and the critics of the Ann Rutledge story. It is not hard to believe that there was some attraction between Lincoln and Ann. She was pretty and intelligent. Lincoln was by no stretch of the imagination pretty,* but he was a rising and much respected young man in New Salem. So it would not be surprising if these two young people living in a frontier settlement were drawn to each other. Was it love? Love, after all, is about the most elusive and subjective element in human life; an emotion that runs the scale from warm friendship to searing passion. (Nobody suggests, incidentally, that Lincoln and Rutledge ever slept together.)

One suspects that the relationship between Lincoln and Rutledge was closer to the friendship end of the scale, particularly if Ann was engaged to the absent John McNamar. But in such a friendship between two young members of the opposite sex, it is likely that each privately speculated from time to time about a deeper relationship.

And it is not hard to imagine that when Ann died unexpectedly, Lincoln grieved. Ann would not need to have been the love of Lincoln's life for him to have felt grief; he might have felt the same for any of the friends he had made in New Salem who died young, or as thirty years later, he would grieve with the mothers who lost their sons in battle.

---

*According to tradition, Lincoln was once accused during a debate of being two-faced. He is said to have replied, "I leave it to my audience. If I had another face, do you think I'd wear this one?"

7

WAS DR. MUDD AN ACCOMPLICE TO LINCOLN'S ASSASSINATION?

The trial of the assassins of President Abraham Lincoln took place from May 9 to June 30, 1865, in a room on the third floor of the Washington Penitentiary. John Wilkes Booth, the man who had killed Lincoln at Ford's Theater, was not there; two weeks before the trial began he was pursued by Union soldiers to a Virginia tobacco shed, where he was shot to death. But the eight persons who were accused of conspiring with him sat in the penitentiary in a prisoners dock along one wall, manacled and separated by guards.

Most of the accused were shabbily dressed men from the margins of society; reporters described them as ruffians of low intelligence. But one man struck the onlookers as different. The well-dressed Dr. Samuel A. Mudd appeared to be a gentleman. A reporter said, "He has a sort of homebred intelligence in his face, and socially is as far above his fellows as Goliath of Gath above the rest of the Philistines."*

The thirty-one-year-old Mudd was indeed different. He was

---

*Another prisoner who stood out from the others was the lone female, Mary Surratt, who was found guilty and executed. As in the case of Dr. Mudd, there is a lively debate about whether or not she was guilty.

born to a prominent planter family in Maryland, and was a college graduate and a medical doctor. Before his arrest, he lived with his wife and four children on a sizable tobacco farm thirty miles south of Washington. What did this gentleman physician-farmer have to do with John Wilkes Booth and the assassin's circle of malcontents and drifters?

The bare facts in the case are these: At about 4:00 A.M. on the morning of April 15, 1865, the assassin John Wilkes Booth and his young coconspirator David Herold came to Mudd's door. The two were fleeing Washington, where six hours before Booth had fired a bullet into the back of the president's head. Booth was injured; he had broken his leg when he leaped from the presidential box to the stage at Ford's Theater. Mudd took Booth to an upstairs bedroom, where he found that the patient had fractured his leg above the ankle. Mudd made a makeshift splint, and had his hired man fashion a pair of crutches. Mudd provided a razor, soap, and hot water so that Booth could shave his mustache. While Booth rested, Mudd and Herold rode out to see if they could obtain a carriage for the injured man to ride in, but they were unsuccessful. At about 5:00 P.M. Herold and Booth rode away on horseback from the Mudd home.

Mudd was later arrested by federal troops. He was put on trial with the other accused conspirators, and found guilty. Sentenced to life, he was taken to Fort Jefferson, a grim island prison in the Dry Tortugas off the coast of Florida. When yellow fever broke out in the prison population, Mudd acted with great heroism, taking over command of the prison hospital after the institution's doctor died. For this act Mudd was pardoned in 1869 by President Andrew Johnson. The presidential pardon, however, did not address the issue of Mudd's guilt or innocence.

Mudd returned to his family, his farm, and his medical prac-tice in Charles County, where he died in 1883. Mudd main-tained to the end of his life that he was innocent of anything except performing his duty as a physician. His descendants have taken up the cause, writing books and petitioning to have his conviction overturned. The 1936 movie *Prisoner of Shark Is-land* depicts Mudd as an innocent victim. The Michigan legisla-ture, at the urging of Mudd descendants who had settled in that state, passed a resolution stating that the doctor was not guilty. Presidents Jimmy Carter and Ronald Reagan expressed the same opinion.

But despite the sentiment of family, Hollywood, the Michigan legislature, and two past presidents, was Samuel Mudd involved in the assassination of Lincoln?

MUDD'S POLITICS

Mudd's tobacco farm was located in Charles County in southern Maryland. Although Maryland remained in the Union, many Charles County residents were strongly sympathetic to the Confederacy. Did Mudd share that sentiment? His accusers say he was virulently opposed to the Union and to Abraham Lincoln. They cite reports that during the war he harbored Confederate fugitives and guerrillas on his farm. Early in the war he wrote an angry letter to a Northern magazine, lashing out at Lincoln and expressing confidence in a Southern victory. An acquaintance of Mudd's, Daniel J. Thomas, testified at the trial that shortly before the assassination, Mudd expressed treasonous opinions in the course of a conversation. According to Thomas, Mudd said that "Abraham Lincoln was an abolitionist, and that the whole Cabinet were such; that he thought the South would never be subjugated by abolitionist doctrine, and he went on to state that the President, Cabinet, and other Union men in the State of Maryland would be killed in six or seven weeks."

His accusers also cite Mudd's record as a slaveholder. His former slaves testified that he would sometimes discipline them by threatening to send them to the Confederacy. In a fit of anger he shot one of his slaves in the thigh. After his imprisonment, he complained bitterly when he was guarded by Black troops.

Mudd's defenders admit that early in the war he was indeed a secessionist, like most of his Charles County neighbors. And they concede he did briefly provide a hiding place on his farm for some fugitives, including his brother-in-law Jeremiah Dyer, who, like the others, was on the run from the Yankees. But as the war progressed, Mudd realized that the Southern cause was lost and that the president would offer the best terms to the South. A neighbor said that on the day after the assassination, Mudd described the death of Lincoln as "one of the most terrible calamities that could have befallen this country." Mudd's defenders say that the prosecution witness Thomas was mentally unbalanced and a notorious liar.

THE DOCTOR AND THE ACTOR

The injured man who came to Mudd's door on April 15 was not a stranger. The defenders of Mudd acknowledge that the doctor had met Booth prior to the assassination.

The first time was in November 1864, when Booth was on a visit to southern Maryland. Booth attended a service at a local Catholic church at which Mudd was present, and after the service the two men were introduced to each other by a mutual friend. According to Mudd's defenders, Booth told Mudd that he was in the region in order to buy some land. Mudd offered to show him the area, and Booth stayed overnight at Mudd's home. The next morning the two went to a neighboring farm, where the actor purchased a horse. Mudd then brought Booth back to a hotel in the nearby town of Bryantown, where the actor was staying.

Mudd's accusers say that Booth's purpose in visiting southern Maryland was not to buy property at all but rather to scout out an escape route from Washington to the South and to identify Confederate sympathizers in the region who could shelter him. They say that Booth at that time was plotting to kidnap Lincoln and that he sought Mudd's help in the scheme.

Mudd's defenders reply that it may well have been Booth's purpose to plan a safe route to the Confederacy, but that Mudd was entirely ignorant of the actor's mission and not at all involved in the kidnapping plot. He genuinely believed that Booth was in southern Maryland for the sole purpose of buying land.

Then came a second encounter between Mudd and Booth. The principal source of what occurred is Louis J. Weichmann, a government clerk who became the chief witness for the prosecution at the trial of the assassins. Weichmann said that one winter day, later established as December 23, 1864, he was walking along a Washington street with a friend, John H. Surratt, when they encountered Samuel Mudd and John Wilkes Booth walking together. According to Weichmann, Mudd knew Surratt, and the two greeted each other; Mudd then introduced Booth. The four then went to Booth's rooms at the National Hotel for drinks and cigars. Later they went to Mudd's rooms at another hotel. Weichmann testified that during this time, Booth, Mudd, and Surratt had private conversations from which Weichmann was excluded. At one point Booth, Mudd, and Surratt went into the hallway to talk. At another, Booth made some notations, as if drawing a map, on the back of an envelope.

When he was arrested and put on trial, Mudd denied that the Washington meeting with Booth had ever taken place. But after his trial, when he was a prisoner in the Dry Tortugas, he changed his story and admitted that the gathering, much as described by Weichmann, had taken place, although he said that it had been entirely innocent, and that Booth was once again chatting about buying property in southern Maryland. Mudd said that he had been a "mere looker on" at this encounter.

Mudd's accusers believe there may have been yet another meeting between Mudd and Booth. Two decades after the assassination, Thomas H. Harbin, who claimed to have been a Confederate secret agent, said in a newspaper interview that on December 21, 1864, he slipped from Virginia into Maryland to attend a meeting with Mudd and Booth at a Bryantown tavern. According to Harbin, Mudd had arranged the meeting, the purpose of which was to arrange the capture of Lincoln.

The accusers cite evidence of other connections between Booth and Mudd. One of the conspirators, George A. Atzerodt, wrote a confession in which he charged that Booth had stocked provisions with Mudd as part of the plan to kidnap Lincoln and take him to Richmond. Samuel Arnold, one of the other conspirators, is reported to have told a Union officer that Mudd was one of the residents of southern Maryland whom Booth had drawn into his plots against Lincoln.

In sum, those who believe Mudd was guilty say that he was a key member of the "action team" assembled by Booth to kidnap Lincoln, a scheme approved by the Confederate government in Richmond. They believe Booth intended to take the president through Charles County and then across the Potomac into Virginia. Once in Richmond, Lincoln was to be exchanged for Confederate prisoners of war held in Union hands. The accusers believe that Mudd had been identified to Booth as a man who could be helpful in the scheme, and the actor deliberately sought him out when he visited Charles County in November 1864. They believe that Mudd's purpose in coming to Washington in December 1864 was to introduce Booth to John H. Surratt, a Confederate courier whom Mudd had known for several years. Booth recruited Surratt into his circle of conspirators, which included David Herold, Lewis, Payne, Samuel Arnold,

Michael O'Laughlin, George Atzerodt, and others who were subsequently convicted as Booth's accomplices.

What happened to the kidnapping scheme? With the sudden fall of Richmond to the Union army and the surrender of General Robert E. Lee, the plan became unworkable. At some point thereafter Booth decided to assassinate the president.

THE MAN WITH THE FAKE BEARD

Even though Mudd may have known Booth, did he recognize the actor when the injured man, accompanied by David Herold, appeared at his door on April 15, 1865? What Mudd told the authorities and what his partisans have maintained ever since is that the doctor had no idea who his visitor was. According to Mudd, Herold gave his name as "Henson" and said his companion was "Tyson" or "Tyser." Henson said that they had been riding to Washington when Tyson had fallen from his horse and injured his leg, and that they had gotten Dr. Mudd's name and address from passersby. According to Mudd, Tyson kept to himself and spoke very little; he had a beard, his face was partially concealed by a shawl, and he kept his head turned away. Mudd's wife said that as Tyson and Henson were leaving the home, she got a close look at Tyson and saw that his beard was false.

Mudd's lawyer at the conspiracy trial explained how it could be that Mudd would not recognize Booth:

> [Mudd] had seen him that dark cloudy morning, at daybreak, faint with fatigue and suffering, muffled in his shawl and disguised in a heavy beard; had ministered to him in the dim light of a candle, whose rays struggled with the dull beams of the opening day; had seen him, perhaps, sleeping in the darkened chamber, his mustache then shaved off, his beard still on, his effort at concealment still maintained. . . . Let it be remembered, too, that Booth was an actor, accustomed by years of professional service to disguise his person, his features, and his tones.

Mudd's accusers dismiss this scenario as ridiculous; they believe that Mudd surely recognized Booth as the man who had stayed overnight in his home the previous November and with whom he had met in Washington in December. The accusers say that none of the witnesses who saw Booth when he murdered Lincoln or in the course of his flight from Washington caught sight of a false beard, and no such prop was found among the actor's effects after he was slain. The accusers believe that Mudd made up the lie of the false beard and the aliases to protect himself.

WHAT MUDD SAID TO THE YANKEES

Mudd's defenders say that, at the earliest, the doctor did not learn of the assassination until late on Saturday, April 15, when he went to the nearby village of Bryantown, which by then was swarming with federal soldiers searching for the fugitives. They say that Mudd had no reason to connect the assassination to his morning visitors; in fact, he did not even know that John Wilkes Booth was involved; the rumor circulating in the neighborhood at that time was that the crime had been committed by a local Rebel guerrilla named John Boyle. However, a neighbor testified at the trial that Mudd had stopped by on the way back from Bryantown around sundown on Saturday and conveyed the news of the assassination and the fact that it had been carried out by a man named Booth.

Mudd went to Easter service at a Catholic church the next morning. After the service, Mudd told his cousin, George Mudd, about the visit the day before by the two strangers. Cousin George offered to tell the federal soldiers who were combing the area; Samuel agreed that it would be a good idea. Mudd's defenders say he deserves credit for coming forward with this information; his accusers say that by waiting overnight he was giving Booth time to escape.

George went to the authorities on Monday, and four officers rode out to the Mudd farm on Tuesday, April 18, to interview the doctor; Mudd was repeatedly questioned over the next few days until he was finally arrested and taken to Washington on April 24. His accusers say that his behavior and his statements during this period plainly demonstrate his guilt. Federal officers who interrogated Mudd found him nervous and evasive, as if he were hiding some information. The first officer to question Mudd, Lieutenant Alexander Lovett, testified:

Dr. Mudd appeared to be much frightened and anxious
... his manner was very reserved and evasive ... When
we asked Dr. Mudd whether two strangers had been there,
he seemed very much excited, and he got as pale as a
sheet of paper, and blue about the lips, like a man that
was frightened at something he had done.

Some of Mudd's alleged statements to the authorities were
suspicious. According to the investigating officers, he said that
he had met Booth only once before, when the actor came to
Maryland in November 1864, thus covering up the December
meeting in Washington. He said that Booth had been wearing
a pair of revolvers, but he did not mention the carbines that
Booth and Herold were carrying with them. He said that after
the two fugitives left his house, they headed east in the direction of a local minister's house; but the officers found that in
fact Booth and Herold had headed to the south, and they believed that Mudd's story was "a blind to throw us off our
track."

Then there was the boot. Four days after the Federals first
came to his home, Mudd informed them that he had cut a boot
off his patient's leg in order to treat the fractured bone, and
that the boot was still in the house. The boot was retrieved
from upstairs; inside was the inscription "J. Wilkes" (the last
name was obscured). In explaining why he had not produced
the boot earlier, Mudd said that it had slipped his mind.
Mudd's accusers believe he managed to recall the boot only
after the Yankee officers threatened to search his house.

THE DISPUTED CONFESSIONS

Complicating the Mudd story are allegations that months and
years after Mudd was put on trial, he gave confessions that
indicated his guilt. The first of these alleged confessions was
reported by one of Mudd's guards, Captain George W. Dutton.
According to Dutton, he was with Mudd in July 1865 on board
the ship that was taking the doctor to prison. When Mudd was
informed that the ship's destination was to be the Dry Tortugas,
he supposedly cried out, "Oh, there is now no hope for me."
In this moment of despair, Mudd allegedly confessed to Dutton
that he had indeed recognized Booth when the actor came to

his door on the morning of April 15, but he had lied about that fact. He confessed further that the meeting with Booth in Washington on December 23, which he had previously denied, actually did happen. He said that he came to Washington on that occasion expressly to see Booth and to introduce him to Surratt. He told Dutton that he had lied about his contact with Booth out of fear for his life and for the lives of his wife and children.

One of Mudd's defenders, Theodore Roscoe, argued that this supposed confession was a fabrication created by the government to reaffirm to the public that Mudd was guilty.

The second alleged confession is said to have occurred in 1877, eight years after Mudd's release from prison. Mudd was traveling in a wagon with one Samuel Cox, Jr.; both men were campaigning as Democratic candidates for the Maryland legislature. According to Cox, Mudd confided that he had recognized Booth on April 15, but had believed the actor's story about having broken his leg in a fall from a horse. When he learned later that day that Lincoln had been killed and that Booth was the assassin, he considered turning Booth and Herold over to the authorities but instead upbraided Booth and demanded that he and Herold leave his house. The accusers believe that Mudd did make this confession to Cox, but that even then he was still hiding the full level of his involvement; they doubt that he would have taken the risk of turning the assassins over to the authorities when he himself was so deeply implicated in Booth's schemes.

A FAIR TRIAL?

Mudd's defenders say that the doctor was unfairly convicted. Mudd and the other accused assassins were tried not in a civilian court by a judge and a jury but rather by a special military commission presided over by a panel of nine Union officers. This tribunal, say the defenders, was a kangaroo court determined to avenge the death of Lincoln.

Mudd's accusers reply that the military trial was conducted as fairly as possible under the difficult circumstances. They point out that the prisoners were able to obtain lawyers. Mudd himself was defended by Thomas Ewing, Jr., a general in the

Union army who had previously served as chief justice of the Supreme Court of Kansas.

In 1866 the United States Supreme Court ruled in the *Ex Parte Milligan* case that military trials of civilians were unconstitutional in those instances where civil courts were open and fully able to function. The decision overturned the conviction of one Milligan, a civilian who had been sentenced to death by a military court during the war. Mudd's partisans argue that the *Milligan* decision should be applied to the case of Mudd, who was also a civilian improperly tried by the military. In 1992, the descendants of Mudd made this argument before the Army Board for the Correction of Military Records. The ABCMR agreed, and formally recommended to the Assistant Secretary of the Army that Mudd's 1865 conviction be overturned. The same view prevailed at a mock trial at the University of Richmond Law School in 1992, when a panel of judges declared that Mudd had been wrongly convicted.

Those who believe Mudd was guilty say that the *Ex Parte Milligan* decision does not apply. They cite two habeas corpus appeals filed on behalf of Mudd while he was still imprisoned, which called for his release. The first appeal was turned down by Chief Justice Samuel P. Chase in 1866, the same man who had earlier supported *Milligan*. The second was rejected two years later by a U.S. district judge in Florida on the grounds that the assassination of the president was a crime of such a serious nature that a military trial was justified.

As of this writing the opponents of Mudd have prevailed: the Assistant Secretary of the Army rejected the findings of the Army Board for the Correction of Military Records, stating that since Mudd's two habeas corpus petitions had been examined and turned down by legally constituted federal courts in the 1860s, it was improper for the ABCMR to overturn those decisions.

Weighing the Evidence

Mudd's descendants and his supporters have presented the image of Mudd as entirely innocent. They say he ministered to an injured man on his doorstep, a man who gave a false name and wore a false beard. When he suspected that his patient was not what he seemed, the doctor saw to it that the authorities were informed. But because of the national hysteria over Lincoln's death and the need to find a scapegoat, he was brought before a biased military court and wrongly found guilty.

This image is fundamentally wrong. By his own admission, Mudd lied about the extent of his previous involvement with Booth. Mudd does seem to have been a party to Booth's original scheme to kidnap Lincoln and bring him to the Confederacy. The meetings with Booth in Maryland and Washington seem to have been devoted to furthering that plan. And Mudd's story that he did not recognize Booth—the man he entertained in his Maryland home and with whom he had sipped punch and smoked cigars in Washington—is unlikely, as is the melodramatic story of the alias and false beard. Further, Mudd does seem to have delayed notifying the authorities long enough to have given Booth a head start, and then to have misdirected those authorities about the course of Booth's flight.

So Mudd was clearly no innocent country physician doing his duty for an injured stranger. But that does not mean that Mudd was totally guilty. There is a Mudd family tradition that General Lew Wallace, one of the military judges in the conspiracy trial, privately remarked: "If Booth had not broken his leg, we would never have heard of Mudd." Whether or not Wallace said such a thing (and he in fact denied it), the words pretty well sum up a weakness of the case against the Maryland doctor.

The consensus among historians who have studied the assassination is that Booth determined to kill Lincoln only a matter of days, or perhaps even hours, before he carried out the deed at Ford's Theater. There is no evidence that Mudd knew of the assassination in advance or that he expected Booth to show up at his door, and no evidence that Booth had intended, before breaking his leg, to stop at Mudd's home.

This leaves us with the following likely scenario. Booth arrived unexpectedly at Mudd's door on April 15. Mudd recognized the actor, and probably learned from his lips about the assassination. He treated Booth's injury, and tried to find a wagon to help him escape southward. Later that day, Mudd saw the federal troops around Bryantown, and knew that they were on Booth's trail. Now he faced a quandary. He knew he was in grave danger because of his earlier involvement in the kidnapping plot and because of his aid to the assassin. Should he remain silent and hope for the best, or should he come forward in a way that would minimize his involvement?

Mudd and his wife must have spent an agonizing night trying to decide what to do. The next morning Mudd told his cousin about two strangers who had stopped at his house. When the soldiers arrived two days later, he and his wife spun out the story of the aliases and the false beard. He could not cover up his November meeting with Booth—after all, he had been widely seen with Booth at that time by friends and neighbors— but he did omit his more incriminating December meeting in Washington with the actor.

So how guilty was Mudd? He was actually charged with two crimes. The first was that he, along with the others accused, "did combine, confederate, and conspire together . . . traitorously to kill and murder Abraham Lincoln, then President of the United States aforesaid, and Commander-in-Chief of the Army and Navy thereof." Of this charge of premeditated participation in the assassination, the weight of the evidence is that he was innocent.

But Mudd was also specifically charged with being an accessory after the fact—that he did "advise, encourage, receive, entertain, harbor, and conceal, aid and assist the said John Wilkes Booth." Of that charge the weight of the evidence suggests that he was almost certainly guilty.

What about the legality of Mudd's trial? It may well be that his constitutional rights were violated when he was brought before a military commission. But that does not affect his guilt or innocence. If the Supreme Court had decided to overturn Mudd's conviction in light of *Milligan,* the government would still have been able to try him again in a civilian court with a jury of his peers; under which circumstances he might have been found guilty once again and sent back to his prison cell in the Dry Tortugas.

8

WHY DID CUSTER LOSE?

Custer's Last Stand was, from the perspective of military history, a small-potatoes affair. Only about 2,500 Indians and cavalrymen fought at Little Bighorn, compared to 150,000 Union and Confederate troops at Gettysburg thirteen years before. And whereas Gettysburg marked a turning point in the Civil War, Little Bighorn had no lasting strategic importance; it was only a momentary delay in the dispossession of Native Americans from their lands. Yet Custer's June 25, 1876, battle against the Sioux and Cheyenne has remained as much in the American mind as the great struggle at Gettysburg. Indeed, according to one calculation, Little Bighorn and Gettysburg are the two battles in American history about which the most has been written. Custer, incidentally, was at both battles: he played a minor role in the first, but was indisputably the star of the second.

Why the fascination with the Custer massacre? Part of it is the indelible image of the bold, thirty-seven-year-old General George Armstrong Custer, his long yellow locks waving in the wind, slashing with his sabre at the onrushing savages, while his grim, blue-coated troopers fight for their lives.

But as any Custer buff will tell you, that image is dead wrong. Custer's hair was cut short on that campaign, and he and his men were not wearing sabres or blue uniform jackets. Furthermore the entire Seventh Cavalry Regiment did not perish; only about 40 percent of the officers and men present at the Battle of the Little Bighorn lost their lives. And it was certainly not a massacre in the generally accepted sense, since Custer's men were armed soldiers.

The interpretations of Custer's Last Stand have the same shifting quality. In some he is the hero, in others the villain; in some the men of the Seventh Cavalry are brave, in others they are cowards who bicker among themselves and commit suicide rather than face the enemy.

The primary question is whether or not Custer made a mistake. On its face the question seems absurd. He was, after all, utterly defeated, so there were obviously fatal errors committed. But can these errors be attributed to Custer? Would another commander, using different tactics, have been able to achieve a different result? Did some or all of the blame belong to his subordinates?

Much of the debate also swirls around what happened in the final hour of Custer's life. No soldier survived in the group that Custer led away from the rest of the regiment, so what actually took place during the Last Stand is the subject of endless speculation.

DID CUSTER DISOBEY ORDERS?

In the summer of 1876, Custer's Seventh Cavalry was part of an expeditionary force under the command of General Alfred Terry. Terry's mission was to crush the hostile Sioux and their Cheyenne allies. The army was waging war against the Indians because the Sioux had refused to both cede their land to the United States (land previously guaranteed to them by the same United States) and stay on government reservations.

On June 21, Terry met with Custer and other officers in the cabin of the steamboat *Far West*, moored on a bank of the Rosebud River in Montana. At that meeting, and in written orders delivered to Custer the next day, General Terry directed Custer to take the field with the Seventh Cavalry to find the band of hostile Indians believed to be gathering on one of the network of rivers and creeks in the wild Montana Territory. Terry's best guess was that the Indians were camped on either the Bighorn or the Little Bighorn Rivers. He ordered Custer to proceed along a circuitous route, going far south along the Rosebud Creek, then heading north along the Bighorn River. According to one

officer who was present, Terry stuck pins in a map to show
Custer the route to follow.

The intent was to crush the Indians between two columns,
with Custer's column moving up from the south and pushing
the Indians against Colonel John Gibbon's blocking column to
the north. Terry's orders said: "it is hoped that the Indians, if
upon the Little Big Horn, may be so nearly inclosed by two
columns that their escape will be impossible." Terry seems to
have expected Gibbon to be in position to the north on June
26, and some students of the battle believe he expected the
battle to be joined that day.

Those who believe Custer was responsible for the defeat at
Little Bighorn say that he disobeyed orders from Terry. They
point out that Custer did not follow the circuitous route specified by Terry and that he attacked the village on the twenty-
fifth, not the twenty-sixth. By so doing, say his critics, Custer
ignored both the route and the timetable that his commanding
officer had directed him to follow. They say that this impetuos-
ity was typical of Custer, who earned a reputation for reckless-
ness during the Civil War.

Custer's critics also charge that the publicity-seeking general
had a particular reason for seeking a quick, solo victory. The
Democratic convention was to be held in St. Louis in late June.
News of a stunning victory by Custer, a loyal Democrat, could
have reached the convention just in time for the delegates to
nominate him for the presidency by acclamation.

Custer's champions deny that their man disobeyed orders.
They say that Terry gave Custer wide freedom of action, and
that the twenty-sixth was not a preordained day of battle but
only Terry's estimate of when Gibbon would reach his position.
Similarly, the route was only a suggestion, which Custer was
free to change as circumstances presented themselves. Custer's
defenders say that any sort of tight battle plan was impossible
simply because no one knew where the Indian village was located or when and if Custer would find it.

It made sense for Custer to attack on the twenty-fifth, argue
his defenders, because that is when he came upon the Indian
village after four days on the trail. If he had delayed his attack,
the Seventh Cavalry might have been discovered by the Indians,
who could have fled before he could strike. Indeed, there were
signs that enemy scouts had already spotted his advance.

As proof that Custer had wide latitude to attack when and

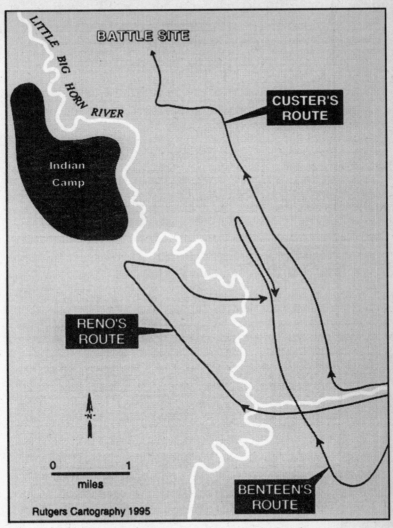

Conjectured Route of the Seventh Cavalry
Battle of the Little Bighorn, June 25, 1876

where he chose, his defenders cite additional language of Terry's orders:

> The Brigadier General [Terry] commanding directs that, as soon as your regiment can be made ready for the march, you will proceed up the Rosebud in pursuit of Indians whose trail was discovered . . . a few days since. It is of course impossible to give you any definite instructions in regard to this movement, and were it not impossible to do so the Department Commander [Terry] places too much confidence in your zeal, energy, and ability to wish to impose on you precise orders which might hamper your action when nearly in contact with the enemy. He will, however, indicate to you his own views of what your action should be, and he desires that you should conform to them unless you shall see sufficient reasons for departing from them.

Custer's defenders also say that there is no real evidence that Yellow Hair was thinking about the presidency, and even less evidence that the Democratic party would ever have considered him.

FORCES DIVIDED

As they advanced toward the Indian camp on the Little Bighorn, Custer's Seventh Cavalry Regiment consisted of roughly six hundred men, including officers, enlisted men, and "others." The others included Indian scouts and civilians, such as mule drivers and a newspaper reporter. At a few minutes after noon on June 25, about fifteen miles away from the Indian village, Custer stopped to subdivide his force into three battalions. The first consisted of three companies, about 125 men, under the command of Captain Frederick W. Benteen. The second, commanded by Major Marcus A. Reno, consisted of three companies, with about 130 men. Custer himself took command of the third and largest battalion, with five companies, about 210 men. He also assigned a force of about 130 under command of Captain Thomas McDougall to guard the train of pack mules that carried the vital reserve ammunition.

Custer dispatched Benteen's battalion off on a scouting expedition to the south. As the Seventh got closer to the village, Custer directed Reno's battalion to attack. Custer then led his battalion ahead, probably (although there is debate about his intent) to strike the Indians from one direction while Reno engaged them from another. McDougall's pack train followed to the rear.

Critics of Custer have said that dividing his regiment in this way was an epic blunder. Each of the battalions was too far away to help the others, and equally far from the reserve ammunition in the pack train to hold out for long against the Indians. Military historian Colonel W. A. Graham put the error this way:

> Not only were all [the parts of the regiment] separated by miles of difficult and enemy-infested country, but no one of the commanders, Custer, Reno, Benteen, or McDougall, knew where either of the others was, or what he was doing. This unfortunate separation, and, as it proved, fatal ignorance of each other's acts and whereabouts, gave to the Sioux, whose horde outnumbered the soldiers at least six to one [sic], every opportunity to beat them in detail; opportunities of which they promptly and thoroughly availed themselves with almost Napoleonic sagacity.

Captain Frederick Benteen put the matter more bluntly. He said the division of the regiment by Custer "was the whole and sole reason that we were so badly beaten."

Custer's defenders say that the decision to split the regiment appears wrong only in hindsight. At the time, given the information possessed by Custer, it was a reasonable battle plan. Sending Benteen's battalion off on a scout would protect the rear of the regiment from enemy attack. Separating Custer's battalion from Reno's would enable the cavalry attack to be launched from two directions. At the Battle of the Washita, eight years before, Custer had won a great victory over the Cheyenne by splitting his regiment and surprising the enemy in much the same way.

What went wrong with the plan, say Custer's defenders, was that the force of Indians camped on the Little Bighorn was much larger and more determined to fight than Custer or any other White officer knew. They speculate that the Indians would have won a victory even if the regiment had remained together.

Custer's partisans say that if he made a mistake, it was in giving command of the battalions to Reno and Benteen, two officers lacking in loyalty or fighting ability.

MAJOR MARCUS A. RENO

A crucial moment in the battle came in the opening moments, when Custer directed Reno to lead his battalion in an attack across the Little Bighorn. When Custer gave this order, he promised to provide support to Reno's attack. He then galloped off with his battalion further downstream, never to return.

After crossing the river and entering the valley with his battalion, Reno found himself facing fire from the enemy. He had his men dismount and form a skirmish line. When the Indians began to close in, he pulled his men back into a stand of timber. After a short time he abandoned this position too, and his force retreated across the river and up a rise of bluffs known ever afterwards as "Reno Hill," about two miles from the village. Reno was later joined on the hill by Benteen's battalion and by McDougall with the pack train.

At that point, about two-thirds of the Seventh Cavalry was on Reno Hill, besieged by Indians. The remaining third—consisting of Custer and his battalion—had disappeared to the northwest. Major Reno, as the ranking officer after Custer, commanded the force on the hill. The Indians attacked his position through the rest of the day and began again the next morning. Then, under the smoke screen of a prairie fire, the enemy dismantled the village and departed toward the Bighorn Mountains to the southwest. It was not until June 27, two days after the battle, that General Terry reached the survivors on Reno Hill. They learned, to their astonishment, that Custer and his batallion had been killed to the last man.

Critics of Reno accuse him of a failure of leadership. They say that he needlessly stopped his attack on the Indians and that his retreat to the stand of timber was unnecessary. Even worse, they charge that his retreat from the timber across the river to the bluffs was hasty and panicked, and resulted in unnecessary loss of life. The critics say that he should have maintained his position longer and withdrawn in orderly fashion. Once on the hill, say Reno's critics, he seemed paralyzed by fear and failed to go to Custer's aid or to permit Benteen to do so. It is alleged that while on the hill he drank to bolster his courage, and that he cowardly proposed escaping from the hill with the able-bodied troops, leaving the wounded behind. One explanation given for Reno's lack of nerve is that early in the fight he was splattered by the brains of an Army scout who was killed by a shot to the head while standing next to him. Others propose that he disliked Custer, and felt no compulsion to come to his assistance.

The central question is whether the outcome of the Little Bighorn would have been different if Reno had fought with greater determination in support of his commanding officer. Reno's critics say that if he had pressed his initial attack on the village, or at least maintained his position in the valley, the Indians would not have been able to leave that part of the battlefield to bring the weight of their numbers against Custer. And if Reno had later left his hill position to come to Custer's aid, Custer's battalion might have been saved. Said historian W. A. Graham: "Had Reno fought as Custer fought, the Battle of the Little Bighorn might have been Custer's last and greatest Indian victory."

But Reno's defenders believe that their man acted correctly; that the number of Indians opposing him was so great that had he continued his initial attack on the village, or had he journeyed from Reno Hill to Custer's side, he and his command would have been slaughtered along with Custer, adding to the magnitude of the defeat. In short, they say, Reno's wise caution ensured that at least part of the Seventh Cavalry survived Little Bighorn. In 1879, a military court of inquiry convened at Reno's request investigated his conduct at the Battle of Little Bighorn and absolved him of blame.

Bitterness against Reno remained, however, and as late as 1926, the fiftieth anniversary of the battle, there was a campaign to keep Reno's name off a monument being erected on the battlefield. At that time, Custer's widow, Elizabeth, referred to Reno as "the one coward of the regiment."

Captain Frederick W. Benteen

It is generally acknowledged that Benteen acted with heroism on Reno Hill. He organized the defenses, brought up the pack train, made sure that ammunition was distributed, and led a counterattack against the Indians. Said one student, "Benteen was a man of magnificent presence and dominating personality; cool, keen, daring, and brave as a lion."

But Benteen's critics say that while the brave lion might have performed ably in the defense of Reno Hill, his actions earlier in the battle contributed to Custer's death. Benteen, it will be recalled, was assigned by Custer to conduct a scouting expedition to the south of the column. Benteen did so, and then returned to the trail leading to the Little Bighorn. But, say the critics, he moved with inexcusable slowness when he should have been dashing ahead to catch up to Custer, and he arrived on the scene too late to help his commander. By one calculation, Benteen was only about a half hour behind Custer when he returned from the scouting expedition but he was an hour and twenty minutes behind by the time he reached the Little Bighorn River, despite the fact that Benteen had received two messages by courier from Custer summoning his help and asking him to bring ammunition packs from the mule train. The last message was scribbled in haste by Custer's aide, Lieutenant William W. Cooke: "Benteen. Come on. Big Village. Be quick. Bring packs. W.W. Cooke P.S. Bring pacs." Benteen's critics say that he ignored this direct order from his commanding officer and instead halted his battalion on Reno Hill. Benteen's critics imagine Custer and his beleaguered troops, surrounded by Indians, muttering to themselves, "Where the hell is Benteen?"

Said one critic of Benteen, historian John S. Gray, "There is no escaping the conclusion that Benteen was delayed, not so much by his brief scouting circuit, as by dawdling after he reached the main trail." Gray charged that for the rest of his life, Benteen lied about his speed on the trail in order to obscure his failure.

Why was Benteen so dilatory? One explanation is that he did not think that there was any large body of Indians in the vicinity. Another is that, like Reno, he personally hated Custer. Benteen found the commander an insufferable braggart; he sarcastically referred to a book written by Custer, *My Life on the Plains*, as "My Lie on the Plains." Another interpretation, more favorable to Benteen, is that he could not obey his orders from Custer to "come on" because he received a countermanding order from Reno, who ordered him to halt at Reno Hill.

How Many Indians?

The question of the number of Indians who faced the Seventh Cavalry at the Little Bighorn is important, since trying to assess Custer's chances of success depends on the number of warriors who opposed him. The problem is that, unlike the Whites, the Indians kept no muster rolls, casualty counts, diaries, or other written documents to serve as guides; as a result, the estimates of Indian strength have varied widely. Immediately after the battle, the survivors interviewed by General Terry came to a rough estimate of 1,500 warriors. A report written by an Army captain one year after the battle estimated that Indians numbered 3,500. In 1881, a survivor guessed that he and his comrades had faced 7,000 warriors. In 1908, another survivor estimated the number to be between 2,500 and 3,000. In a 1926 study of the battle, Colonel W. A. Graham estimated 4,500 warriors.

John S. Gray examined the issue in 1976. Using estimates of the number of lodges, the number of adult males per lodge, and the number of Indians absent from reservations, he arrived at a total of 1,780 warriors, which he rounded off to "less than two thousand fighting Indians."

In regard to casualties, we know with fair precision the number of troopers who perished. Gray tallied 210 dead from Custer's battalion and 53 from the rest of the regiment. But how many Indians? No one knows for certain, but the consensus is that the numbers were not overwhelming.

Weapons, Recruits, Fatigue

Several factors have been suggested as contributing to, or perhaps even causing, Custer's defeat. One of these is weaponry: some students of the battle believe that the Indians were armed with repeating rifles, sold to them by unscrupulous White traders, and that these arms were far superior to the Seventh Cavalry's single-shot Springfield carbines, which are said to have frequently jammed when the cartridge-ejection mechanism failed.

By examining scratch marks on cartridges, Richard Allen Fox, Jr., a University of South Dakota archaeologist who directed a dig at the battlefield in the 1980s, concluded that only a very small percentage of the Springfields jammed—not enough to make a difference in the outcome of the battle. The archaeological evidence also suggests that while some Indians did possess repeating rifles, they were in a minority; others carried lances, bows and arrows, antiquated muzzle-loaders, and carbines taken from dead soldiers. But, said Fox, even the small number of repeating rifles in the hands of the Indians would have proved highly effective in close-range combat.

Another reason sometimes given for Custer's failure is that the Seventh Cavalry consisted of too many raw recruits, inexperienced in combat and deficient in horsemanship and marksmanship. One estimate is that as many as forty percent of the regiment were recruits. But others disagree; a rival estimate is that only three percent were truly raw recruits, as defined by less than three months of service.

Fatigue has also been given as a contributing cause of Custer's defeat. The regiment had been riding hard for days on end, including a night march on the evening before the battle. Alcohol too has been blamed. Writers with a temperance point of view say that officers and men had been drinking heavily before, and perhaps during, the battle. But others dispute the charge. Custer, incidentally, was a teetotaler.

A more difficult issue is how Custer's cavalrymen compared with the Sioux and Cheyenne warriors they faced. The Indians were trained in warfare from childhood, and they were accustomed to the hard life on the plains. In contrast, the frontier army of the 1870s has been described as a miserable collection of unhappy soldiers, beset by desertion, drunkenness, and suicide. In his book *Son of the Morning Star*, Evan S. Connell colorfully described the universe of the troopers:

> Vicious punishment, loneliness, boredom, booze, fleas, maggoty bread, tarantulas, mosquitos, blizzards, deserts, psychotic sergeants, incomprehensible lieutenants and captains and majors and colonels, yipping savages anxious to part your hair.

Weighing the Evidence

So who was to blame for Custer's defeat? Let us begin with Yellow Hair himself. The first question is whether he disobeyed his orders. The weight of the evidence seems to be that he did not. His instructions from Terry clearly gave him ample freedom to depart from them if circumstances warranted. And the circumstances did indeed seem to warrant a quick attack, since it appeared from Sioux pony tracks found near the trail that the Indians had discovered Custer's presence.

The second question is whether dividing his regiment before the battle was a mistake. The inescapable answer is a resounding yes. Had Custer not sent Reno and Benteen away on separate assignments, his force would have been three times larger than it was. This would have reduced the odds against him from ten to one to three to one (assuming an opposing force of two thousand warriors). While this may not have guaranteed victory, it might have at least allowed a less stunning defeat.

Philip Sheridan, the Civil War general who was surely one of the great military men of his age, said as much in commenting on the battle of the Little Bighorn. He observed that if Custer had used more caution, and attacked the village in a group, with proper posting of men on the flank, "all the Indians there could not have defeated him."

When Custer is criticized on this score, his defenders frequently snap back that only in retrospect did Custer's action in splitting the regiment appear to be a grave error. Given the information he had at the time about Indian numbers, his decision seemed judicious. Said historian John S. Gray:

> Custer's decisions, judged in the light of what he knew at the time, instead of by our hindsight, were neither disobedient, rash, nor stupid. Granting his premises, all the rest follows rationally. It was what neither he, nor any other officer, knew that brought disaster.

But there is some evidence that Custer may well have known the strength of the Indian village and simply did not care. His Indian scouts are said to have told him that the force of Indians he would face was vast, but Custer pressed on anyway. When he caught sight of the village himself he is reported to have said, "Boys, hold your horses, there are plenty of them down there for us all."

All of which makes Custer guilty of overconfidence and even arrogance. If so, it was an overconfidence and arrogance shared by other White officers in the army, who generally had contempt for the fighting ability of the Indians, and who believed they could defeat any number of hostiles with ease.

What about Benteen? For all his heroic acts later, Benteen was certainly to blame for being slow in coming to the aid of Custer, at a time when it could have made a difference, and at a time when he had clear orders commanding him to "Come quick."

The case of Reno is more complicated. Certainly he failed to exercise leadership. But it is hard to fault him for halting his attack on the village early in the battle, since the force he encountered was formidable—in fact the same force that later crushed Custer. What about the accusation that, later in the battle, Reno should have abandoned his defensive position on the bluffs and gone to the aid of Custer? It would have been a brave thing to do, but it would also have exposed his soldiers to the same fate as Custer's. If he had exercised the same prudence as Reno, Custer might have survived the battle. But then, if Custer had been more prudent he would not have been Custer, the dashing boy general.

It's interesting to compare Custer with General Charles Lee, the hapless subject of chapter 2. Custer is condemned for being too impetuous, Lee for being too cautious. The lesson seems to be that the real standard for judging military performance is not temperament, but whether one wins or loses.

What about the other factors suggested as contributing to Custer's downfall—malfunctioning weapons, large numbers of recruits, alcohol, fatigue, and so on? Some of these played a part; yet there were countless other engagements between the army and the Indians on the Western frontier in which the same factors were operating, and in which the Indians customarily lost.

This suggests that there might be another answer to the question of who deserves the blame for the disaster at Little Bighorn. Custer biographer Robert M. Utley observed, "The simplest answer, usually overlooked, is that the Army lost largely because the Indians won." In other words, it is somewhat insulting to the determination and skill of the Indians who fought at Little

Bighorn to assume that it was only through some failing of the Whites, and not through the military ability of the Indians, that Custer lost.

And indeed, the Indians were well prepared for battle on that occasion. Their advantage was more than just numbers. The Sioux and Cheyenne—tribes whose leaders included the legendary figures Sitting Bull, Crazy Horse, and Gall—demonstrated great fighting prowess. The fact that Whites were trying to throw them off sacred land strongly motivated them to fight with ferocity, as did the immediate threat posed by Custer to their wives and children in the village.

Postscript:
What Happened to Custer?

What happened after Custer and his force separated from Reno? The last soldier to see Custer alive (or at least the last solider who lived to tell about it) was the courier who carried the "Come quick" message from Custer to Benteen. The courier recalled seeing Custer and his 210-man battalion entering a ravine now known as Medicine Tail Coulee. Later the next day, a scouting party from General Terry's column found the bodies of Custer and his battalion on a rugged, ten-acre stretch of ground northwest of the coulee. What happened in the interval between those two sightings constitutes the final puzzle at the center of the Battle of the Little Bighorn.

There are three main sorts of evidence that have been employed to solve this mystery. The first of these are the accounts of the Indians, as recorded by White men who interviewed them in the years after the battle. But there is difference of opinion about the reliability of Indian testimony. In describing what happened, each Indian usually spoke of his or her own actions on that day, not the larger issues of troop movements and topography that obsessed the White interviewers. To make matters worse, the interviewers framed the questions and recorded the answers to fit their preconceived notions of the truth. Some students of the battle dismiss the Indian accounts; others place greater weight on them.

The second form of evidence comes from archaeology. Recent excavations at the Custer battlefield have unearthed bullets, cartridges, arrowheads, and other artifacts that have been used to determine the positions of Indians and cavalrymen. But there are critics who claim that the battlefield artifacts were too disturbed by souvenir hunters in the century before the archaeological digs began to be of much use.

The third source is the record of where individual soldiers died. After the battle the corpses of Custer's men remained pretty much where they had fallen. The bodies were then identified by the survivors and buried. Reburials followed later. The records of the burials and the placement of grave markers on the battlefield make it possible to speculate on the movements of the companies. But once again there is criticism of the validity of burial evidence. It is claimed, for example, that the identification of the dead and where they had fallen was often careless.

Using these sorts of evidence, there have been endless debates about the sequence of events and how the companies of cavalrymen and their Indian enemies disported themselves over the topography of the battlefield. One recent author, archaeologist Richard Allen Fox, Jr., said that most of the attempts to divine what happened fall under what he calls the "fatalist" school, which holds that as Custer's "Come quick" order suggests, the general rapidly encountered an enormous body of Indians, who drove his battalion to a desperate defensive position. In some versions of this scenario, the outnumbered troopers fought heroically to the last man, as in the illustrations of the Last Stand that adorned nineteenth-century saloons. In other variants, the rush of Indians came so suddenly that there was no time for any sort of heroics or defensive maneuvers. Another version posits that Custer's men were so frightened that they committed mass suicide. But in all variants of the fatalist scenario, Custer's defeat was inevitable. Interpreting the archaeological evidence, Fox painted a different picture. He argued that Custer (or if he died early, one or more of his officers) was actually on the offensive for much of the time, sustaining fairly light casualties and still expecting to be able to defeat the Indians. According to Fox, Custer's "Come quick" message was not a cry of panic but the words of a confident commander who wanted reinforcements and ammunition to ensure his victory over the Indians.

What went wrong? Fox believed that at a crucial moment in the battle, one company of troopers—Company C—was directed to charge Indians who had infiltrated close to Custer's position. But C Company's attack disintegrated in the face of an Indian counterattack. The panic of C Company spread to the right wing of the battalion, and most of the soldiers in that wing were soon slaughtered trying to run away. The collapse of the right wing placed the left wing in an exposed situation, and they too were eventually overwhelmed. In brief, Fox believed that Custer's battalion fell victim to "combat shock"—a sudden battlefield condition in which a unit's organization and fighting will collapse. The implication is that the battle might have gone otherwise.

From the mass of evidence and interpretations, the following seems reasonably certain:

➤ Custer divided his battalion into two wings in order to maneuver against the Indians; one under the command of Captain George Yates and the other under Captain Myles Keogh.

➤ Once Major Reno retreated across the river and up the bluffs, the mass of Indians who had been fighting him moved downstream to attack Custer's battalion. Whether they came in an enormous rush or gradually infiltrated his position slowly is unclear.

➤ There were most likely several "Last Stands," rather than just one. Clusters of bodies were found within a radius of 1,500 yards on spots known as Custer Hill, Custer Ridge, Calhoun Ridge, Calhoun Hill, the South Skirmish Line, and the Ravine.

➤ The end came relatively quickly, probably within an hour of when Custer and his battalion entered Medicine Tail Coulee.

As for General George Armstrong Custer—aka Yellow Hair, the Son of the Morning Star, the Boy General—he was found dead with bullet wounds in his head and in his side. Like the rest of his troopers, his dead body had been stripped of clothing. One of the survivors of Reno's command said that in the distance, the naked bodies of the cavalrymen looked like white boulders strewn on the Montana prairie.

9

⸺⬥⸺

DID LIZZIE BORDEN KILL
HER PARENTS?

Thursday, August 4, 1892, began as an unpromising day at the home of Andrew J. Borden at 92 Second Street in the manufacturing town of Fall River, Massachusetts. An oppressive heat wave had borne down on the town for most of the week, and that morning brought no relief. To make matters worse, for the past few days members of the household had been sick to their stomachs.

Despite the heat and the illness, Mr. Borden left the house shortly after 9:00 A.M. to conduct some business downtown. A bank president and real estate owner about seventy years old,* Borden was one of the wealthier residents of the town. Left behind in the house were his daughter Lizzie, thirty-two, his wife Abby, about sixty-three, and the family maid, Bridget Sullivan, about twenty-six. The Bordens had another daughter, Emma, forty-two, who was out of town visiting friends. The

---

*How old was Andrew Borden? The experts differ widely. Edwin H. Porter and Robert Sullivan (see Selected Bibliography) say that at the time of his death, Andrew was seventy. David Kent says seventy-two; Edward D. Radin, "nearing seventy." Similar confusion exists about the age of Andrew's wife, Abby, whose reported age at death has ranged from sixty-three to sixty-seven. All of which tends to shake one's confidence in the reliability of historical "facts."

three women, Lizzie, Abby, and Bridget, went their separate ways to do household chores in different parts of the house; Lizzie to do ironing and sewing, Abby to do some dusting and then make the bed in the guest room, and Bridget to wash the first-floor windows inside and out.

At about 10:45 A.M., Andrew Borden returned. He was greeted by Lizzie, who told him that Abby had gone off to visit a sick friend. Andrew settled down for a nap on the couch in the sitting room. The maid went upstairs to her attic room for a rest. Lizzie, according to her account, went to the barn in the backyard.

At about 11:10, the maid heard Lizzie urgently calling her to come downstairs. "Come down quick!" Lizzie yelled, "Father's dead! Somebody's come in and killed him." Before Bridget could go to look at the corpse, Lizzie dispatched her out of the house to get help.

Father had indeed been killed. Neighbors and police found him sprawled out on the couch. His face had been chopped into a bloody pulp; one severed eye hung out of its socket.

A short time later, the body of Abby Borden was found on the floor of the guest bedroom on the second floor. She lay face down, her head a mass of wounds and blood. Based on medical evidence, Abby had been killed about an hour and a half before her husband. Whoever had murdered Abby and Andrew Borden had used a sharp instrument, most likely an axe or a hatchet.

When news spread of the double murder, crowds gathered outside the Borden home. The police searched the house and questioned the surviving family members, the neighbors, and the maid. At length, the police became convinced that the murderer was Lizzie. She was indicted by a grand jury, and went on trial in New Bedford, Massachusetts, in June 1893. The jury found her innocent of the crime. She spent the remaining thirty-four years of her life in Fall River, the subject of whispers and suspicion.

The murder and the trial caused a sensation, a sensation that has continued for over a century. Certainly there have been other equally brutal murders before and since, but there is something compelling about the idea that a respectable husband and wife could be hacked to death in their house on a summer morning without any apparent motive and without anyone seeing the killer. And even more compelling is the idea that the murderer might have come from within that respectable family; a churchgoing, quiet spinster named Lizzie Borden.

The case has produced, by one count, nearly twenty full-length books, sixty-six assorted articles, essays, and chapters in books, eleven plays, one opera, one made-for-television movie, and even a ballet—the highly regarded *Fall River Legend* by Agnes de Mille. These works fall into two camps: those that say Lizzie Borden did it and those that say she didn't.

Let us proceed to examine the pieces of evidence that have been debated ever since that stiflingly hot day in 1892.

POISON

Shortly after the murder, Eli Bence, a clerk at a Fall River drugstore, came forward to say that on Wednesday, August 3—the day before the murder—Lizzie Borden had come into the shop to buy prussic acid, a deadly poison. Lizzie told the clerk that she wanted to use the substance to clean her sealskin cape. Bence refused to sell it to her, and told her it could only be dispensed by a physician's prescription. Two other men in the store at the time confirmed Bence's account. Lizzie herself denied that she had been to the drugstore. (At the jury trial, the judge refused to permit Bence to testify on the grounds that the evidence was not germane to the charge.)

Lizzie Borden's accusers use the druggist's account as evidence that Lizzie was planning to poison someone in the house. Indeed, the accusers note that in the days immediately preceding the murder, Andrew, Abby, and Bridget had come down with an illness that caused them to vomit.

Lizzie's defenders explain the family's sickness by the fact that for several days the family had been eating leftover fish and mutton. Given the heat wave and the primitive form of refrigeration in common use at the time, the defenders say that the food had probably spoiled.

THE NOTE

Lizzie Borden said that on the morning of the murder, someone had come to the house with a note for Abby, summoning her to visit a sick friend. Lizzie told this story to Bridget, her father,

the neighbors, and the authorities. The police searched the
house, even piecing together scraps of paper found in the wastebasket, but they could find no note. No one corroborated the
story of the note; neither the person who wrote it nor the person
who delivered it ever came forward.

Lizzie's accusers say she fabricated the business about the
sick friend in order to convince her father and Bridget that
Abby Borden had left the house, when in fact Abby was lying
dead on the floor of the guest bedroom. The prosecution lawyer
in Lizzie's trial said to the jury: "No note came; no note was
written; nobody brought a note; nobody was sick . . . I will stake
the case on your belief or disbelief in the truth or falsity of
that proposition."

Lizzie's defenders argue that there was indeed a note. As to
why it disappeared, they suggest that Abby threw it in the
stove fire after she read it. Why didn't the writer come forward?
The defenders suggest it might have been written by an immigrant who was reluctant to become involved with the law.

THE SPATTERING BLOOD

The murder of Abby and Andrew Borden was gruesome work:
the murderer hacked away at their heads at close range, with
blood gushing forth from the wounds. Expert witnesses (including a physician from Harvard Medical School, Dr. Edward S.
Wood), testified that judging by the position of the bodies and
the nature of the wounds the murderer would most likely have
been spattered with blood. The defenders of Lizzie Borden say
that when neighbors and police saw her on August 4, she had
no blood on her, and she therefore could not have been the
killer.

Lizzie's accusers cite the testimony of doctors who examined
the bodies of Abby and Andrew that the direction in which
blood spatters is unpredictable. Dr. Wood said that while it was
likely that the assailant would have been spattered, that was
not necessarily the case. Moreover, if the victims died from
blows to the brain, the amount of blood that would spurt from
severed arteries would be reduced.

If blood did spurt in her direction, the accusers have suggested that Lizzie could have avoided it by wearing an apron,
by holding up a newspaper in front of her, or (when murdering

her father) by standing behind the door next to the sofa. A television version of the case had Lizzie taking off her clothes to commit the murders in the nude, a clever way to avoid blood stains and to boost television ratings.

The accusers make the obvious point that after committing each murder, Lizzie could have cleaned herself and changed her clothes. But Lizzie's defenders reply that there was simply no time for that to happen, at least after Andrew's murder. He arrived home around 10:45 A.M.; by 11:30 A.M. the police and neighbors had arrived at the house. Lizzie's defenders narrow the time considerably. Although Andrew arrived home around 10:45, it took some time for him to settle in for a nap and for Bridget to go upstairs to her room. At the other end, Bridget said she was called downstairs by Lizzie at around 11:10, and the police received a telephone call alerting them to the crime at 11:15—all of which would have given Lizzie only fifteen minutes or so to commit the murder, wash the blood from her body and her hair, change her clothes, wash the blood off the axe and hide it, and hide her bloody clothes. One of her defenders calculates that at the most, Lizzie had less than ten minutes for this purpose.

One final point in regard to blood. On the petticoat Lizzie said she wore on the morning of the crime, Dr. Wood found a spot of blood one-sixteenth of an inch in diameter, located six inches from the bottom of the skirt. Lizzie's defenders say that since Lizzie was having her period at the time of the murder, it was undoubtedly a drop of menstrual blood. The accusers cite Dr. Wood's testimony: "The fact that it was plainer and more extensive on the outside of the skirt, indicates that it came onto the skirt from the outside and not from the inside."

THE BURNED DRESS

The experts did not find any blood on the dress that Lizzie said she had worn on the day of the murders. But did they examine the right dress? On Sunday, August 7, three days after the murders, Lizzie was observed burning a dress in the kitchen stove. At the trial, Lizzie's sister, Emma, explained it this way:

My sister had a Bedford cord dress, light blue with a darker figure in it, which was made by Mrs. Raymond the dressmaker in the first week of May ... At the time the dress was made, the painters were painting the house, and as a result, Lizzie, when wearing it shortly after it was made, stained it with paint. There were paint marks along the front, and on one side toward the bottom, and on the wrong side of the skirt.

In separate testimony the dressmaker confirmed that she had made a Bedford cord garment in May, and that it had been stained by paint.

Emma said that on Saturday, two days after the murders, she came across the dress in a closet and said, "Lizzie, you have not destroyed that old dress yet. Why don't you?" The next morning, while Emma was washing the dishes, Lizzie came into the kitchen with the dress over her arm and said, "I think I shall burn this old dress up," and proceeded to place it in the stove.

Lizzie's accusers say that this was obviously the dress Lizzie wore when she murdered her parents, and the stains were blood, not paint. Lizzie must have known that it was an inappropriate time to dispose of a dress. Indeed, a neighbor who was in the kitchen at the time testified that she warned Lizzie not to put the dress in the stove. In a 1974 book on the case, *Goodbye Lizzie Borden*, Massachusetts Supreme Court Justice Robert L. Sullivan expressed his skepticism:

> What are the odds against Lizzie Borden, amid the excitement and confusion, the searches and outright suspicion of the days following the murders, singling out the Sunday morning after the murders to tidy up her wardrobe? And what are the odds against Lizzie Borden on that day choosing as a method of tidying up her wardrobe the unheard of method—unheard of in that frugal family—of burning in the kitchen stove a soiled dress only ten weeks old?

THE HATCHET

When the police searched the basement, they came across several axes and hatchets, evidently used to cut wood for the kitchen stove. The accusers say that one of the hatchets, found in a box on a shelf, was probably the murder weapon, for the following reasons:

➤ The three-and-a-half-inch blade fit the wounds in the skulls of Abby and Andrew Borden.

➤ The handle was broken off near the hatchet head; judging by the color of the exposed wood, the break had been made recently. The handle may have broken while in the course of killing Andrew, or perhaps the murderer deliberately broke off the handle and got rid of it (perhaps burning it in the kitchen stove) to hide bloodstains.

➤ The hatchet was covered with ashes, and there was a pile of ashes in the basement. Presumably the murderer had washed the blood off the hatchet, and while it was still wet, rolled it in the ash pile.

If this hatchet was the murder weapon, the fact that it remained in the house would support the accusers' claim that the murder was committed by Lizzie.

Lizzie's defenders argue that the hatchet was a common, widely available type that could have been left by a murderer from outside the household, and that a medical test of the weapon performed by Dr. Wood found no trace of blood. At the trial, one of the policemen who came to the Borden home after the murders testified that the broken handle was found together with the hatchet blade—contradicting other policemen's testimony that the handle was missing. The defenders use this contradiction to cast doubt on the evidence of the hatchet.

LIZZIE'S ALIBI

Lizzie and her defenders present the following alibi for the morning when the murders took place: For the first part of the morning, during which time Abby was killed, roughly from 9:00 to 10:45 A.M., Lizzie occupied herself by eating, ironing, reading a magazine, and sewing. Most of this time she was in the kitchen on the first floor or in her bedroom on the second, although she also went down to the basement, evidently to use the house's only toilet.

At about 10:45, Lizzie's father arrived home. After Andrew lay down for his nap, Lizzie went out to the barn. She was planning to go on a fishing trip, and she wanted to see if she could find some lead to use for sinkers. She climbed up the steps to the loft where she thought the lead was kept. She looked for lead, and possibly ate some pears she took from the trees in the backyard. Altogether she stayed for somewhere between twenty minutes to half an hour in the barn loft. When she came back inside she discovered her father's dead body on the sofa.

The accusers of Lizzie Borden try to pick apart this alibi, concentrating on the trip to the barn. Shortly after the murders were discovered, a Fall River policeman with a musical name, William H. Medley, went up to the loft to investigate. Medley testified at the trial that the floor of the loft was covered with a layer of dust that had not been disturbed. Medley's account was confirmed by another officer. Both policemen testified that the loft was suffocatingly hot; hardly a place to spend twenty minutes. The accusers also ask why Lizzie suddenly became concerned about sinkers for a fishing line, since, according to her testimony, she had not gone fishing for the past five years and did not have any hooks or lines.

Lizzie's defenders provide evidence to confirm she was in the barn when she said she was. An ice cream peddler, Hyman Lubinsky, testified that he had ridden his wagon past the Borden home that morning and had seen a woman walking from the direction of the barn to the house. He said he knew Bridget Sullivan, and it was not she; the defenders say it therefore must have been Lizzie. The stable owner who boarded the horses Lubinsky used said that the peddler had left the stable a few minutes after 11:00, which would have enabled him to pass the Borden home just about the time Lizzie would have been coming from the barn.

The defenders also cite the trial testimony of witnesses who said that curiosity seekers had been in the loft before officer Medley climbed up to investigate, which would negate the claim that the dust on the loft floor was undisturbed.

The Sisters' Quarrel

After she was indicted for murder, Lizzie Borden was confined in a jail in a nearby town. The matron of the jail, Hannah Reagan, testified that on August 24, 1892, she overheard a conversation between Lizzie and her sister Emma, who had come to pay a visit. According to Reagan, the two sisters had argued like this:

LIZZIE: Emma, you have gave me away, haven't you?"

EMMA: No, Lizzie, I have not.

LIZZIE: You have, and I will let you see. I won't give in one inch.

The accusers cite this incriminating exchange as proof that Lizzie was guilty.

The defenders claim that no such conversation ever took place, and that Reagan's story was a lie she had been pressured into telling. Lizzie's lawyer and other witnesses said that Reagan had attempted to retract her account, but that her police superiors had refused to let her. One defense witness said she had heard Reagan say of the quarrel, "It is all a lie from beginning to end." But Reagan stuck by her account of the quarrel.

The Motive

One of the police officers who arrived at the Borden home on the morning of the murders asked Lizzie if she had any idea who murdered her father and mother. Lizzie replied, "She's not my mother, sir. She is my stepmother. My mother died when I was a child." The accusers of Lizzie Borden seize on this remark as emblematic of the hatreds within the Borden household that drove Lizzie to murder.

Lizzie's mother died when Lizzie was two, and her father took Abby as his second wife about two years later. Several witnesses testified at the trial that Lizzie and Emma despised Abby. According to one witness, Lizzie referred to Abby as "a mean good-for-nothing," and said, "I don't have much to do with her; I stay in my room most of the time." The witness also quoted Lizzie to the effect that she and Emma avoided having meals with their parents as much as possible. A woman who shared a cabin with Lizzie on a steamship returning from a trip to Europe in 1890 said that Lizzie repeatedly expressed her dislike of Abby and her reluctance to return to her unhappy home.

At the root of the hatred Lizzie felt for Abby, say the accusers, was money. Although he lived in a modest house and was extremely frugal, Andrew Borden was one of the richest men in Fall River. Lizzie's accusers say she feared her father would leave his worldly goods to Abby. He had already bestowed on his wife a half-interest, worth one thousand five hundred dollars, in a house where Abby's stepsister lived. Emma testified that this arrangement created trouble between the Borden parents and daughters. The accusers speculate that Lizzie struck when she did because her father was about to give more property to Abby or make out a will leaving his wealth to her.

There have been several other motives suggested by Lizzie's accusers. Victoria Lincoln, who grew up in Fall River and claimed to have heard hints from people who knew the Bordens, theorized that Lizzie suffered from a type of epilepsy. When Lizzie killed Abby, says Lincoln, Lizzie was in the midst of a seizure.

Novelist Evan Hunter advanced the intriguing theory that Lizzie was having a lesbian affair with the maid, Bridget. Lizzie murdered Abby, says Hunter, because her stepmother came across the two together in bed. In a 1993 article in *American Heritage*, Marcia L. Carlisle proposed that Lizzie had been sexually abused by her father, and that this produced in her a rage that resulted in his murder. In support of this thesis, Carlisle pointed to modern cases of patricide that have been committed by the victims of incest.

Lizzie's defenders reject these arguments. In regard to money, they note that Andrew had been generous with his daughters and had provided them with rental property equal to what he had given Abby. Bridget Sullivan testified on the stand that the family usually took meals together and that relations were congenial:

Q: You never saw anything out of the way?

A: No sir.

Q: You never saw any conflict in the family?

A: No sir.

Q: Never saw the least—any quarrelling or anything of that kind?

A: No sir, I did not.

The defenders characterize Lizzie as a dutiful, affectionate daughter to Andrew. She had given him a ring, which he was wearing when he was murdered.

And finally, the defenders point out, Lizzie Borden was an entirely respectable young woman. She was the secretary of the Christian Endeavor Society of the local Congregationalist Church and a member of the board of directors of a charity hospital. To imagine such a person chopping her parents to death with a hatchet is, to say the least, improbable.

If Lizzie Didn't Do It, Who Did?

Those who believe Lizzie Borden was innocent seek another culprit. The most common theory is that it was an outsider who sneaked into the house to murder the Bordens. Several neighbors and passersby testified that they had seen strangers:

➤ Sarah B. Hart said that she and her sister had seen a young man leaning on a fence outside the Borden home prior to 10:00 A.M.

➤ Delia S. Manley said that she had also seen a young man on the street near the Borden home that morning.

➤ Charles N. Gifford and Uriah Kirby said they had seen a stranger on the next block the day before the murder.

➤ Mark P. Chase said he had seen a man in a buggy on the Borden's street the day of the murders.

➤ Benjamin Handy said he had seen a suspicious young man walking down the Borden's street on the morning of the murders.

And there were other, sensational stories of bloody men clutching hatchets on the outskirts of Fall River.

Who was this stranger? Presumably he was not simply a robber, since no money or jewelry was missing from the house. He must have been either a maniac with no motive, or an enemy of the Bordens. Lizzie herself had told her neighbor, Miss Alice Russell, on the night before the murder, "I feel afraid sometimes that Father has got an enemy, for he has so much trouble with his men that come to see him." Lizzie said she had overheard her father quarreling with an unnamed man over Andrew's refusal to rent the man property. One Mary A. Durfee said that before the previous Thanksgiving she had seen Andrew arguing loudly with a man on his steps. There had in fact been a burglary of the Borden home early in the summer.

The accusers of Lizzie Borden dismiss these accounts of a mysterious stranger. The prosecution at the trial produced neighbors who said they had seen no strangers around the Borden home that morning. And even if they did, say the accusers, it would be natural to see passersby on a busy street close to downtown. The accusers also point to the fact that the police investigation failed to turn up anybody outside the family who might have committed the murder of Andrew Borden, whether tenant, hired hand, or business associate. And in regard to the early summer burglary, the accusers suggest that Lizzie performed it herself; an early sign of her hostility to the family.

If not a stranger, could some member of the household other than Lizzie have committed the crime? One of Lizzie's defenders, Edward D. Radin, advanced the hypothesis that the murderer was Bridget Sullivan, the only other person home that morning with Lizzie and the two victims. Radin said that instead of washing windows, Bridget struck down Abby in the early morning; and instead of later going to her room to lie down she axed the sleeping Andrew once Lizzie had gone out to the barn. Bridget left the Borden home later that day; she could have hidden the bloody hatchet in the belongings she took with her. As to the motive, Radin speculated that Bridget may have been angered when Abby, knowing the maid was feeling ill, ordered her nonetheless to wash the windows. Bridget then had to murder Andrew because he had overheard her quarrel with Abby.

Another possible culprit is Lizzie's uncle, John Vinnicum Morse. Morse, the sixty-nine-year-old brother-in-law of Andrew Borden, had gone to the Midwest as a young man to make his fortune. He had returned from Iowa to Massachusetts three years before the murder. On the day before the murder he had come for an overnight visit to the Borden home. He had gone out the morning of the murder to visit other relatives in Fall River. Lizzie's defenders point to the curious fact that he came to visit the Borden home without bringing any luggage or change of clothing. One of Lizzie's defenders, David Kent, argued that Morse's alibi for the morning of the murder was suspicious precisely because it was so good:

> Amazingly, he could trace his movements minute by minute and street by street, including the number of the trolley he had ridden and the number on the cap of the conductor who had driven it. His remembrances would suit a casebook on alibis.

Another suspect is Lizzie's older sister, Emma Borden. Her alibi was that she had been gone for two weeks before the murders visiting with friends in Fairhaven, Massachusetts, and was summoned back to Fall River after the murders by a telegram. Writer Frank Spiering speculated that in reality, Emma secretly came back from her trip on the morning of the murders, and with Lizzie's connivance, committed the killings. But Emma's Fairhaven friends stated that she was with them at the time.

Over the years other assorted theories, mostly unsupported by evidence, have been advanced—for example, that the murder was committed by a boyfriend of Bridget's, or that Abby was murdered by Andrew, who was then killed by Lizzie to cover up her father's crime, or that Andrew had a crazed, illegitimate son who did the deed.

Weighing the Evidence

The primary support for the defenders' claim that Lizzie was innocent of the murder of her father and stepmother is the fact that all the evidence against her is circumstantial: there is not a single eyewitness to link her to the murder. Besides this, the following claims by the defenders carry the most weight:

➤ Lizzie was a respectable young woman, hardly the type to commit a bloody murder of this sort.

➤ She would have probably been spattered by blood, and would have had very little time to clean herself and hide the weapon.

➤ Strangers were seen in the vicinity of the house on the morning of the crime.

➤ The murder weapon was never positively identified.

➤ The ice cream vendor lent some support to Lizzie's alibi that she was in the barn at the time of her father's murder.

The best argument on the other side of the case is simply that it is hard to imagine how anyone other than Lizzie could have committed the crime. If an outsider had been involved, he would have had to sneak into the house without being detected by Lizzie, who was moving about inside, or by Bridget, who spent most of the morning washing the windows. The intruder would have to have tracked Abby to the guest bedroom, and after killing her, hidden somewhere in the house for ninety minutes or so until Andrew returned. After killing Andrew, he still would have faced the challenge of escaping undetected from the house, while somehow hiding the murder weapon on his person.

The only other person in the house at the time was Bridget, and it is difficult to imagine that she killed two people simply because she was disgruntled at having to wash the windows. The notion that John Vinnicum Morse should be suspected precisely because he had a good alibi is also far-fetched, as is the completely unsubstantiated charge that Emma came home undetected to commit the murder.

The overwhelming weight of the evidence is that Lizzie Borden murdered her father and her stepmother. It was Lizzie and Lizzie alone who had the means, the motive, and the opportunity. She tried to purchase poison the day before the crime, she probably invented the story about the note from the sick friend, she burned a dress in the kitchen stove, she was hostile to her stepmother.

Whether Lizzie committed the murders out of a desire to inherit the family wealth, or because of some psychological or physiological trauma, or out of some combination of rational calculation and irrational rage, is not clear. What is clear is that, except in regard to the number of wounds, the old nursery rhyme is dead correct:

Lizzie Borden took an axe
And gave her mother forty whacks.
When she saw what she had done,
She gave her father forty-one.

There is one final, chilling mental image. In her testimony at the trial, Bridget recalled how on that fatal day she had come from the sitting room to the front door to let Mr. Borden into the house after he'd returned from downtown. The door was hard to open, and Bridget swore as she struggled to unlock it. From somewhere upstairs, she heard Lizzie laughing. Was Lizzie amused by the stuck door, or was she laughing at the thought that she had just murdered her stepmother, and was now about to do the same to her father?

10

WHO BLEW UP THE
USS *MAINE*?

The night of February 15, 1898, was hot and sultry in Havana, the capital of the Spanish colony of Cuba. The battleship USS *Maine* was moored to a buoy in the harbor, two hundred yards from the nearest ship. At ten minutes after nine the bugler played taps, the signal for the crew to go to sleep in their hammocks slung below decks. In his cabin, Captain Charles Dwight Sigsbee finished a report to the Department of the Navy and then started work on a letter to his wife. Sentries stationed around the ship watched for signs of any intruders.

The *Maine* had been in Havana for the past three weeks. Ostensibly the ship was paying a courtesy visit, but the real purpose, on the order of President William McKinley, was to protect American lives and property in Cuba. The situation on the island was unstable. For years, Cuban guerrillas had been fighting to win independence. Their Spanish masters had fought back savagely, sweeping the countryside and imprisoning rebel sympathizers in concentration camps. The American press, and in particular the jingoistic New York *Journal* and the New York *World*, filled their pages with lurid accounts of Spanish cruelty and Cuban suffering. Under pressure from the United States, the Spanish government had moderated its policies somewhat and was making concessions to the Cubans, but relations with the United States were still strained.

At 9:40 P.M., as Sigsbee was sealing the letter to his wife, he heard what he later described as "a bursting, rending, and crashing sound or roar of immense volume, largely metallic in character." The lights went out and the cabin filled with smoke.

When Sigsbee made his way to the deck, he found that his ship was burning and sinking into the harbor. He and most of his officers survived that night; their quarters were toward the stern of the ship, away from where the explosion occurred. But the crew, whose quarters were in the forward section, were decimated by the explosion and were trapped as the vessel sank. Out of the 354 officers and men on board that night, 266 died.

Immediately after the disaster Captain Sigsbee sent a telegram to the Secretary of the Navy, describing what had happened. Although he privately believed that his ship had been sunk through sabotage, he urged caution. "Public opinion should be suspended until further report," he wrote in the telegram. But public opinion in the United States, exemplified by the yellow journalism of the *World* and the *Journal*, was that the disaster had been caused by Spanish treachery.

The Navy Department established a court of inquiry consisting of four naval officers, who were sent to Havana. The investigation lasted one month, during which time testimony was taken from the surviving officers and crew of the *Maine*, from eyewitnesses who saw the disaster from nearby ships, and from divers who inspected the wreck resting on the floor of the harbor, thirty-six feet below the surface. The final report was three hundred pages long, with diagrams and photographs. The court concluded that the loss of the *Maine* was caused by the explosion of a mine.

The court issued its report in late March, and a few weeks later the United States declared war on Spain. The conflict may well have happened even without the sinking of the *Maine*, but popular outrage, expressed in the slogan "Remember the *Maine*," unquestionably contributed to the outbreak of hostilities.

Another opportunity to investigate the *Maine* came in 1911, thirteen years after the end of the war. For the practical purpose of removing an obstruction from Havana Harbor and for the symbolic one of reclaiming the seventy or so bodies that had never been recovered, the Army Corps of Engineers set about uncovering the ship. A cofferdam was erected in the harbor around the wreck, the water was pumped out, and the damaged areas of the ship were cut away. The undamaged aft section was sealed with concrete and wood, and then refloated, towed out to sea, and ceremonially sunk. The human remains found on the ship were buried at Arlington National Cemetery. The work took almost one year to complete.

While the project was going on, a specially appointed board, consisting of four naval officers and an army officer, assembled in Havana to try to reopen the question of how and why the *Maine* had been destroyed. The evidence used by the 1911 board was far superior to that used by the 1898 court of inquiry, since this time the damaged *Maine* could be closely examined and photographed. The board (known as the Vreeland board after its senior member, Rear Admiral Charles E. Vreeland) released its report in December 1911. Although the board disagreed with the 1898 court of inquiry report on important details, it agreed that the *Maine* had been sunk as a result of a mine. Neither report was able to determine who set the device.

There were voices of dissent as early as 1898. The Spanish authorities in Cuba conducted their own investigation after the sinking, and concluded that the ship had been destroyed by an internal accident rather than external sabotage. This view was echoed by naval authorities in England, France, and Germany, as well as by antiwar Americans. A contrary view was expressed by Captain Sigsbee himself, who in magazine articles and a book argued that his ship had been sunk by a mine. Over the years an occasional article or book appeared arguing one way or the other about the cause of the disaster.

In 1974, the eighty-fifth anniversary of the Spanish-American War, retired Admiral Hyman G. Rickover read an article in a Washington newspaper about the *Maine*. Rickover was a controversial figure, the tempestuous father of the nuclear submarine service. He was intrigued with the mystery of the *Maine*, and at his request, two civilian engineers employed by the navy, Ib S. Hansen and Robert S. Price, examined the material on the incident that had come out of the 1898 and 1911 investigations, and particularly the 1911 photographs. Hansen and Price's report, "The U.S.S. *Maine*: An Examination of the Technical Evidence Bearing on Its Destruction," was included as an appendix to Rickover's 1976 book, *How the Battleship Maine Was Destroyed*. The conclusion of Rickover, Hansen, and Price was that the *Maine* sank because of an internal accident, and not as the result of a mine explosion.

And so the debate stands: on one side are those who believe it was an accident and on the other are those who believe it was sabotage. The most recent study is Michael Blow's 1992 *A Ship to Remember: The Maine and the Spanish American War*. Blow, whose grandfather survived the *Maine* explosion, examined the evidence and then threw up his hands:

> Like the identity of Jack the Ripper in London, the killing of John F. Kennedy in Dallas, and the Tonkin Gulf "incident" of August, 1964—the mystery of the *Maine*—the "crime" of the nineteenth century—will forever remain unsolved.

The mystery of the *Maine* is indeed difficult to untangle, but let us attempt to delve into the depths of the harbor of Havana to determine what happened.

THE MINE

The 1898 court of inquiry primarily based its finding that the *Maine* had struck a mine on the fact that a portion of the keel (the underside of the ship) had blown thirty-four feet upward with such force that it had smashed through the main deck, forming an inverted metal V. The members of the court believed that the keel could have penetrated upward only from an external explosion below the ship. The court fixed the center of this external explosion at frame 18. (The frames were the vertical ribs of the ship, which ran from the bow to the stern, three to four feet apart. Frame 18 was located fifty-nine feet from the bow.) The board concluded that the explosion of the mine at frame 18 had touched off another explosion in one of the ship's magazines, where powder and shells were stored.

The 1911 Vreeland board stated that the inverted V at frame 18 was caused by the internal magazine explosion, and not by the mine. The board believed that the location of the mine explosion was further aft, between frames 28 and 31, on the port side, and that the magazine that was touched off was directly above. This magazine, designated as A-14-M, held powder and shells for the six-inch deck guns. The evidence for the Vreeland board's conclusion came from the fact that an area of about one hundred square feet on the underside of the ship around frames 28-31 had been pressed inward.

In sum, the 1898 court of inquiry and the 1911 Vreeland board disagreed on where the damage had occurred, but they agreed that the primary cause of the disaster was an undersea mine, which had caused an explosion in one or more of the ship's internal magazines.

Critics of this official view say that the evidence of the mine explosion is not convincing. Hansen and Price argued that the damage to the bottom plating between frames 18 and 31 does not bear out the existence of a mine. They said that the plates had been bent smoothly, with none of the mangling or rupturing of the exterior that would be expected from a mine powerful enough to touch off an internal magazine. Indeed, the inside portion of the plating was more mangled than the outside, which is exactly the opposite of what one would expect to find if there had been an external explosion.

But how then explain the denting inward of the ship's underside? Hansen and Price confessed that "a simple explanation is not to be found," but they suggested several possibilities. One was that the bottom plating had been pressed inward when the ship struck the bottom of the harbor as it sank; another was that the pressure of the internal explosion pushed the unreinforced bottom plating of the ship outward, forcing the water away, and that the rush of the water returning and flooding into the ship caused the plating to be pushed inward.

Critics of the mine theory believe that the official inquiries were flawed. For example, the 1898 physical investigation of the wreck was hampered by the divers' inexperience and by the fact that the ship had sunk in dark, filthy water that made it impossible to see the extent of the damage. And even if the water had been crystal clear, much of the hulk was hidden by the thick mud at the bottom of the harbor.

Captain Sigsbee was permitted to attend meetings of the 1898 court and to question witnesses. Since it was in Sigsbee's interest to prove that his ship was sunk by a mine and not through his own negligence, the critics say that his presence as an interrogator was improper. The critics also say that the 1898 court and the 1911 board failed to interview outside technical experts.

A more serious criticism is that the atmosphere of the time made a fair verdict impossible. Admiral Rickover said of the 1898 report:

The court's verdict of an external explosion was one that could be expected. The strained relations between the two nations, the warlike and patriotic atmosphere in Congress and the press, and the natural tendency to look for reasons for the loss that did not reflect upon the Navy might have been predisposing factors in the court's finding.

Critics also believe that the 1911 Vreeland board was biased. The Spanish-American War had been over for only thirteen years, and the American officers on the board were reluctant to find that the nation had made a mistake in going to war over the *Maine*.

OTHER MINE THEORIES

Those who believe the *Maine* was sunk by a mine point to the fact that when the vessel arrived in Havana Harbor on January 25, a Spanish pilot came on board and directed the ship to the mooring location at buoy number four. The mine advocates say that this was a remote, seldom-used spot, and that the *Maine* was deliberately placed there either because a mine was already located there or because it provided a good location for planting one.

The defenders of the official verdict of sabotage paint a scenario of how a mine could have been planted at buoy four while the *Maine* was moored there. The harbor was filled with lighters—small freight-carrying boats. One of those lighters could have been rigged to conceal a mine. When the lighter came close to the *Maine,* saboteurs could have released the mine, dropping it down into the water. The mine could have been attached to the lighter by insulated wire on a reel, which played out as the mine sank. The other end of the wire could have remained on the lighter when it docked or else could have been brought on shore. The saboteurs could have carefully observed the *Maine* as it slowly moved around buoy number four with the motion of the wind and the water. When the ship was directly over the mine, the saboteurs could have set it off by sending an electric charge down the wire. Captain Sigsbee, who advanced this interpretation, said that lighters frequently passed near his ship, and that on the night the explosion occurred the *Maine* had swung to a northwest position, which it had not occupied before.

The mine advocates say that the device could have been quite crude—even a barrel filled with explosive powder would have sufficed. Sigsbee estimated that as few as twelve men could have constructed the mine, launched it, and detonated it. Another possibility is that the mine was not intended for the *Maine* but was simply part of the harbor defenses employed by the Spanish authorities. It might have been a contact mine that came loose from its regular location and drifted into contact with the ship.

Several witnesses, both on the *Maine* and farther away, testified that they heard two explosions. The first was described as a short blast; the second, as louder and longer. Some witnesses said they saw the prow lift with the first explosion, as if from a blast underneath the ship. Those who believed the *Maine* was sabotaged believe that the first explosion was the mine; the second, the magazines.

Critics attack the mine theory on several grounds. The most common observation is that no person or persons came forward to admit (or take credit for) this historic act of sabotage. Even if the perpetrators covered up their crime at the time of the disaster, say the critics, surely one of them would have talked to the press after the Spanish-American War was over, or else made a deathbed confession that would be reported later.

The critics also say that using a mine would have been impractical in the small, crowded harbor because of the possible damage to other ships and buildings. The critics disagree that buoy four was a remote and seldom-used location; quite to the contrary, they believe it was a desirable berth frequently used by other ships. The critics also deny that the Spanish would have mined the inner harbor. It would have been much simpler to lay mines in the narrow channel that separated the harbor from the sea; mines were also made unnecessary by the fact that Havana was protected by well-armed forts overlooking the harbor.

On technical grounds, the critics of the sabotage theory say that the mine would have to have been very powerful and placed with great accuracy directly under a magazine. The critics observe that the mines used by the Spanish were too crude and ineffective to accomplish that end, and they cite episodes during the Spanish-American War when U.S. warships struck

Spanish mines without suffering any damage. Hansen and Price said that the damage found on the bottom of the *Maine* was slight, indicating that the mine explosion, if there was one, would have been insufficient to set off the magazines.

And if there was a mine, say the critics, it would have to have been constructed on extremely short notice, since the Spanish authorities were given only a few days' warning that the *Maine* was sailing to Havana. The critics cite the fact that in modern warfare, it takes months to train personnel in underwater demolition and additional time to plan an attack on a specific target.

The critics say that if a mine had exploded, a water geyser would have erupted upward at the time of the explosion and quantities of dead fish would be floating in the vicinity. No geyser and no fish kill were reported at the time of the *Maine* incident. The defenders of the official verdict say that neither the water column nor the dead fish are necessary results of a mine explosion. The critics charge that no fragments of the mine or connecting wires were ever found; the defenders say they could have sunk into the deep mud at the bottom of the harbor or been reeled in by the saboteurs.

What about the testimony of two explosions and the lifting of the prow? The critics say that the disaster occurred so suddenly that the recollection of witnesses is suspect. Moreover, a single explosion could sound like two, since the noise would travel at different speeds through the air and the water. There could have been two or more explosions caused by separate magazines on the ship exploding one after the other. The apparent lifting of the prow could be caused by an internal explosion.

One other possibility has been offered: could the *Maine* have been sabotaged by some means other than a mine? Specifically, could a person on board the ship—a visitor from Havana or a crew member—have planted a bomb at some vulnerable point? Both the critics and the advocates of the mine theory say this is unlikely. Morale was high among the crew, and visitors who came on board ship were escorted wherever they went. The munitions lockers and other compartments were kept locked. After the *Maine* was sunk, divers found the ship's keys in the captain's quarters, precisely where they were supposed to be kept.

WAS IT AN ACCIDENT?

If not a mine or a bomb, what did cause the explosion of the magazines? Possible causes of the disaster suggested at one time or another are the ship's boilers, electrical system, torpedoes, and stored paint and solvent. But these possibilities can be dismissed. While the ship was moored in the harbor all but two of the boilers were shut down, and those two were in the aft portion of the ship, away from the center of the explosion. The electrical system was insulated to prevent explosion. The torpedoes had been disarmed. Inflammable material such as paint had been stored carefully.

The most likely culprit, say those who believe in an accident, is a fire in a coal bunker adjacent to magazine A-14-M. The *Maine* carried eight hundred tons of coal in bunkers below deck near the magazines. A fire could have developed in the bunkers, producing heat and flame that could have set off a magazine. Critics of the sabotage theory believe that was exactly what happened; that the coal bunker known as A-16 caught fire through spontaneous combustion, and that the heat from that fire caused an explosion in magazine A-14-M, which was located on the other side of the wall. Hansen and Price's original report presented six reasons why this scenario is a likely one:

1. Frequent bunker fires did occur on warships of that period. 2. The brand of bituminous coal in the A-16 bunker is known to have caused fires by spontaneous combustion. 3. The coal had been in bunker A-16 since loading at Newport News, Virginia, about three months earlier. 4. The bulkhead between the bunker (A-16) and the six-inch reserve magazine (A-14-M) was a single steel plate, probably one-fourth-inch thick. 5. Tanks of both brown powder and black saluting powder were stored in the six-inch reserve magazine right against the bulkhead or at least very close to the bulkhead. 6. Ventilation of the bunkers was natural through a vent pipe to the forward stack. This stack was not in use, thus perhaps making the ventilation insufficient to prevent a rise in bunker temperature.

Those who believe the explosion was accidental criticize Sigsbee as a lax commanding officer who did not take proper precautions to ensure the safety of his ship. In 1886, Sigsbee had commanded the USS *Kearsage;* an inspection team found the ship shabby and admonished Sigsbee for not enforcing ordnance regulations and for not properly drilling his detachment of marines. Sigsbee's champions reply that the *Kearsage* was a very old ship that had just come through a storm at the time of inspection.

Another incident took place in 1897, when Sigsbee took command of the *Maine.* He was sailing the ship in the East River of New York when an excursion steamer with tourists aboard suddenly appeared in front of the ship. To avoid striking the steamer, Sigsbee veered sharply, and collided with a barge and a pier. The ship suffered slight damage. Sigsbee was actually given a commendation for his handling of the incident. But the critics believe these episodes demonstrate carelessness and a lack of concern for detail. The implication is that Sigsbee was negligent in his care of the *Maine* as it stood on duty in Havana Harbor.

A different view was presented in the testimony of Sigsbee, his officers, and his defenders. They depicted a commander who took every precaution. As part of the ship's routine, lights were extinguished, the galley was sealed off, and cigarettes were doused whenever the magazines were opened. Crews inspecting the magazines wore antistatic slippers to prevent sparks. As part of the ship's construction, electric lamps were sealed in glass and no steam pipes ran through the magazines. The temperature in each magazine was checked and recorded daily, and never reached a dangerous level. Particular caution was taken with the coal bunkers. All bunkers were ventilated through air tubes and were inspected daily. Bunker A-16, in fact, had been inspected on the day of the explosion by the engineering officer on duty. Fire alarms had been installed in every bunker to warn of danger. Officers and crew walking below deck past the magazines and bunkers routinely put their hands against the walls, so that if a fire was burning it would have been detected. On the day of the explosion, no heat was reported in the walls of bunker A-16.

ASSORTED SUSPECTS

If the *Maine* was destroyed by a mine, who placed it there? The culprits most frequently mentioned by the mine advocates are the Spanish who ruled Cuba and their Cuban-born sympathizers who resented American interference. The Spanish authorities were forced to permit the *Maine* to enter Havana Harbor as a courtesy gesture, but underneath, runs this argument, they seethed with anger at the American intrusion into internal affairs. They treated Captain Sigsbee with diplomatic courtesy, while secretly plotting to blow up his ship.

At the 1898 court of inquiry, an anonymous Spanish-speaking witness testified that while traveling on a ferry the morning of the day the tragedy occurred, he overheard a conversation between three Spanish officers and a civilian discussing plans to blow up the *Maine*. The court also heard testimony that a letter had been sent to the American consulate in Havana with the details of a plot. In the days before the explosion a flyer was circulated in Havana calling on those loyal to Spain to strike a blow at the "Yankee pigs" and the battleship from their "rotten squadron."

If it was not the Spanish, perhaps it was the Cuban insurgents, trying to create an incident that would bring the United States into war with Spain. The British historian Hugh Thomas, in his 1971 *Cuba: The Pursuit of Freedom*, suggested this as a possibility, but admitted there was no evidence.

In calling for war against Spain, the Foreign Relations Committee of the United States Senate said that even if the mine had been set by the Cuban rebels, the Spanish still bore the blame for not providing greater protection for the *Maine:*

> The destruction of the *Maine* was compassed either by the official act of the Spanish authorities or was made possible by a negligence on their part so willing and gross as to the equivalent in culpability to positive criminal action.

Could Americans have blown up the *Maine?* A common rumor in Havana at the time of the explosion was that the ship had been destroyed by the United States in order to provoke a war with Spain. And indeed, there was a group of American intellectuals, politicians, military men, and adventurers (including Assistant Secretary of the Navy Theodore Roosevelt, who fits all of those categories) who welcomed war with Spain as a way to make the United States a global power. One American mentioned as a possible conspirator in the destruction of the *Maine* was the millionaire William Astor Chanler, who ran guns

to the Cuban rebels. Even William Randolph Hearst, publisher
of the yellow New York *Journal*, was accused of arranging the
destruction of the *Maine* in order to boost his newspaper's
circulation.

The critics of the mine theory reject all of this as unsupported
speculation. They argue that the Spanish had everything to lose
and nothing to gain by attacking an American ship, since it
would be likely to bring the United States into a war on the
side of the Cuban rebels. That, in fact, is precisely what happened, and the conflict resulted in the loss of Spain's empire.
As to the Cuban rebels, the critics argue that the task of constructing a mine and planting it under the eyes of the Spanish
authorities would have required a level of expertise quite beyond them. And, say the critics, it is ludicrous to imagine that
Americans would blow up one of their own ships and kill their
fellow countrymen.

Weighing the Evidence

There is no shade of gray in the mystery of the *Maine*. Either
it was destroyed by sabotage or by an accident. Stripping away
all the rhetoric, the hearsay evidence, the patriotic sentiment,
and the hypothetical scenarios, the whole debate comes down
to a few feet of dented metal on the underside of a wrecked
battleship. When the Vreeland board examined this dented portion in 1911, it saw proof that a mine had exploded underneath
the *Maine*. Sixty-five years later, Hansen and Price looked at the
photographs of the same dented metal and concluded that the
Maine had been sunk by an internal accident, and the denting
of the ship's bottom had been caused by some other factor, such
as the impact of the bottom of the harbor on the sinking ship.

One wishes for some scrap of evidence that could confirm
the existence of a mine: a confession by one of the conspirators,
a piece of the mine in the harbor mud, a witness who saw a
passing lighter drop the mine into the water. But none of this
exists. In the absence of such proof, the weight of the evidence
is that the *Maine* was destroyed by a fire in a coal bunker,
which touched off magazine A-14-M.

The destruction of the *Maine* is one of those events that re-

minds one of Benjamin Franklin's line about unexpected historical consequences from a small act: "for want of a nail the shoe
was lost; for want of a shoe a horse was lost; and for want of
a horse the rider was lost." A retired army lieutenant colonel,
L. Van Loan Naisawald, speculated in a 1972 article that if it
had been known at the time that the *Maine* was destroyed due
to an accident, the Spanish-American War might never have
been fought, which in turn would have meant that the United
States would never have gained the Philippines and therefore
become a power in the western Pacific, and thus would not
have come into the confrontation with Japan that resulted in
Pearl Harbor.

That fire in the *Maine*'s coal bunker was perhaps more costly
than anyone could have imagined in 1898.

11

DID SHOELESS JOE THROW
THE WORLD SERIES?

Joseph Jackson (1889–1951) was a country boy from South Carolina who got his start in baseball as a teenager playing for the amateur Textile League team at the cotton mill where he worked. His talent got him into the minor leagues and then into the majors. At one game early in his career he played in his stocking feet because he had blisters from breaking in a new pair of cleats. A reporter covering the game made up the nickname Shoeless Joe, which seemed to fit Jackson's country boy manner. So did the fact that he could neither read nor write and the fact that he favored a custom-made bat he called "Black Betsy."

The country boy sure could play baseball. Ty Cobb called him "the greatest natural hitter I ever saw." In his first full season in the majors, Jackson achieved a .408 batting average; his career average was .356, the third highest in baseball history. In 1915 his contract was bought out by the hot Chicago White Sox. By the 1919 season, Jackson was one of the most famous players in the nation and a favorite of the fans, although he was sometimes teased for being illiterate. "Hey, Jackson, can you spell 'cat'?" a fan yelled at him during one game. "Hey mister, can you spell 'shit'?" Jackson shouted back derisively.

Jackson's downfall came with the 1919 World Series between the American League White Sox and the National League Cincinnati Reds. The underdog Cincinnati team won, five games to three. (The best of nine games was required for victory that year.) Even as the Series was being played, rumors circulated that some of the White Sox players had conspired with big-time gamblers to lose the Series. In 1921, eight Chicago players—Jackson, pitcher Eddie Cicotte, outfielder Oscar "Happy" Felsch, first baseman Arnold "Chick" Gandil, shortstop Charles "Swede" Risberg, third baseman George "Buck" Weaver, pitcher Claude "Lefty" Williams, and utility infielder Fred McMullin—were banned forever from professional baseball by the stern verdict of the baseball commissioner, Kenesaw Mountain Landis:

> No player [wrote Landis] who throws a ball game, no player that undertakes or promises to throw a ball game, no player that sits in conference with a bunch of crooked players and gamblers where the ways and means of throwing a game are discussed and does not promptly tell his club about it, will ever play professional baseball!

The other seven "Black Sox" as they came to be known have faded from memory, but Jackson has not. A half-century after his death he remains a hero to many baseball fans. Shoeless Joe is a central character in the popular movie *Field of Dreams*, where he serves to embody the simple, joyous nature of baseball.

Appealing fictional characters based on Shoeless Joe appear in the novel and movie *The Natural* and the Broadway musical *Damn Yankees*. The South Carolina legislature has passed resolutions stating that Jackson was innocent of wrongdoing. His hometown of Greenville, South Carolina, recently named a ball field in his memory. The Shoeless Joe Jackson Society lobbies to have Jackson voted into the Hall of Fame. Former baseball commissioner A. B. "Happy" Chandler said, "I never in my life believed him guilty of a single thing." One of Jackson's most fervent supporters is Donald Gropman, author of *Say it Ain't So: The True Story of Shoeless Joe Jackson*, who stated flatly, "I maintain that Jackson was literally innocent of guilty involvement in the Black Sox scandal."

But those who believe Jackson to be guilty say that while he may have been a country boy and a fabulous player, his corruption and greed brought dishonor to the national pastime.

THE FIX

The ringleader in the fix of the 1919 Series was first baseman Chick Gandil, a player who had frequently consorted with gamblers. As it became certain in the closing weeks of the 1919 season that the White Sox would win the American League pennant, Gandil approached some of his teammates with the proposal that they could make a considerable amount of money by throwing the Series. On September 21, while the White Sox were in New York to play the Yankees, a group of players met in Gandil's room at the Ansonia Hotel and agreed to the fix. A week and a half later, when the team was in Cincinnati for the start of the Series, the group met at the Stinton Hotel with a representative of the gamblers to discuss the arrangements and the amount of the payoff.

Those who believe that Jackson was innocent say he did not go to the meetings at the Ansonia or the Stinton and did not attend any of the other sessions between the players and the gamblers. Indeed, they say, Jackson never gave his assent to participating in the fix. According to this interpretation, Jackson was approached twice in private by Gandil and asked to throw in his lot with the other conspirators. The first time was in Boston where the team had gone to play the Red Sox, the second time was on a small wooden bridge near the White Sox stadium in Chicago. Both times, say his supporters, Jackson turned Gandil down because he did not want to play crooked ball.

Jackson's champions cite as evidence Shoeless Joe's testimony before a Cook County grand jury a year after the Series. The grand jury was investigating rumors of a fix, and Jackson was answering questions posed to him by Hartley Replogle, an assistant state attorney:

Q: Who mentioned it [the fix] first to you?

A: Gandil.

Q: Who was with you?

A: We were all alone.

Q: What did he say?

A: He asked me would I consider $10,000 to frame up

something and I asked him frame what? And he told
me and I said no.

Q: What did he say?

A: Just walked away from me, and when I returned here
to Chicago he told me that he would give me twenty
and I said no again, and on the bridge where you go
into the club house he told me I could either take it
or let it alone, they were going through.

Q: What did they say?

A: They said, "You might as well say yes or say no and
play ball or anything you want." I told them I would
take their word.

Q: What else did you say?

A: Nothing.

Attorney Alan Dershowitz, a champion of Jackson, interpreted this passage to mean that "Jackson was approached by a
teammate and offered ten thousand dollars to throw the World
Series. He declined. A short time later the offer was renewed,
this time for twenty thousand dollars. Jackson refused again."
Jackson's supporters offer additional evidence that their man
did not participate in the fix. Jackson himself claimed that before the Series began he went to see the team manager, William
"Kid" Gleason, and the team owner, Charles Comiskey, to ask
if he could be benched, but he did not tell them the reason.
They refused his request.

Jackson said that after the Series he went to Comiskey to tell
him what he knew, but that he was refused admission to the
owner's office. Once back at his home in Savannah after the
season ended, Jackson, with his wife's help, wrote a letter to
Comiskey saying that the Series had been fixed. He offered to
provide more information. Comiskey never replied to the letter.
Still later, Jackson met in Savannah with Harry Grabiner, secretary to Comiskey, to negotiate his contract for the upcoming
1920 season. Jackson said that he asked Grabiner what he
should do with five thousand dollars he had received as a payoff from the other players, and that Grabiner told him, "Why,
keep it."

This scenario raises two questions about Jackson's behavior.
The first is why Jackson, if he was innocent, was given a five

thousand dollar payoff. Jackson supporter Donald Gropman believed that the corrupt players wanted to maximize the amount
of money they received from the gamblers, so they falsely
named Jackson as one of the White Sox who would have to be
paid off. The players' original intention was to keep Jackson's
share for themselves without telling him, but they changed their
minds and gave Jackson a portion, theorized Gropman, either
out of remorse or out of fear that if he ever learned of the deal
he would make a claim for the money.

To support this argument, Gropman cited testimony given by
the gambler Bill Burns that at the meeting with the players at
the Stinton Hotel, Lefty Williams said he was "representing"
the absent Jackson. Lefty Williams himself stated that he had
never talked with Jackson about throwing the game and had
never gotten Jackson's permission to use his name with the
gamblers. Jackson gave the same story—he had never given his
assent to be represented by Williams.

The second question is why Jackson accepted the five thousand dollars if he was not involved in the conspiracy. His defenders answer that he did not expect to receive any money,
and that he was genuinely taken by surprise when Lefty Williams offered him an envelope containing cash. He said he tried
to refuse, but Williams pressed it on him. Williams himself supported this interpretation when he testified that he came to Jackson's hotel room and threw the money on the bed, saying,
"There is your dough, there is the dough that we got."

So in sum, say his supporters, Jackson never agreed to the
fix, never asked for the money he was paid, and was rebuffed
when he tried to inform the team owner and turn over the
money.

Those who believe Jackson was guilty paint a different picture. They believe that Jackson did agree to participate in the
fix, and although he may not have been at the Stinton Hotel
meeting in Cincinnati, he was probably present at the earlier
meeting with the corrupt players at the Ansonia Hotel in New
York. Jackson's accusers point out that both White Sox pitcher
Eddie Cicotte and gambler Bill Burns identified Jackson as one
of the conspirators, and Lefty Williams admitted that he had
delivered the five thousand dollars to Shoeless Joe. But the main
evidence for Jackson's guilt, they believe, can be found in his
own testimony to the grand jury. In an early part of his testimony, as we have seen above, Jackson seemed to say that he

had turned down Gandil's invitation to participate in the fix. But in a later part of this long and rambling interrogation, state attorney Replogle brought Jackson back to the issue, and this time Jackson gave more detail about his involvement:

Q: Did anybody pay you any money to help throw that series in favor of Cincinnati?

A: They did.

Q: How much did they pay?

A: They promised me $20,000, and paid me five.

Q: How much did he [Gandil] promise you?

A: $20,000 if I would take part.

Q: And you said you would?

A: Yes, sir.

DID JACKSON PLAY TO WIN?

Jackson's critics say that he did not perform up to his potential in the Series, particularly in his fielding; that he missed some easy catches and threw wide from the outfield. And while he may have gotten hits, those hits, they argue, came in non-clutch situations that had no effect on the outcome.

Those who believe Jackson was innocent see his performance otherwise. His .375 batting average and twelve hits was the best record of any Chicago or Cincinnati player in the Series, and he threw out five Cincinnati runners. Jay Bennett, who analyzed Jackson's Series performance in an article in *American Statistician*, declared that Jackson did hit well in clutch situations, and concluded that Shoeless Joe "made a greater contribution to his team's chances for victory than any other batter in the Series." Bennett further found that all the other seven Black Sox, through their poor playing, helped ensure a White Sox defeat.

As proof that it was other players and not Shoeless Joe who deliberately brought about the White Sox defeat, Jackson's supporters cite a play that occurred in the fourth game of the Series. The score was tied 0-0, when a Cincinnati batter hit a single to the outfield. Jackson caught the ball and threw it to home plate to get out a Cincinnati player running from second base. Eddie

Cicotte, the White Sox pitcher who was in on the fix, deflected the ball with his glove, so that the runner scored.

In his grand jury testimony, Shoeless Joe stated that "I tried to win all the time":

Q: Did you bat to win?

A: Yes.

Q: And run the bases to win?

A: Yes, sir.

Q: And field the balls at the outfield to win?

A: I did.

Q: Did you do anything to throw those games?

A: No, sir.

Q: Any games in the series?

A: Not a one. I didn't have an error or make no misplay.

THE MEN BEHIND THE SCENES

Those sympathetic to Jackson tend to be highly critical of Charles Comiskey, the owner of the White Sox, whom they depict as a notorious tightwad and tyrant. Most clubs gave players a meal allowance of four dollars per day; Comiskey gave only three dollars. Most clubs washed uniforms for free; Comiskey tried to charge the players. Even by the standards of the era, before today's multimillion dollar contracts, Comiskey paid low salaries. Jackson's maximum salary was six thousand dollars, while less talented players on other teams made ten thousand dollars. Requests for raises were refused, despite the fact that the franchise was hugely profitable. Jackson, like other players in that era, could be dropped from the team for any reason with only ten days' notice.

One often-repeated story holds that Comiskey promised one of his pitchers a ten thousand dollar bonus if he won thirty games. But when the pitcher achieved twenty-eight wins, Comiskey is supposed to have benched him. On another instance Comiskey promised his players a bonus if they won the 1917 pennant, but when they did the only bonus he provided was a case of cheap champagne.

But Comiskey's worst crime, his critics believe, was his handling of the Black Sox case. He was not particularly interested in uncovering the truth, it is charged, but instead sought to cover up the scandal to preserve his reputation and his asset, the team. He refused to talk to Jackson about the fix, yet for public relations purposes he made a sham offer of a twenty thousand dollar reward for information about the scandal, hiring a detective to investigate.

Comiskey's chief advisor in these machinations was his high-priced Chicago lawyer, Arthur Austrian. Jackson's supporters say that when rumors of the fix became too loud to cover up, Comiskey shielded himself by having Austrian throw the players to the wolves. When Eddie Cicotte came to Comiskey late in the 1920 season to confess, Comiskey sent him to Austrian, who persuaded the pitcher to tell all he knew to the grand jury. And when, in the wake of Cicotte's confession, Joe Jackson told Comiskey that he wanted to talk about what happened during the Series, the owner sent him, too, to Austrian.

Jackson's champions regard his meeting with Austrian as a setup. They believe that Austrian told Jackson that if he tried to deny his involvement in the fix, no judge or jury would believe him, but if he falsely confessed to being involved, he would be let off with no penalty and could return to playing baseball. After coaching him in what he should say, Austrian immediately turned Jackson over to the grand jury—and then left him there.

Jackson's supporters say that Austrian had improperly created the impression that he was acting on Jackson's behalf, while in reality his only loyalty was to his client, Charles Comiskey. The lawyer never told Jackson to consult his own attorney, never warned him of the consequences of signing a statement waiving his immunity from prosecution, and never advised him of his legal rights.

The state's attorney, Hartley Replogle, and the judge presiding over the grand jury, Charles MacDonald, have also been accused of misleading Jackson into believing that by making a confession his troubles would end. Shoeless Joe later testified that Austrian, Replogle, and MacDonald "told me I could tell my story and then go anywhere I liked." But in the end, Jackson was indicted by the grand jury and suspended by Comiskey. Jackson's supporters say he was easy prey for the lawyers: the illiterate center fielder was entirely ignorant of legal matters,

and to make matters worse had been drinking heavily the day
he went to the grand jury.

Supporters of Jackson also lash out at Commissioner Kenesaw
Mountain Landis, who permanently banned Jackson and the
other Black Sox from baseball, and subsequent commissioners
who have refused to reconsider the banishment.

There is one other big shot who, incidentally, walked away
unscathed: Arnold Rothstein, the New York City gambler who,
from behind the scenes, orchestrated the fixing of the World
Series. Rothstein was never indicted and never convicted. But
he did not come to a happy end; Rothstein was shot and killed
by a rival gambler in 1928.

The Legal Record

Shoeless Joe Jackson went through two jury trials. The first was
the celebrated 1921 case in which he stood accused with the
other Black Sox before a Cook County jury. The second trial
occurred in 1924, when Jackson sued the White Sox for back
salary on the grounds that he had been improperly dropped
from the team because of the scandal.

In both trials, Jackson was vindicated by the jury. In the 1921
case, all the accused players were found not guilty. In the 1924
trial, the jury decided that Jackson had been wrongly suspended, and awarded him $16,711.04 compensation for having
his contract illegally voided by Comiskey. As part of its decision, the jury in the second trial issued a "special verdict,"
which consisted of answers to questions posed by the judge.
Question 6 asked: "Did the Plaintiff Jackson unlawfully conspire
with Gandil, Williams and other members of the White Sox
Club, or any of them, to lose or 'throw' any of the base ball
games of the 1919 World's Series to the Cincinnati Baseball
Club?" To this question the jury unequivocally answered no.

But those who believe Jackson to be guilty say that the 1921
and 1924 jury decisions are not conclusive. Prior to the first
trial, much of the evidence against the players, consisting of
original copies of grand jury testimony and other documents,
mysteriously vanished from the prosecution's files. And because
Illinois had no statute specifically making it illegal to throw an
athletic event, the judge instructed the jury that the state had
to prove that the defendants had conspired to "defraud the

public"—a difficult charge to prove. Jackson's accusers also say that the 1921 judge and jury were warmly sympathetic to the players. (Commissioner Landis's order banning the Black Sox came despite the not-guilty verdict.)

In 1924 the jury was again favorably disposed. But this time the judge was not. He overruled the jury's award to Jackson and briefly jailed him for committing perjury. The case was eventually settled out of court.

"SAY IT AIN'T SO"

Did Shoeless Joe confess his guilt to a kid in a crowd? Shortly after Jackson testified to the grand jury in 1920, a story by baseball writer Hugh Fullerton appeared in the *New York Evening World*. Fullerton described how a shamefaced Jackson emerged from the courthouse under guard. A gang of street kids awaited him. One of the boys, braver than the others, cried out, "It ain't so, Joe, is it?"

> Jackson gulped back a sob, the shame of utter shame flushed his brown face. He choked an instant, "Yes Kid, I'm afraid it is," and the world of faith crashed around the heads of the kids. Their idol lay in dust, their faith destroyed. Nothing was true, nothing was honest. There was no Santa Claus. Then, and not until then, did Jackson, hurrying away to escape the sight of the faces of the kids, understand the enormity of the thing he had done.

The story of the encounter between Shoeless Joe and the kid has entered American folklore, with the twist that the kid's question is now remembered as "Say it ain't so, Joe."

Jackson's defenders believe the whole thing never happened. They argue that Fullerton hated Jackson, and was trying to make him look bad. Jackson himself said later it wasn't true:

> I guess the biggest joke of all was that story that got out about "Say it ain't so, Joe." It was supposed to have happened ... when I came out of the court room. There weren't any words passed between anybody except me and a deputy sheriff ... He asked me for a ride and we got in the car together and left. There was a big crowd

hanging around in front of the building, but nobody else said anything to me.

But Jackson's accusers accept the story as genuine. According to the writer John Lardner:

The authenticity of this incident seems pretty well established by the fact that four different men mentioned it in four different stories within three hours of the time that Jackson left the hearing.

Weighing the Evidence

Joseph Jackson led a reasonably comfortable life after his banishment from professional baseball. He returned to the South, where he owned several small businesses and was a player and coach with local teams. In 1949, *Sport* magazine published an interview with the aging former baseball star. Jackson told the interviewer that he had never been involved in the fix. He said he had been named as one of the Black Sox only because he had been the roommate of one of the crooked players. He never mentioned receiving any money. "Oh, there was much talk those days," he said to the interviewer, "but I didn't know anything was going on." Without any intended irony, the article was entitled "This is the Truth!"

But of course, it was not the truth. Jackson's own sworn testimony to the grand jury three decades before confirms that he did indeed know what was going on. Jackson's supporters try to twist the transcript's words. They read Joe's statement about his encounters with Gandil as proof that their man flatly rejected the first baseman's overtures, and they invent a tortured explanation about why he was given money and why he took it. But a fair reading of the transcript indicates that Jackson did not turn Gandil down but instead knowingly accepted the offer to participate in the fix in exchange for a payoff. It could be argued that Jackson's statement "I told them I would take their word" is ambiguous, but there can be little doubt about what Jackson meant when, later in the interrogation, he answered,

"Yes, sir," to the question of whether he had agreed to take part.

At still other places in the transcript, there is ample proof that Jackson knew he had done something wrong. He said that he told Gandil that he wanted to quit, he said that he felt ashamed for what he had done, he said he felt that he had been cheated, and that when he received the payment, his wife "felt awful bad about it, cried about it a while."

The argument of Jackson's modern-day supporters that the transcript was a false statement created by conniving lawyers who bamboozled a confused and drunk Jackson does not wash. Even if Comiskey sought to protect himself and even if Jackson had been denied his full legal rights against self-incrimination, the evidence of the transcript stands.

But how then to explain the fact that Jackson played so well in the Series, at least in his hitting? The answer seems to be that throwing a World Series is not a simple, easily defined task. The conspiracy had to be kept secret from other players and from the crowds of spectators and reporters who watched every movement on the field. The moves of the players in on the deal could not be choreographed in advance; they had to make mistakes as the occasion arose without making it seem obvious. To make matters even more complicated, the gamblers who bankrolled the scheme tried to squeeze the players. They failed to deliver the money as promised, saying that it was out on bets. The players became disgruntled, and they sent a message to the gamblers by winning the third game of the Series. By the end of the Series the whole affair had turned sour. The players were arguing among themselves, and the gamblers were issuing threats of violence.

In such an atmosphere of secrecy, anger, and confusion, it is not hard to imagine how Jackson could agree at the start to throw the game, but then play as he normally would when he stepped up to the plate.

Many of the arguments used by Jackson's champions to prove his innocence could be applied to other members of the Black Sox conspiracy. Just like Jackson, many of the others felt remorse at what they had done, were not paid what they had been promised, and claimed that they played their best. The evidence against Fred McMullin was so weak that he was not put on trial with Jackson and the other Black Sox in 1921. Buck Weaver seems to have backed out of the conspiracy in its early stages and received not a dime. So why is Jackson the only one for whom so vociferous a public campaign has been waged? Probably because he was the best player among them, and the only one who could have made it to the Hall of Fame.

Should Jackson be forgiven after all these years and allowed his place in Cooperstown? Have the successors to Commissioner Landis been too harsh in refusing to relent? Perhaps. And yet, there is a certain majesty to the fact that when standards crumble elsewhere, professional baseball will not abide players who do not perform to the best of their ability.

12

WERE SACCO AND VANZETTI GUILTY?

On Thursday, April 15, 1920, a murder-robbery occurred in the town of South Braintree, Massachusetts, ten miles outside Boston. At about three o'clock in the afternoon, a paymaster and a guard employed by the Slater & Morrill shoe factory were gunned down by a gang of robbers who grabbed the $15,776.51 company payroll and escaped in a stolen car. The crime was vicious; witnesses saw a robber mercilessly pump bullets into the already fallen guard.

Three weeks after the crime, the police arrested two Italian immigrants, Nicola Sacco and Bartolomeo Vanzetti. Sacco was a worker at a shoe factory in Stoughton; his friend Vanzetti was a fish peddler in Plymouth. Both were adherents of the revolutionary doctrine of anarchism.

Sacco and Vanzetti were put on trial in a Dedham, Massachusetts, court and, on July 14, 1921, were found guilty. After repeated appeals were turned down, the two were executed in the electric chair on August 23, 1927, seven years after the crime.

For a majority of Americans during the 1920s, the Sacco-Vanzetti case was exactly what it appeared to be: two criminals had been properly convicted and punished. But for a few people at the time of the trial, and later for millions of angry men and women around the world, the case was a miscarriage of justice and a disgrace to the United States. Defense committees were formed, resolutions were adopted, and pamphlets were written all with one claim: Sacco and Vanzetti were innocent men who, because they were foreigners with unpopular beliefs, had been railroaded by the established order in Massachusetts. Intellectuals like Felix Frankfurter, Albert Einstein, and H. G. Wells wrote on behalf of Sacco and Vanzetti. During the last days before the executions, there were mass demonstrations in Boston, New York, London, Berlin, Johannesburg, Copenhagen, Sydney, Buenos Aires, and elsewhere. In Paris, a mob attacked the American embassy. Communists organized much of this international protest, but it attracted liberals and conservatives as well.

At the funeral service in Boston, an orator expressed the sense of outrage:

> Massachusetts and America have killed you—murdered you because you were Italian anarchists. Two hundred and fifty years ago the controlling people in this state hanged women in Salem—charging them with witch-craft. . . . The minds of those who have killed you are not blinded. They have committed this act in deliberate cold blood . . . You, Sacco and Vanzetti, are the victims of the crassest plutocracy the world has known since ancient Rome.

The battle between the defenders and accusers of Sacco and Vanzetti has continued in the years since the crime in hundreds of books, articles, novels—and even a musical score. Most of these support the view that Sacco and Vanzetti were innocent, but there is a persistent school that supports the view that one or both were guilty as charged. Over and over again, the students of the crime have taken the reader down the dusty factory street in South Braintree to watch the robbery unreel, or into the swelteringly hot courtroom in Dedham to search the faces of the judge and jury for prejudice.

"THOSE ANARCHISTIC BASTARDS"

The crime for which Sacco and Vanzetti were accused occurred at about the time of the so-called Red Scare—a period just after World War I when Americans saw evidence of alien, radical subversion in terrorist bombings and labor unrest. In January 1920, anticommunist raids authorized by the U.S. Department of Justice took place around the nation. Over six thousand suspected radicals were arrested, and hundreds were eventually deported. The defenders of Sacco and Vanzetti believe that in such an atmosphere, it was impossible for two Italian anarchists to obtain a fair trial.

In support of their belief, the defenders of Sacco and Vanzetti point to Webster Thayer, the judge who presided at the trial and who imposed the death sentence. The evidence is strong that Thayer personally believed that Sacco and Vanzetti were guilty. He reportedly said to an acquaintance, "We must protect ourselves against them, there [are] so many reds in the country," and on another occasion, "Did you see what I did with those anarchistic bastards the other day?"

Other participants in the case have been accused of prejudice. The district attorney who presented the prosecution's case, Frederick Katzmann, is depicted as a ruthless lawyer who coerced witnesses to change their testimony and who even fabricated evidence. The jury members at the Dedham trial are said to have been biased against the foreign defendants. The foreman is alleged to have remarked, "Damn them, they ought to hang them anyway."

Those who believe that Sacco and Vanzetti were guilty respond that by the time of the 1921 Dedham trial, the passions of the Red Scare had cooled and the two defendants received reasonably fair treatment. These accusers concede that Thayer was biased, but they argue that he was enough of a jurist to separate his personal prejudices from his courtroom behavior. They point to the fact that at the Dedham trial, Thayer specifically instructed the jury not to be influenced by the politics or foreign birth of the defendants.

As for District Attorney Katzmann, the accusers of Sacco and Vanzetti admit that he was a clever lawyer-politician who would use the standard tools of his trade to win a conviction. But they deny that he would falsify evidence. The accusers point out that neither Thayer nor Katzmann introduced Sacco and Vanzetti's radicalism into the trial at Dedham: that explosive issue was raised by the defense. As for the jury, the accusers cite the testimony of the jurymen in the years after the trial that they based their verdict on the evidence.

But the accusers of Sacco and Vanzetti concede that the attitudes of the Massachusetts establishment did harden in the six years between the trial and the executions. During that period the defense turned up much suggestive new evidence, leads on other possible culprits, affidavits from witnesses who changed their stories, and examples of Judge Thayer's bias. At the same time the clamor for a commutation of the sentence or for a new trial increased. But Judge Thayer coldly turned down all motions for a new trial, and a special advisory committee appointed by the governor of Massachusetts to study the case seems to have proceeded from the assumption that Sacco and Vanzetti were guilty. The modern-day accusers of Sacco and Vanzetti recognize that the more the international protest movement on behalf of the two men grew in size and anger, the more official Massachusetts closed ranks. But the accusers believe this does not negate the guilt of Sacco and Vanzetti.

EYEWITNESSES

Of the dozens of people who claimed to have seen some aspect of the crime, seven testified at the trial that they saw Sacco; four said they saw Vanzetti. The following were the witnesses against Sacco:

➤ Lola Andrews, a passerby, said she spoke to Sacco, who was working under a car on Pearl Street in South Braintree, where the robbery occurred, later that day.

➤ William S. Tracy, a businessman, said he saw Sacco and another man lounging in front of a Pearl Street store around noon.

➤ William J. Heron, a railroad detective, said he saw Sacco and another man in the waiting room of the South Braintree station shortly after noon.

➤ Lewis Pelser, a worker at a factory overlooking the scene of the crime, said he saw Sacco shoot the payroll guard, shoot at the paymaster, and shoot at the factory window where Pelser was watching.

➤ Mary E. Splaine, a factory bookkeeper, said she saw Sacco lean out of the car as it drove away from the crime.

➤ Frances J. Devlin, another bookkeeper, said she saw Sacco

shoot into a crowd of onlookers as the car drove away from the crime.

➤ Carlos E. Goodridge, a salesman, said he was coming out of a Pearl Street poolroom when he saw Sacco in the car as it drove by. Goodridge said Sacco pointed a gun at him.

The following witnesses identified Vanzetti:

➤ John W. Faulkner, a textile worker, said he spoke to Vanzetti on a train to Braintree on the morning of the crime.

➤ Harry Dolbeare, a piano repairer, said he saw Vanzetti in a car with other Italians in South Braintree in the morning.

➤ Michael Levangie, a railroad gate-tender in South Braintree identified Vanzetti as the driver of the getaway car as it drove past his shack.

➤ Austin T. Reed, a gate-tender at a rail crossing outside South Braintree, said he stopped the getaway car at the crossing, and that Vanzetti pointed his finger at Reed and said, "What to hell did you hold us up for?"

The defenders of Sacco and Vanzetti attempt to discredit these witnesses by showing the contradictions in their testimony, their hesitation and doubt about their identification, and in some cases, their dubious character. In regard to the witnesses against Vanzetti, it has been argued that Levangie could not have seen the accused at the wheel, since Vanzetti did not know how to drive, and Reed could not have heard him speaking so plainly, since Vanzetti had a thick accent. Faulkner's testimony that he saw Vanzetti on the train was contradicted by the conductor and by ticket agents. Dolbeare did not come forward with his evidence until he was called as a potential juryman at the Dedham trial, and it is alleged that he testified mainly in order to escape jury duty.

The witnesses against Sacco are even more flawed. Lola Andrews, for example, changed details of her story at various times and failed to identify a photo of Sacco. A defense witness said that Andrews complained to him that the prosecution was pressuring her to identify Sacco and Vanzetti, but that she was unable to do so. Andrews's former landlady and others who knew her testified that the woman was a liar. A woman who had been with Andrews on that day in South Braintree said they had not spoken to the man under the car. A year after the trial, Andrews signed an affidavit saying she had lied at the trial when she identified Sacco; she then retracted her affidavit, saying she had signed it under pressure. Carlos E. Goodridge, the witness at the poolhall, was discovered to be a convicted thief who was using an alias. Three of Lewis Pelser's fellow workers claimed Pelser hid under a bench when the shooting started and did not witness the crime. Pelser, who had a drinking problem, subsequently behaved like Lola Andrews—he retracted his testimony, and then retracted his retraction.

ALIBIS

When questioned about his whereabouts on the day of the crime, Vanzetti said he had been selling fish from his pushcart in Plymouth. The following witnesses appeared on his behalf:

➤ Joseph Rosen, a peddler, said he had sold Vanzetti some fabric that day.

➤ Alfonsina Brini, a friend of Vanzetti's, said she had seen Vanzetti with Rosen, and then saw Vanzetti selling fish.

➤ LeFavre Brini, the fifteen-year-old daughter of Alfonsina, said she was given fish by Vanzetti.

➤ Angel Guidobone, a friend of Vanzetti, said she purchased fish from him.

➤ Melvin Corl, a fisherman, said he spoke to Vanzetti for about an hour and a half while he, Corl, was painting his boat.

➤ Frank Jesse, a boatbuilder, said he saw Vanzetti speaking to Corl.

At the time of his arrest, Sacco was vague about where he had been on the day of the robbery, at first saying that he had probably been at the 3-K shoe factory where he was employed. But the payroll records of the factory indicate that he was not at work on that day. Sacco then claimed that on that day he had gone to Boston to arrange for a passport to return to Italy. The following witnesses corroborated his story:

➤ Dominick Ricci, a carpenter, said he saw Sacco at the train station in the morning waiting for the Boston train.

➤ Angelo Monello, a contractor, said he saw Sacco in Boston's North End.

➤ Albert Bosco, an editor; Felice Guadagni, a journalist; John Williams, an advertising agent; and Antonio Dentamore, a bank employee all said that at one time or other they met Sacco in a Boston restaurant.

➤ Giuseppe Andrower, an Italian passport official, said he saw Sacco in the embassy.

➤ Carlos Affe, a Boston grocery store owner, said he conducted business with Sacco.

The accusers of Sacco and Vanzetti point out that most of the witnesses who corroborated their alibis were Italians, most were friends of the defendants, and many had leftist connections. For example, Williams was an active member of the radical labor union, Industrial Workers of the World; Ricci and Affe were anarchists. The defenders respond that one would expect men of like belief and background to associate with one another.

The accusers try to discredit the alibi testimony by asking how witnesses testifying more than a year later could be sure it was on April 15, 1920, and not some other date, when they saw Sacco in Boston and Vanzetti in Plymouth. In one instance, however, there was some confirming evidence. Bosco, Guadagni, and Dentamore all said they were able to remember it was April 15 when they met Sacco because they had discussed a banquet in the North End that day for a well-known Italian newspaper editor. Years later, the appeals committee appointed by the governor of Massachusetts expressed doubt about the testimony, since records indicated that the editor had been feted in May; however, an edition of a Boston Italian-American newspaper from April 1920 was produced that contained a notice of another banquet for the same editor that had taken place on April 15.

THE MORELLI GANG

South Braintree witnesses established the fact that five men committed the crime. The accusers believe that two of them were Sacco and Vanzetti and that the others were friends of theirs: Mike Boda, Ferruccio Coacci, and Ricardo Orciani are the names most often mentioned by students of the crime. The shadowy Coacci had been deported to Italy for radical activities just before Sacco and Vanzetti's arrest; Orciani was not indicted because his factory record showed he had been at work on the day of the crime; Boda managed to flee to Italy before he could be apprehended. If this group did not commit the South Braintree robbery, who did? The defenders of Sacco and Vanzetti argue that it was the Morelli gang from Providence, Rhode Island.

In 1925, one Celestino Medeiros, a young Portuguese hoodlum who had been convicted of the murder of a bank cashier and who was in jail while his conviction was being appealed, confessed that he had committed the South Braintree robbery along with a gang of Italians from Providence. He refused to name his confederates, but said that Sacco and Vanzetti were not among them. It was discovered by one of Sacco and Vanzetti's attorneys that there was in fact a gang of Italian criminals in Providence, led by Joseph Morelli and his brothers. One of the gang's specialties was stealing from freight cars, and in the past they had pilfered merchandise shipped from South Braintree shoe factories. They may have thus had a contact in South Braintree who could have provided them with details of the delivery of the Slater & Morrill factory payroll.

Witnesses from the underworld were found who stated that Medeiros had told them it was the Morelli gang that had pulled off the job. Another bit of confirming evidence is that Joseph Morelli bore a strong resemblance to Sacco. The defenders have identified other members of the gang whose features corresponded to witness accounts and who might have been available on the date of the crime.

The accusers of Sacco and Vanzetti dismiss Medeiros, calling him a minor crook of weak intelligence who possibly thought that he could gain some legal and financial support from the Sacco-Vanzetti defense committee. They also cite inconsistencies in his testimony. He claimed, for example, that the payroll was in a large sack, when in fact it was in two metal boxes. He also said that the gang arrived in South Braintree around noon, but it had been established by witnesses that the robbers had arrived in town much earlier in the day.

SACCO'S PISTOL AND THE BALLISTIC EVIDENCE

Shortly after the South Braintree robbery, four ejected shells of the type used in a .32-caliber automatic pistol were found near the scene of the crime. The shells were of different manufacture: two were Peters, one a Remington, and one a Winchester. When Sacco was arrested three weeks later, he had in his possession a .32-caliber Colt automatic pistol and an assortment of .32-caliber cartridges that included sixteen Peters, three Remingtons, and six Winchesters.

In the course of the autopsy performed on the slain payroll guard, the county medical examiner found four bullets in the body. He marked each of these bullets with a Roman numeral in the order in which he removed them from the corpse—I, II, III, and IIII. Bullet III, which was evidently the one that proved fatal, was an obsolete type of Winchester that had not been manufactured since 1917. The Winchester cartridges in Sacco's possession were of the same obsolete type.

At the Dedham trial, the prosecution produced experts who said that based on ballistic evidence, bullet III could have come from Sacco's automatic. In the years after the trial, the tools for analyzing ballistic evidence became more sophisticated. In 1927, an expert using an improved type of microscope stated that both bullet III and one of the shells found at the crime scene (known as "shell W") definitely matched test shells and bullets fired from Sacco's pistol. This was confirmed by other ballistics tests in 1961 and 1983. The 1983 test produced another conclusion: the Peters shells found at the crime scene and those in Sacco's possession were manufactured on the same milling machine.

All of these findings are used by the accusers to prove that Sacco participated in the South Braintree crime.

The defenders of Sacco and Vanzetti refute this evidence on several points. They argue that if Sacco's assortment of cartridges matched that found at the crime scene, it was simply a coincidence. The brands were common, even the obsolete Winchesters. And if the Peters shells were manufactured on the same machine, this too proves nothing. During the trial, the defense introduced its own experts who stated flatly that bullet III was not fired from Sacco's pistol. But as time went on and the ballistics evidence seemed more firm, and as shell W was also identified as coming from Sacco's automatic, the defenders of the two anarchists took a new tack, arguing that fraud had been practiced: that the prosecution had dishonestly substituted a bullet from a test firing of Sacco's gun in place of bullet III, and at the same time added shell W to the shells found at South Braintree.

As evidence of this deception, the defenders present several arguments. First, the Roman numeral scratched in the base of bullet III appears to be different from those that the medical examiner scratched in the other bullets he removed from the corpse. The counterargument is that whatever minor differences there were probably came from the fact that bullet III was slightly deformed because it struck a bone.

Second, the defenders point out that while bullet III may have come from Sacco's gun, the bullets marked I, II, and IIII removed from the slain guard came from some other pistol. So if bullet III is genuine, there must have been two gunmen who shot the guard; one who fired bullets I, II, and IIII; and the other who fired bullet III. But most witnesses to the shooting saw only one gunman standing over the guard and firing at close range. The counterargument is that the moments of the shooting were chaotic, and no witness saw the entire event.

Third, the defenders say that District Attorney Katzmann desperately wanted a conviction, so he took the risk of making a substitution. The counterargument is that at the time of the alleged substitution, the case had not taken on the world-shattering dimensions of later years, and that Katzmann would not have risked his career for so minor a conviction. Moreover, it was not until years after the Dedham trial that improvements in ballistics technology made it possible to state with a degree of certainty that bullet III and shell W came from Sacco's pistol.

VANZETTI'S REVOLVER

When Vanzetti was arrested he had in his pocket a .38-caliber Harrington & Richardson revolver. He had no extra bullets for it—only those in the revolver. The payroll guard who was murdered at South Braintree was said to have owned the same kind of pistol. It was not found on his body, and the accusers of Sacco and Vanzetti say that the robbers must have taken it away with them. It was this gun, they say, that Vanzetti was carrying when he was arrested.

Like so much else in this case, the story of the gun is tangled. About three weeks before he was killed, the guard had taken the pistol to a repair shop in Boston, where the hammer was replaced. At the trial, the prosecution said that Vanzetti's pistol had a new hammer, thus proving it was taken from the guard; the defense said the pistol did not have a new hammer, proving it did not come from the guard. The defense further developed an alternative history for Vanzetti's revolver, saying it had originally belonged to a man in Maine, and was not the one owned by the payroll guard. To complicate the matter still further, there is some debate about whether the guard's gun was a .38 or a .32 revolver and whether or not the guard was even armed that day. The one person who could have cleared up this whole debate was the company paymaster, but he was murdered along with the guard on April 15.

About all that can be said is that Vanzetti's pistol was the same kind thought to have been carried by the murdered payroll guard.

The Shoemaker and the Fish Peddler

Much has been made by the defenders of Sacco and Vanzetti of the noble character of the two men. During the seven years the two spent in prison, they projected themselves as innocent victims of persecution. In his letters and in the testimony of his supporters, Sacco emerged as a simple, hardworking man who loved his family. Vanzetti was a much more remarkable personality. Although English was not his native language, he wrote and spoke with extraordinary eloquence. The following words in rough English, which were attributed to Vanzetti by a newspaper reporter who interviewed him on death row, have been compared to the Gettysburg Address in their spare beauty:

If it had not been for this thing, I might have live out my life among scorning men, I might have die, unmarked, unknown, a failure. Now we are not a failure. This is our career and our triumph. Never in our full life can we hope

to do such work for tolerance, for joostice, for man's understanding of man, as now we do by an accident.

Our words—our lives—our pains—nothing! The taking
of our lives—lives of a good shoemaker and a poor fish
peddler—all!

The moment that you think of belong to us—that last
agony is our triumph!

Those who believe Sacco and Vanzetti to be guilty say that
Vanzetti may not have actually said these words; that they were
mostly invented by the newspaper reporter. And even if Vanzetti did say it, eloquence is not proof of innocence. The accusers also point to the circumstances of the arrest of Sacco and
Vanzetti, which took place at night on a Brockton streetcar.
They were under suspicion because they had earlier that evening been in the company of Mike Boda, who was thought by
police to have something to do with the South Braintree crime.
When they were arrested, Sacco and Vanzetti were armed with
pistols. The police claimed that the two men made a motion as
if to draw those weapons. When later questioned by District
Attorney Katzmann on such issues as their whereabouts on the
day of the South Braintree crime, where they obtained their
weapons, and whether they knew other suspects, Sacco and
Vanzetti seem to have prevaricated, or at least they gave accounts that they later changed. These circumstances were used
at the trial and have been used since then as evidence that Sacco
and Vanzetti behaved as if they were guilty of some wrongdoing.

The defenders say Sacco and Vanzetti carried guns only because it was customary for Italian immigrants to do so at the
time and the story that they attempted to draw those weapons
was a police lie. If they seemed to act as if they were in fear,
it was because as anarchists they legitimately feared official persecution for their beliefs. Indeed, a fellow anarchist had died in
police custody in New York a short time before.

And what about anarchism? The defenders of Sacco and Vanzetti emphasize the utopian aspects of that creed, saying that it
represented a belief in human freedom and economic justice.
The accusers say that a key tenet of anarchism was the belief
that violence against the oppressive capitalist order was justified
in order to hasten the revolution. Sacco and Vanzetti, say their
accusers, would have regarded the theft of a payroll and the

slaying of a guard and a paymaster not as a crime but as a heroic battle within the international class war.

Weighing the Evidence

The defenders of Sacco and Vanzetti have much in their favor when they claim that the two anarchists were elsewhere when the robbery-murder was committed in South Braintree on April 15, 1920. Only a minority of the eyewitnesses placed them at the crime scene, and the credibility of some members of that minority is deeply flawed. It is true that the alibi witnesses produced by Sacco and Vanzetti's defense are also weak; most of them were friends and fellow radicals. But if the burden of proof is on the prosecution, then one would conclude that at least on the testimony of the witnesses, the case is unproved.

It also seems to be true that there was a degree of prejudice against Sacco and Vanzetti. While the trial was not the kangaroo court that the defenders describe, Judge Webster Thayer's remarks outside the courtroom about "anarchistic bastards" would seem to justify a new trial with a different judge. So too would other nagging facts—such as the confession of Medeiros and the retractions signed by two prosecution witnesses.

So the accusers of Sacco and Vanzetti do not seem to have a convincing case except for one thing—the ballistics evidence. The following points have been established about Sacco's gun and ammunition:

➤ The assortment of cartridges in Sacco's possession matched the assortment found at the crime scene.

➤ The Peters cartridges owned by Sacco were evidently manufactured on the same machine as the ones found at the crime scene.

➤ The Winchester bullets owned by Sacco were of the same obsolete type as the one found at the crime scene.

➤ Most importantly, one of the bullets and one of the shells fired during the crime probably came from Sacco's pistol.

This evidence outweighs all the weaknesses of the other, circumstantial evidence. It had a dramatic effect on those who saw
it. One of the Dedham jurors was asked years later which evidence impressed him the most:

> The bullets, of course. That testimony and evidence on it
> sticks in your mind. You can't depend on the witnesses.
> But the bullets, there was no getting around that evidence.

The comparison microscope, which was developed after the
trial, made it possible to compare, with great precision, the bullet and shell that came from the crime scene with those obtained
in test firings from Sacco's gun. Essentially, the microscope
fuses the image from half of one bullet (or shell) to half of the
other, so that the viewer can see if distinctive marks on one are
continued on the other. Photos of bullet III and a test bullet
taken through the comparison microscope are indeed striking.
One observer said that it is like being able to produce an exact
match between two different photos of a landscape of muddy,
crisscrossed paths.

William E. Young and David E. Kaiser, two recent defenders
of Sacco and Vanzetti, admitted the importance of the ballistics
evidence, saying that "if bullet III is genuine Sacco is probably
guilty." Young and Kaiser, like other partisans of Sacco and
Vanzetti, then tried to prove that bullet III is not genuine. But
the evidence they provide—the suspicious scratch marks, the
witness accounts of one gunman, and the supposed duplicity
of the district attorney—fail to provide convincing proof.

So the probability is that Sacco was one of the participants
in the South Braintree murders. But what about Vanzetti? No
evidence comparable to bullet III and shell W exists to connect
him to the crime. There are some tantalizing hints that suggest
he was in fact innocent. For example, three men who were
active in the defense of Sacco and Vanzetti in the 1920s—attorney Fred Moore and Italian anarchists Carlo Tresca and Gio-
vanni Gambera—are reported to have privately spoken to the
effect that Sacco was guilty and Vanzetti innocent. And during
the long years in prison, Vanzetti was much more vehement
than Sacco in denying his involvement in the crime and in
fighting for a new trial. Even as he was brought into the death
chamber, Vanzetti continued to declare his innocence. In con-

trast, Sacco shouted, "Long live anarchy!" as he was put to death.

The question of Vanzetti's innocence has produced a split in the ranks of the accusers. Two authors, Francis Russell and James Grossman, were drawn to the conclusion that Vanzetti was not guilty. But another, David Felix, argued that if we accept Sacco's guilt, then the testimony of the South Braintree witnesses must have been accurate. How can we then assume, asked Felix, that only the witnesses against Vanzetti were lying and only Vanzetti was framed by the prosecution? Said Felix, "on the basis of the known facts and simple reasoning, the student of the case is forced to conclude that the guilt-innocence division creates many new problems and leaves the old ones unresolved."

But without the same hard, physical evidence that tips the scale against Sacco, the case against Vanzetti simply cannot be proved. In sum, the probability is that Sacco was guilty and Vanzetti was innocent.

Of course, we can never know with certainty whether Sacco and Vanzetti were among the gang of robbers who killed the paymaster and the guard in Braintree on April 15, 1920. For three-quarters of a century, the case has continued to divide the defenders and the accusers of the two anarchists. We can sympathize with the Bostonian who remarked that one reason why the afterlife might be attractive is that he could finally learn the truth about the good shoemaker and the poor fish peddler.

13

WHO KIDNAPPED THE
LINDBERGH BABY?

"Mrs. Lindbergh, do you have the baby?" Betty Gow anxiously asked Anne Morrow Lindbergh. It was shortly after 10:00 P.M. on the evening of March 1, 1932, at the estate of the famous aviator Charles Lindbergh and his wife Anne in rural Hopewell, New Jersey. The nursemaid Gow had discovered that the Lindbergh's twenty-month-old baby, Charles Jr., was missing from his nursery crib. Summoned by the nursemaid, Charles and Anne rushed into the room and found the window of the nursery open and an envelope, which turned out to contain a ransom note, resting on the sill. So began the Lindbergh kidnapping case, arguably the most famous and controversial crime of the twentieth century.

Colonel Lindbergh paid a ransom of fifty thousand dollars one month after the kidnapping, but the baby was not returned. The body of the child was later found in the woods about two miles from the Lindbergh home; Charles Jr. had apparently died on the night of the crime and was dumped there.

Two and a half years after the kidnapping, the police arrested Bruno Richard Hauptmann, a German immigrant carpenter who lived in the Bronx with his wife and son. Hauptmann was brought to trial in Flemington, New Jersey, and found guilty of murder-kidnapping. He died in the electric chair on April 3, 1936.

Over the years there have been serious doubts about whether Hauptmann was guilty, and the case has been debated in books and in the courts. His most fervent advocate was his widow, Anna, who campaigned fiercely for over sixty years to clear her husband's name, even after a lawsuit that she initiated against the state of New Jersey was dismissed without comment by the U.S. Supreme Court in 1986. Other early supporters of Hauptmann were his attorney, Lloyd Fisher, who continued to fight after other defense lawyers gave up, and Harold Hoffman, a governor of New Jersey in the 1930s who expressed public doubts about the verdict.

Was the conviction and execution of Bruno Richard Hauptmann a miscarriage of justice?

THE RANSOM MONEY

Hauptmann's troubles began when he used a ten-dollar bill from the Lindbergh ransom money to purchase gas at a Manhattan service station. An attendant at the station wrote down the license plate number on the bill, and the police tracked the registration to Hauptmann and arrested him. After his arrest, lawmen found $13,760 in ransom bills hidden behind the walls of his garage. It was possible to identify the ransom money because the serial number of the bills had been recorded before the ransom was passed. The bills were also noticeable because they were gold certificates, which became rare after the United States government introduced a new form of currency in 1933.

Those who believe Hauptmann was guilty regard his possession of the ransom money as compelling evidence that he was the kidnapper. But Hauptmann's defenders provide the following explanation of how he came to have the money, based on his own testimony:

Hauptmann, they say, had entered into a business partnership with a fellow German immigrant named Isidor Fisch. Just before Fisch left for a trip back to Germany in late 1933, he asked Hauptmann to keep some property for him, including a shoe box. (A friend of Hauptmann's later testified that he had seen Fisch bring the shoe box to Hauptmann's apartment.) Hauptmann placed the box on an upper shelf in a kitchen broom closet and forgot about it. In August 1934, Hauptmann was doing some work in the kitchen when he came across the shoe box, which was wet from a leak in the ceiling. He opened up the box and discovered to his astonishment that it contained about fourteen thousand dollars. He didn't know it was part of the Lindbergh kidnap money, but he did know that Fisch—who had since died in Germany—owed him money from their joint business ventures. Hauptmann decided to keep the money for himself. Hauptmann's defenders say that taking this money was his one illegal act. They believe that Fisch was most likely a money launderer, who bought the ransom money at a discount from the real kidnappers.

But those who believe Hauptmann is guilty ridicule the "Fisch Story" as an improbable lie. They argue that Hauptmann actually spent some of the money before he claimed to have opened the shoe box. The key proof they offer is the testimony of Cecile Barr, a cashier at a Manhattan movie theater. Barr said that on a night in November 1933—nine months before Hauptmann said he opened the shoe box—a man Barr subsequently identified as Hauptmann paid for a movie ticket with a five-dollar bill that turned out to be from the ransom.

THE LADDER

On the night of the kidnapping, a homemade, portable ladder consisting of three sections held together by pegs was discovered on the grounds of the Lindbergh estate; it had evidently been used to take the baby from the second-floor nursery. After Hauptmann was arrested, police searching his Bronx apartment found that part of a plank used in the flooring of the attic had been sawed off and removed. An expert from the U.S. Department of Agriculture, Arthur Koehler, concluded that the wood grain and nail holes in one of the side rails of the ladder (known as "rail sixteen") proved that the rail was made from the missing attic plank.

Koehler provided more evidence to link the ladder to Hauptmann. Through an analysis of unique characteristics of the wood in other sections of the ladder, he claimed that the material had been purchased from a lumberyard in the Bronx, not far from where Hauptmann lived. He also said that tools belonging to Hauptmann—a chisel, a saw, and a wood plane—had been used in the construction of the ladder. A sketch resembling the ladder was found in a notebook seized from Hauptmann's home.

Hauptmann's defenders attack this evidence as fabrication. They note that it was not until a week after the police occupied the Hauptmann apartment that the attic plank was discovered to be missing. They charge that the police themselves sawed off the board and then tampered with either the remaining section of the planking or with the original rail sixteen to make the rail in the ladder appear to match the attic plank. To support their claim, the defenders cite one of the defense witnesses at the trial who said he had examined rail sixteen early in the investigation and saw only one nail hole in it; the rail exhibited at the trial had four nail holes, demonstrating that the evidence had been faked.

Hauptmann's defenders also argue that the wood in the ladder does not, in fact, match the attic plank. Three men with experience in woodworking and carpentry testified for the defense at the trial; they claimed that, based on patterns in the grain, thickness of the board, and markings on the plank, rail sixteen did not come from Hauptmann's attic. The defenders say that a narrow strip of wood that would have gone between the attic wood and rail sixteen was missing, making it impossible to match the grain. One witness added that the evidence linking Hauptmann's woodworking tools to the ladder was inconclusive.

Hauptmann himself said that he had not made the sketch in his notebook and that the ladder was too crude to be made by a professional. "If I made that ladder," he said to a reporter, "I would be a second-rate carpenter."

JAFSIE AND OTHER WITNESSES

A key witness in the case was a retired school principal living in the Bronx, Dr. John F. Condon. Shortly after the kidnapping, the seventy-two-year-old Condon wrote a letter to a local paper offering to serve as go-between. He was contacted by a man who said he was a member of the kidnapping gang. The Lindbergh family and the police believed that the man was in fact the kidnapper because a letter he sent to Condon had a symbol of two interlocking circles—the same symbol used as an identifying mark on the ransom note left in the nursery.

Condon spoke to this man, who called himself "John," on the telephone, received letters from him, and met him on two occasions at night in Bronx cemeteries. At their last cemetery meeting, on April 2, 1932, Condon handed over the ransom to John while Colonel Lindbergh waited in a nearby car. At the trial, Condon identified Hauptmann as John.

The defenders of Hauptmann depict Condon as a blustering, melodramatic, publicity-seeking character (he gave himself the code name "Jafsie," from his initials) who had seen John only at night. When he was first called to identify Hauptmann in a police lineup, he seemed to express doubt.

The other main witnesses for the prosecution were the following:

➤ Amandus P. Hockmuth lived in Hopewell where the road to the Lindbergh estate intersected the county highway. He testified that on the day of the kidnapping, he saw Hauptmann drive by in a car with a ladder in the backseat. Hauptmann's defenders argue that the eighty-seven-year-old Hockmuth was nearly blind.

➤ Millard Whited, a logger who lived in the vicinity of the Lindbergh estate, said that he had seen Hauptmann in the area a few days before the kidnapping. Hauptmann's defenders say that the illiterate Whited was a disreputable local character who was given money by the police for his testimony.

➤ Joseph Perrone was a Bronx taxi driver who identified Hauptmann as the man who had given him a dollar one night in the Bronx to take a letter to Condon during the negotiation over the ransom. The defenders say that Perrone was a weak character who, like other defense witnesses, wanted to be involved in solving the crime of the century.

➤ Charles A. Lindbergh himself testified that while he was waiting in the car the night Condon passed the ransom to John in the Bronx cemetery, he heard the kidnapper calling out, "Hey, Doctor!" to Condon. Lindbergh identified the voice as Hauptmann's. The defenders of Hauptmann ask how Lindbergh could make this identification on the basis of a shout heard in the dark more than two years before.

➤ Cecile Barr was the movie cashier who identified Hauptmann as the man who paid for a movie ticket with a
Lindbergh bill. The defenders ask how Barr could remember one customer out of the thousands she sold tickets to.

At the trial, the defense produced witnesses who claimed that
Hauptmann had been elsewhere on the key evenings in the
kidnapping saga.

➤ *The night of the kidnapping.* Anna Hauptmann testified
that her husband picked her up from the Bronx bakery
where she worked and that they spent the rest of the
evening at home. Other witnesses agreed that Hauptmann
had been at the bakery.

➤ *The night the ransom money was passed from Condon to
John.* Anna and another family friend, Hans Kloppenburg,
said they had spent a congenial evening at home with
Hauptmann.

➤ *The night Cecile Barr sold the movie ticket.* This date
happened to be Hauptmann's birthday. Anna and family
friends said they had all been at home in the Bronx cele-
brating with him, so that he could not have slipped out
to a Manhattan movie theater.

Nothing so much symbolizes the conflicting testimony of witnesses as the case of Carlstrom and Larson. Elvert Carlstrom
was one of the defense witnesses who claimed to have seen
Hauptmann at the Bronx bakery on the night of the kidnapping.
But the prosecution produced another witness, Arthur Larson,
who said that on that evening he and Carlstrom had been out
of town.

BOAD, REDY, HAUS

The ransom note left in the nursery and other notes and letters
allegedly sent to Lindbergh and Condon from the kidnapper
contained some curious misspellings: *boat* was written as
"boad," *signature* as "singnature," *ready* as "redy," *good* as
"gut," and *house* as "haus." Dollar amounts were written with

the dollar sign at the end—for example, 50,000$. From these peculiarities it was theorized that the writer was German.

When Hauptmann was arrested, the police kept him up for hours writing words and sentences down on paper. This body of writing is known as the "request" writing because it was requested by the police. In addition, the lawmen collected examples of Hauptmann's handwriting from before the arrest—his notebooks, letters, and automobile license application. This material is referred to as the "conceded" writings, since it was conceded by the defense that it was written by Hauptmann.

These three bodies of written evidence—the kidnapping letters, the request writing, and the conceded writing—have been the subject of fierce debate between those who believe Hauptmann to be guilty and those who believe him to be innocent. During the trial, the prosecution presented eight handwriting experts who identified Hauptmann as the man who wrote the ransom notes. The experts claimed, for example, that in a 1931 entry in his notebook, Hauptmann spelled *boat* as "boad," the same error that appeared in one of the notes given by the kidnapper to Condon.

The defense presented one expert who said that the handwriting on the notes was not Hauptmann's. Why only one? The accusers say that other experts retained by the defense refused to testify because they thought the writing did match; the defenders say that Hauptmann's legal team could not afford to hire more than one expert.

Hauptmann's defenders say that the request writing was flawed by the fact that Hauptmann had been deliberately forced by the police to write words as they had been spelled in the ransom documents. Moreover, say the defenders, the circumstances of the request writing—Hauptmann was exhausted and was given different pens—might have distorted his natural handwriting and created some artificial similarities with the kidnap letters. Hauptmann's defenders add that the prosecution's handwriting experts were as eager as other principals in the case to see to it that the defendant was convicted, and that they were thus biased in their analysis of the handwriting. They say, for example, that Hauptmann spelled *boat* correctly in the conceded writings, but that the prosecution experts negligently read the "t" as a "d."

A significant piece of writing cited by those who believe Hauptmann to be guilty is Dr. Condon's phone number and

address, which had been written on the door trim inside a closet
in Hauptmann's home. When he was arrested by the police,
Hauptmann admitted that he had written the information about
Condon there. Hauptmann's supporters assert that the closet
writing was planted by a newspaper reporter trying to create a
story, and that Hauptmann confessed to writing it because he
was confused after the brutal police interrogation.

HAUPTMANN'S JOB AND FINANCES

Around the time of the kidnapping, Hauptmann was working
as a carpenter on a construction job at the Majestic Apartments
in Manhattan. One important question is whether he was working there on March 1, when the kidnapping took place.

The defenders of Hauptmann make much of the fact that
Joseph Furcht, the manager of the construction job, told a reporter that on March 1 Hauptmann had worked from 8:00 A.M.
to 5:00 P.M. which would have made it difficult for the carpenter
to drive to New Jersey that night. But Furcht soon thereafter
changed his story, saying that he had only guessed that Hauptmann had worked on that day, and was not really sure.

The defenders of Hauptmann say that Furcht changed his
story under pressure from the police. The defenders say further
that the actual payroll records for the period March 1 to March
15, which would show that Hauptmann had indeed worked at
the Majestic on the day of the kidnapping, were confiscated and
suppressed by the authorities. But Hauptmann himself said on
the stand that although he reported to work on the morning of
March 1, he left when he was told there was no work for him
that day. The timekeeper of the construction project at the Majestic said Hauptmann did not start work until March 21.

One fact not in dispute about Hauptmann's employment at
the Majestic is that he quit his job there in early April, the time
when the fifty-thousand-dollar ransom was paid. Despite the
fact that the country was in the midst of the depression, Hauptmann did not again seek regular work as a carpenter. The accusers of Hauptmann point out that although he did not hold a
steady job, he lived comfortably and was able to afford such
luxuries as a trip for Anna and himself to Florida and a trip
for Anna to visit relatives in Germany.

At the trial, an accountant from the U.S. Treasury Department testified that he had examined Hauptmann's personal finances and concluded that his assets could only be explained by the fact that at some point around April 1932 Hauptmann acquired approximately fifty thousand dollars.

Hauptmann's defenders say that the accountant's estimate was deliberately distorted, and that what money Hauptmann did have came from freelance carpentry work, from his business partnership with Fisch, and from good investments in the stock market.

THE BODY IN THE WOODS

On May 12, 1932, seventy-two days after the kidnapping, a truck driver parked by the side of the road and walked into the woods to relieve himself. When he had gone in about seventy-five feet, he came across the badly decomposed body of an infant. The site was not far from the Lindbergh home. The infant was identified as the Lindbergh baby by the clothing, teeth, hair, and other signs. A burlap sack was found nearby, presumably the one used to take the baby from the nursery. An autopsy identified the cause of death as a skull fracture.

Some of the defenders of Hauptmann say that the body was not that of the Lindbergh baby; that the body of another child was placed in the woods to mislead the authorities. If true, the charge of murder lodged against Hauptmann would obviously carry little weight. But why would someone place such a decoy? One explanation is that local bootleggers did so to stop the police from searching cars and trucks in their quest for the kidnappers, a practice that was disrupting the traffic in illegal liquor.

Others among Hauptmann's defenders are willing to concede that the body found in the woods was actually Charles Lindbergh, Jr., but they point to the mishandling of the body of the infant as an illustration of how the authorities bungled the entire case. A detective examining the body in the woods accidentally poked a hole in the corpse's head with a stick. The county physician who was supposed to conduct the autopsy tried to cover up the fact that the autopsy had actually been performed by his friend, the local undertaker.

How did the baby die? At about the time of the kidnapping, Colonel Lindbergh heard the sound of wood cracking. In fact, one of the rungs on the kidnapping ladder was broken. It may be that the kidnapper fell while carrying the baby down the ladder, accidentally killing the child. Another hypothesis is that the kidnapper deliberately killed the infant with a blow to the head.

IF HAUPTMANN DIDN'T DO IT, WHO DID?

The defenders of Hauptmann say that it is far-fetched to imagine that a Bronx carpenter could have known enough about the physical layout of the Lindbergh estate and the lives of the people in the household to have carried out the kidnapping. How could Hauptmann have known that the baby was kept in the nursery on the corner of the second floor, or that the Lindberghs would be staying there on a Tuesday? The house had only recently been completed, and the family usually stayed there only on weekends, spending the rest of the week at the home of Mrs. Lindbergh's parents in Englewood, New Jersey. But because the baby had a cold, the Lindberghs postponed their departure and were staying an extra two days at the estate.

Hauptmann's defenders believe that the crime was most likely an inside job, carried out by members of the household. Betty Gow, the nursemaid, resided at the home of Anne Lindbergh's parents in Englewood. She was called to the Hopewell estate on Tuesday because the baby was sick. Before leaving Englewood she left a telephone message for her boyfriend, Henry "Red" Johnson, saying she would have to break their date. Johnson telephoned Betty Gow at Hopewell that evening. The defenders suggest that Johnson, a Norwegian sailor, may have been involved with the kidnapping.

Another suspect often named by Hauptmann's defenders is Violet Sharpe, a maid at Englewood who committed suicide by taking poison about two months after the kidnapping. Other servants who have come under suspicion are Oliver and Elsie Whately, who worked in the Lindbergh household, and Charles Ellerson, a chauffeur at the estate of Anne Lindbergh's parents. At the trial, Hauptmann's attorney suggested that one of the servants could have taken the child from his crib, walked down the main stairs, and handed the child to an accomplice waiting at the front door.

Other possible culprits have been suggested from time to time:

➤ *J. J. Faulkner.* On March 1, 1933, a man who signed his name "J.J. Faulkner" exchanged $2,980 in gold notes at a Federal Reserve bank; the notes turned out to be part of the Lindbergh ransom money. Faulkner was never found, and it was generally agreed that his handwriting did not match Hauptmann's.

➤ *Charles Lindbergh.* It is sometimes claimed that Lindbergh himself was the kidnapper. The argument is that Lindbergh was fond of practical jokes and decided to trick his wife by removing their son from the nursery, but the ladder broke and the baby was killed. To cover up this grotesque error, Lindbergh faked a kidnapping.

➤ *Elizabeth Morrow.* One writer, Noel Behn, believed that the child was killed by Anne Morrow Lindbergh's sister, Elizabeth. The mentally ill Elizabeth, he said, was jealous of Anne's marriage to the hero aviator. The Lindberghs invented the kidnapping story to cover up this family scandal.

➤ *Jafsie.* The defenders of Hauptmann suggest that the principal prosecution witness, Dr. John F. Condon, may have orchestrated an enormous swindle and kept the bulk of the Lindbergh money for himself

➤ *The Italian gang.* Dr. Condon said that when he'd spoken to "John" on the telephone, he'd heard someone in the background speaking in Italian. The defenders say this demonstrates that there were others involved, perhaps a gang of Italians.

➤ *Paul Wendel.* A New Jersey county detective, Ellis Parker, claimed that one Paul Wendel, a disbarred Trenton lawyer, had committed the crime. Parker produced a confession signed by Wendel, but Wendel said the confession was a fake that he had been coerced into writing.

In these interpretations, Hauptmann is sometimes regarded as a simple extortionist who pretended to be the kidnapper. His defenders theorize that he learned about the identifying symbol of the two interlocking circles on the nursery ransom note and used the symbol to pass himself off as the kidnapper in order to collect the ransom money.

The accusers of Hauptmann dismiss these alternative explanations as red herrings. In regard to Violet Sharpe, for example, the accusers say that she had a hidden history of sexual immorality and was afraid that this information would come out in the kidnapping investigation, causing her to lose her job. In regard to the "Italian gang," the accusers say that perhaps Hauptmann was calling from a public phone, and the voices were from passersby.

As for how Hauptmann could have known about the Lindbergh household, the accusers speculate that he might have learned the location of the nursery by observing the house from the surrounding woods. And they speculate that Hauptmann had no idea that the Lindberghs were usually gone from the estate on weekdays; it was pure, dumb luck for Hauptmann that the Lindberghs happened to be home when he arrived to kidnap the child.

"GOD WILL BE JUDGE BETWEEN ME AND YOU"

The defenders of Hauptmann make much of the fact that throughout the ordeal of his arrest, trial, and imprisonment on death row, he never wavered in claiming his innocence, even when he was beaten by police, when the governor of New Jersey offered to commute his sentence to life in prison, and when a newspaper chain offered to provide funds to support his wife and son. In a letter written from death row before he was to be executed, Hauptmann addressed New Jersey attorney general David Wilentz, who had prosecuted him at the trial:

> Mr. Wilentz, with my dying breath, I swear by God that you convicted an innocent man. Once you will stand before the same judge to whom I go in a few hours. You know you has done wrong on me, you will not only take my life but also all the happiness of my family. God will be judge between me and you.

And then there was Anna, who for the rest of her life unwaveringly maintained that her husband was innocent. When, just before Hauptmann was scheduled to die, the governor suggested her husband might be hiding the truth, she reportedly cried out: "No, no, no! That isn't so. Richard did tell the truth. He is telling the truth."

The defenders speak of the attractive parts of Hauptmann's character; that he was a loving husband to Anna and an affectionate father to his young son. The defenders note that his desire to come to America was so strong that he twice stowed away on a ship from Germany to the United States.

The accusers of Hauptmann offer a different portrait. They describe him as a strong-willed, devious criminal who felt himself superior to those around him. During one exchange in the trial, Attorney General Wilentz said to Hauptmann: "You are having a lot of fun with me, aren't you? . . . You think you are a big shot, don't you? . . . You think you are bigger than everybody, don't you?"

The accusers cite the fact that Hauptmann had a criminal record in Germany, where he had been convicted of grand larceny, petty theft, receiving stolen property, and armed robbery; crimes for which he had served three years in prison. Among his crimes were burglarizing the house of the local mayor by using a ladder to climb in a second-story window and using a gun to rob groceries from two women pushing baby carriages.

Hauptmann's defenders reply that these crimes were committed in the chaos of devastated Germany right after World War I, when Hauptmann was a penniless discharged veteran.

Weighing the Evidence

The following are the strongest points in support of Hauptmann's innocence:

➤ The failure of the prosecution to link Hauptmann with the scene of the crime. The testimony of Hockmuth, Whited, and others that they saw Hauptmann near the Lindbergh estate is unconvincing.

➤ The steadfast refusal of Hauptmann to yield an inch on claiming innocence, even when to do so could have saved him from the electric chair.

➤ The nagging question of how a Bronx carpenter could have known so much about the layout and routine of the Lindbergh estate.

These are fairly weak arguments in the face of the evidence against Hauptmann, except for one thing: the Fisch story. It is not impossible that Hauptmann came into possession of the money the way he said he did—by opening a shoe box left in his care by Isidor Fisch.

If one believes that the ransom money in Hauptmann's garage came from Fisch, then it is possible to see the rest of the case against Hauptmann as a frame-up or a case of mistaken identity. The reasoning runs as follows: The kidnapping and death of the Lindbergh baby was a shock to Americans and a challenge to law enforcement authorities. A culprit had to be found and convicted. When Hauptmann was linked to the crime because of his possession of the Fisch money, the authorities fabricated evidence and bullied or bribed witnesses. The public accepted it all because, as Ludovic Kennedy, one of Hauptmann's defenders, observed:

Public prejudice then was so strong, the desire for a scapegoat so universal, that people were blinded: Lindbergh . . . was the hero who could do no wrong, Hauptmann the immigrant with the criminal record.

Another of the defenders, Anthony Scaduto, said that it need not have been a wide-ranging conspiracy: only ten or so prosecution witnesses would have to have distorted their testimony out of a sense of public duty.

The Lindbergh case is thus much like an optical illusion that changes from a goblet to two faces in profile while you stare at it. Kennedy put it this way:

In the last analysis, belief in Hauptmann's guilt or innocence depends entirely on the view one takes of why he hid the ransom money in his garage. Everything else flows from it. Was it, as people at the time believed (and wanted to believe), because he was a principal participant in the crime? Or was it, as he always claimed, because he found the money in a parcel left by Fisch?

But if one does not believe the Fisch story, then the web of evidence presented by the accusers forms an overwhelming case against Hauptmann. In particular:

➤ Rail sixteen of the ladder does seem to have been constructed from wood in Hauptmann's attic.

➤ Hauptmann's handwriting does seem to match the ransom letters.

➤ John F. Condon was a blustering, vain character, but his identification of "John" as Hauptmann seems to have been honest, and was reenforced by cab driver Perrone.

➤ By his own testimony, Hauptmann did not work at the Majestic Apartments on March 1, except for a brief visit in the morning, and quit at about the same time the ransom was paid.

➤ Hauptmann admitted that he had written Condon's phone number and address on a closet door in his apartment.

➤ The claims of conspiracy are improbable. Faking evidence and coercing witnesses would require an extraordinarily wide-ranging conspiracy between the New Jersey State Police, the FBI, and the New York City police, along with help from employees of the U.S. Department of Agriculture and the Internal Revenue Service.

So in sum, while the Fisch story could be true, the weight of the other evidence is crushing. As far as human reason can determine, Bruno Richard Hauptmann was guilty as charged in the murder-kidnapping of Charles Lindbergh, Jr.

14

⎯⎯◆⎯⎯

WAS THERE A COVER-UP AT PEARL HARBOR?

It was the worst defeat in American military history. On the morning of December 7, 1941, the United States Army and Navy bases on the island of Oahu, Hawaii, were attacked by planes from a Japanese carrier task force. Over the span of two hours, the U.S. Pacific fleet stationed at Pearl Harbor lost eighteen ships, including eight battleships, three cruisers, and three destroyers. One hundred and eighty-eight planes were destroyed, most of them on the ground. The dead numbered 2,433; the wounded, 1,178.

In his declaration of war delivered the next day to Congress, President Franklin D. Roosevelt declared that because of Japanese treachery, December 7 was a day that would "live in infamy." But in the opinion of some Americans, the United States government deserves a share of that infamy.

In 1944, journalist John T. Flynn, a member of the isolationist America First Committee, published a pamphlet entitled *The Truth About Pearl Harbor*. Flynn's thesis was that the blame for the attack rested with the maneuverings and miscalculations of the American government. Flynn's pamphlet was the opening salvo in a critical interpretation of Pearl Harbor that has come to be known as the "revisionist" school, because it seeks to revise the accepted view of the events that took place at Pearl Harbor. Flynn's pamphlet was crude; later generations of revisionists—historians and writers such as Harry Elmer Barnes, Charles Beard, and John Toland—have presented more sophisticated arguments. But the thesis remains the same: America was brought into the war by its own government.

The revisionist school has been attacked by an opposing group, which defends Franklin Roosevelt and the American government; among this group are Gordon W. Prange, Roberta Wohlstetter, and Henry C. Clausen.

Most of the ammunition in this debate between the revisionists and their opponents comes from the eight official government investigations of Pearl Harbor, including an eight-month probe in 1945–46 by a joint congressional committee. These reports have produced thousands of pages of testimony and source documents for the combatants to argue over, as well as a common jargon about hotly debated items like the "Purple Code," the "Winds message," and the "three little ships."

"Your Boys Are Not Going to Be Sent Into Any Foreign War"

The revisionists pin the blame for the Pearl Harbor attack directly on President Franklin D. Roosevelt. They argue that Roosevelt was convinced that the defeat of Nazi Germany was in America's vital interest. Short of war, Roosevelt had done everything he could to achieve that end, sending ships, armaments, and supplies to Britain. By mid-1941, say the revisionists, FDR had become convinced that the United States had to take up arms in the war against Hitler and made secret commitments to that effect.

But, say the revisionists, antiwar, isolationist sentiment was strong in America at that time, and Roosevelt knew that there would be fierce opposition to an American declaration of war. In order to be reelected in 1940, Roosevelt made a pledge to American mothers and fathers: "I have said this before, but I shall say it again and again and again and again, 'Your boys are not going to be sent into any foreign war.'"

So Roosevelt knew that America had to be attacked in order to justify entering the conflict. Hitler had avoided any hostile acts that could constitute an act of war despite provocative actions by the American navy in the Atlantic. Roosevelt thus decided, the revisionists argue, that the United States had to enter the war by the "back door"—that is, by bringing on an attack from Japan that would rally public opinion behind American entry into the world conflict.

The revisionists argue that President Roosevelt learned that Pearl Harbor would be the target and suppressed any warning that might have prevented the attack from happening. Some revisionists go even further and say that FDR deliberately set up Pearl Harbor as an irresistible, vulnerable target; it was in fact Roosevelt himself who ordered the Pacific Fleet moved from the safety of the West Coast to the more exposed Hawaiian Islands. The revisionists identify others who were part of Roosevelt's conspiracy: commonly mentioned are Secretary of the Navy Frank Knox, Army Chief of Staff General George C. Marshall, Chief of Naval Operations Admiral Harold R. Stark, and Secretary of War Henry L. Stimson.

The revisionists place much importance on a diary entry by Roosevelt's Secretary of Labor, Frances Perkins. Describing Roosevelt's attitude at an emergency evening cabinet meeting following the Pearl Harbor attack, Perkins wrote: "In spite of the horror that war had actually been brought to us, he had, nevertheless, a much calmer air. His terrible moral problem had been resolved by the event."

The defenders of FDR reply that if the president appeared calm, even relieved, at the cabinet meeting, it was because the uncertainty he faced had indeed been resolved. They concede that the president believed that American intervention was probably the only way to ensure the defeat of Hitler and the survival of democracy in the world. They also concede that Roosevelt was enough of a politician to realize that a declaration of war without any attack by Germany or Japan would raise enormous public opposition, and that he probably hoped for a hostile act by one of the Axis nations that would justify a declaration of war.

But, say his partisans, Roosevelt did not secretly commit the United States to war and did not want the devastating attack that occurred at Pearl Harbor. FDR had a lifelong affection for ships and the sea and a devotion to the American navy (he had been Assistant Secretary of the Navy in Woodrow Wilson's administration). The defenders of Roosevelt aver that he never would have knowingly sacrificed the navy, especially since the attack at Pearl Harbor caused such severe damage to the American war effort.

The defenders state that Roosevelt, along with other government and military officials, thought that if the Japanese attacked, it would most likely come in the Dutch East Indies, which held the oil supplies the Japanese war machine desperately needed. If an American facility was to be attacked, the conventional wisdom was that it would fall in the Philippines, not at Pearl Harbor.

While Roosevelt clearly favored the Allies in their war against the Axis powers, say his defenders, he was as shocked and outraged by Pearl Harbor as his countrymen were.

WAS JAPAN FORCED TO ATTACK?

The revisionists believe that American diplomacy toward Tokyo as orchestrated by Roosevelt was designed to make war with Japan inevitable. They argue that the United States should have been more tolerant of Japanese expansion in Asia; after all, the United States, Britain, and other European powers had grabbed land in Asia before the turn of the century—the United States acquired the Philippines in 1898. And even if Japan was an aggressor in its war with China, the United States would realize no benefit by taking sides.

But as the revisionists see it, Roosevelt rejected all attempts for a peaceful resolution and instead pressed the Japanese with unreasonable demands until Tokyo's only recourse was to strike. Beginning in 1939, the United States put economic pressure on Japan to stop its expansion in Asia, culminating in 1941 with a freeze on Japanese assets in the United States and a total ban on the exportation of oil to Japan. These acts, say the revisionists, constituted a direct threat to Tokyo.

In March 1941, Japanese diplomats went to Washington to negotiate a solution. The revisionists say that the Japanese were prepared to make generous concessions to maintain peaceful relations, but Roosevelt's government refused to compromise. When the Japanese prime minister, Prince Konoye, requested a personal meeting with Roosevelt, the president demanded impossible preconditions that prevented the meeting from happening. The revisionists believe that Konoye was genuine in wishing for peace, and that by rejecting him Roosevelt paved the way for Konoye's resignation and replacement by the warlike General Hideki Tojo and the militarist faction.

The revisionists say that Roosevelt rejected other peace overtures by the Japanese, including the last-minute offer of a modus vivendi (a temporary agreement to continue working together) by the Japanese that would have made further negotiation possible. In response to the modus vivendi, the Americans presented Japan with a "ten-point note" demanding that the Japanese give up the gains they had made by conquest and that they pull their troops out of China. According to the revisionists, the American government knew that the ten points would never be accepted by the Japanese, and that it constituted an ultimatum.

The defenders of Roosevelt reply that the United States was not intentionally trying to force a war. Indeed, they say that FDR was much more moderate than some of his advisors in his attitude toward Japan, and that it was not until Japan invaded French Indochina in July 1941 that the United States hardened its position. The defenders say that the modus vivendi offered by the Japanese was far too one-sided for the United States to accept, and that the ten-point note was simply a restatement of American goals and not an ultimatum.

WHAT WASHINGTON KNEW

In mid-1940, American cryptographers cracked the secret diplomatic code used by the Japanese government. The diplomatic code was dubbed "Purple" by American intelligence, and the device used to decode it was called "Magic." Other, lower-level Japanese codes had previously been cracked by the Americans.

The revisionists believe strongly that by decoding Japanese secret messages, the United States received plain and direct warning that Pearl Harbor was to be attacked, and even knew that the attack would come on December 7 at around 7:00 A.M. Pacific time. The fact that Pearl Harbor was to be the target, say the revisionists, was revealed by messages sent from Tokyo to a Japanese spy in Hawaii. These messages, beginning on September 24, 1941, instructed the agent to furnish reports on the layout of Pearl Harbor, on defenses, and on the movement of ships in and out of the base.

The revisionists say that the specific warning about the date and time of the attack could be deduced from the intercepted diplomatic messages sent from Tokyo to Japanese negotiators in Washington. By November, these messages made it clear that the Japanese government regarded the negotiations as largely futile. One message said that any agreement had to be arrived at by the end of November: "After that things are automatically going to happen." The most significant messages were sent in the week before Pearl Harbor:

➤ A message intercepted on December 2 instructed Japanese embassy personnel to burn their papers and to destroy most of their code machines.

➤ A message intercepted on December 6 instructed Japanese diplomats in Washington to deliver a strongly worded fourteen-point statement to the American government.

➤ A second intercepted message on December 6 contained thirteen of the fourteen points. These thirteen points constituted a list of grievances against the United States government.

➤ A message intercepted on the morning of December 7 contained the fourteenth point: a stinging statement that negotiations were being broken off.

➤ The final message intercepted on the morning of December 7 instructed the diplomats to deliver the fourteen-point statement to the American secretary of state at 1:00 P.M. eastern standard time. This was a significant hour: 1:00 P.M. in Washington was 7:00 A.M. in Pearl Harbor, just about the time when the attack began.

Besides these coded messages, there were other warnings of Japanese intent. In January 1941, the American ambassador to Japan, Joseph C. Grew, warned the State Department that he had heard rumors that if relations with the United States collapsed, Japan would attack Pearl Harbor. A spy in the employ of the British, Dusko Popov, said later that he had warned the Americans in mid-1941 that the Japanese were interested in military defenses on Hawaii.

And what of the Japanese fleet? The revisionists charge that American intelligence, which monitored the movements of Japanese warships, must have known of the task force heading toward Hawaii.

The revisionists charge that Roosevelt and his circle of conspirators knew from these and other warnings when and where the attack would come. They cite the testimony of the courier who brought the decoded Japanese message breaking off negotiations to the White House on the evening of December 6. According to the courier, Roosevelt was with his aide, Harry Hopkins. Roosevelt read the message, and said to Hopkins, "This means war," adding that the United States could not strike the first blow, but had to wait for the surprise attack to fall.

If America's leaders knew from these warnings and decoded messages that a sneak attack would occur, and that the most likely place and time would be Pearl Harbor on the morning of December 7, why did they fail to warn the military authorities in Hawaii? The answer, say the revisionists, was that Roosevelt and his inner circle wanted Pearl Harbor kept ignorant of the attack: if any signs of preparation were revealed, Japanese admiral Chuichi Nagumo, who commanded the task force advancing toward Pearl Harbor, would have called off the attack and turned his warships back to Japan.

FDR's defenders reply that this view is too simplistic, because it focuses on those intelligence clues that could be seen in retrospect to provide a warning of a sneak attack at Pearl Harbor. These clues, the defenders believe, were just one rivulet in an enormous flow of sometimes contradictory intelligence data pouring into Washington. For example, although the decoded messages indicated that the Japanese wanted information about Pearl Harbor, other messages showed that the Japanese were interested in the defenses of American bases in the Panama Canal, San Diego, San Francisco, the Caribbean, the Philippines, and elsewhere. In the opinion of historian Roberta Wohlstetter, the information about Pearl Harbor was lost in the "noise" of intelligence. Only in hindsight can one separate the reliable, important warnings from the rest.

As to why American intelligence did not detect the enemy fleet, the defenders of FDR note that the move was conducted with extraordinary secrecy. The Japanese ships kept complete radio silence as they crossed the remote northern Pacific, and the secret of the planned attack was shared only by an inner circle of top commanders in Japan. The defenders also dismiss the idea that the Japanese carrier task force would have turned back if the Americans got wind of the attack. They argue that the Japanese fully expected that they would meet resistance, and were astonished when it turned out that they had achieved a complete surprise.

ADMIRAL KIMMEL AND GENERAL SHORT

The chief American army officer in Hawaii at the time of the attack was Lieutenant General Walter C. Short, commander of the Hawaiian Department; his navy counterpart was Admiral Husband E. Kimmel, commander in chief of the U.S. Pacific Fleet. After the attack both men were reduced in rank and removed from command. The revisionists charge that Kimmel and Short were made the scapegoats for Roosevelt's conspiracy; that they acted as well as could be reasonably expected in view of the fact that they were deliberately kept in the dark about the Japanese threat to Hawaii.

What did Admiral Kimmel and General Short actually know? As the secret intelligence that negotiations were breaking down began to accumulate in Washington, two messages were dispatched on November 27 from the high command in Washington. One was sent from Admiral Stark, the chief of Naval Operations in Washington, to Admiral Kimmel and other Pacific commanders:

> This dispatch is to be considered a war warning. Negotiations with Japan looking toward stabilization of conditions in the Pacific have ceased and an aggressive move by Japan is expected within the next few days. The number and equipment of Japanese troops and the organization of naval task forces indicates an amphibious expedition against either the Philippines Thai[land] or Kra peninsula or possibly Borneo. Execute an appropriate defensive deployment preparatory to carrying out the tasks assigned in WPL 46 [the Navy war plan]. Inform district and army authorities. A similar warning is being sent by War Department.

The "similar warning" was a message from Chief of Staff George C. Marshall to General Short:

> Negotiations with Japan appear to be terminated to all practical purposes with only the barest possibilities that

the Japanese Government might come back and offer to continue. Japanese future action unpredictable but hostile action possible at any moment. If hostilities cannot, repeat cannot, be avoided the United States desires that Japan commit the first overt act. This policy should not, repeat not, be construed as restricting you to a course of action that might jeopardize your defense. Prior to hostile Japanese action you are directed to undertake such reconnaissance and other measures as you deem necessary but these measures should be carried out so as not, repeat not, to alarm civil population or disclose intent. Report measures taken. Should hostilities occur you will carry out the tasks assigned in rainbow five [the Army war plan] so far as they pertain to Japan. Limit dissemination of this highly secret information to minimum essential officers.

The revisionists deride these messages as hopelessly inadequate. The message to Admiral Kimmel, they point out, said nothing about the danger to Pearl Harbor, but instead indicated the blow would fall in the western Pacific, thousands of miles from Hawaii. The message to General Short instructed him not to alarm the civilian population, which the revisionists argue made it difficult for him to take any decisive measures. General Short interpreted the message to mean that he should guard against sabotage and one of the actions he took in response to the message was to group his aircraft together for security. This protected them from sabotage but made them more vulnerable to an aerial bomb attack. Short informed his superior, General Marshall, that he had grouped his planes, but he received no reply back that his course of action was ill-advised.

The revisionists also point to the fact that although "Magic" decoding machines were made available to the American commander in the Philippines, Douglas MacArthur, and to the British government in London, none were assigned to Pearl Harbor. The revisionists use this as proof that Admiral Kimmel and General Short were deliberately kept ignorant of the threat of attack.

The defenders counter that the November 27 messages constituted a clear warning of impending war, and that Kimmel and Short should have taken them more seriously. If the messages did not warn specifically about an air attack at Pearl Harbor, it was not out of any intent to lull the commanders into a false sense of security but because the Washington brass genuinely thought the attack would come in the western Pacific, far from the Hawaiian Islands.

The opponents of the revisionist view also point out that there had been other warnings over the months before the attack urging general preparedness on the part of all American commanders in the Pacific. As to why there were no decoding machines at Pearl Harbor, they say that because "Magic" was top secret, the government tried to severely limit access to only those posts where it was thought to be most critically needed.

Finally, they say that even if Short and Kimmel were not being kept properly informed, they were military commanders and as such should have maintained a continued state of readiness. They neglected to take some elementary defensive measures at Pearl Harbor. For example, the radar equipment was not manned at the time of the attack, long-range reconnaissance flights were not carried out, intelligence information was not shared between the army and the navy on the island, and no joint defense was planned. This, say Roosevelt's defenders, is proof of the failure of Kimmel and Short.

GENERAL MARSHALL'S HORSEBACK RIDE

As described above, messages were intercepted by American intelligence on the morning of December 7, instructing the Japanese diplomats to deliver the fourteen-point note to the secretary of state at 1:00 P.M., Washington time. Coupled with the messages that preceded it, this message convinced two army intelligence officers in Washington that an attack would commence at that hour. Starting at about 9:00 A.M., the intelligence officers tried to get in touch with Chief of Staff George C. Marshall. Marshall could not be reached for some time because he was out horseback riding in Virginia. Marshall did not arrive in his office until 11:25 A.M. After conferring with his navy counterpart, Admiral Stark, Marshall finally drafted a message to American bases in the Pacific, warning them to be on the alert. Radio contact with Hawaii was not functioning, so the message was sent out at 12:18 P.M. by Western Union. By the time it reached Hawaii, the attack had already begun.

The revisionists regard this delay as proof of the reluctance of Roosevelt's commanders to warn Pearl Harbor. Why, they ask, would Marshall be out riding a horse when his country was in the midst of a crisis? Why was the message sent by Western Union instead of directly by scrambler telephone? Another piece of the puzzle is that several years later, in his testimony at congressional hearings on the Pearl Harbor attack, Marshall could not recall where he had been on the night of December 6. Said the revisionist Harry Elmer Barnes of Marshall's behavior:

> As conduct on the part of a trained soldier, assumedly dominated by the ideals and professional stereotypes of those high in his profession, and having the supreme military responsibility for the protection of his country, it would seem both fair and reasonable to contend that Marshall's conduct can be explained on only three grounds: mental defect, deliberately treasonable behavior, or carried out under orders from President Roosevelt. The last seems the only plausible and sensible interpretation.

The opponents of this view admit that Marshall had acted unwisely, but they deny that he was purposefully trying to delay the warning about the Japanese attack.

THE WINDS MESSAGE

One of the hottest arguments between the revisionists and their opponents concerns Captain Laurence F. Safford, who in 1941 was a naval intelligence officer stationed in Washington. Safford later testified that a few days before the attack his intelligence group had intercepted a "winds" message broadcast from Tokyo.

The winds messages were a form of code designed to alert Japanese diplomats when other forms of communication could not be safely used. For example, the phrase "east wind rain" spoken in a Japanese shortwave news broadcast was supposed to warn Japanese embassy officials that relations with the United States were coming to a crisis and that all secret papers should be destroyed.

Safford claimed that the message was passed along to the top command in Washington and that it constituted a clear warning that war was about to break out. But most of the other intelligence officers who worked with Safford denied that the message he described arrived before the attack. One of the officers who at first corroborated Safford's story, Lieutenant Commander Alwin D. Kramer, later denied it. The revisionists use this as a prime example of the manner in which genuine warnings about Pearl Harbor were suppressed. They say that Safford was telling the truth, and that Kramer was pressured by the navy to change his testimony.

The defenders of Roosevelt say that Safford was sincere in his belief that the message had come in but his memory was simply incorrect, probably because he was trying to recall events years after the fact. Even assuming for the sake of argument that Safford was correct, argue FDR's champions, the winds message merely duplicated other secret Japanese messages received by intelligence that warned of worsening relations and ordered the destruction of secret papers. The winds message said nothing about an attack on Pearl Harbor, and, according to this interpretation, was therefore of little importance.

THE THREE LITTLE SHIPS

As proof that President Roosevelt wanted to create an incident that would bring America into the war, the revisionists cite the curious episode of the "defensive information patrol." On December 2, 1941, Admiral Stark ordered the U.S. Navy base in the Philippines to send out three ships "to observe and report by radio Japanese movements in west China Sea and Gulf of Siam." The ships could have Filipino crews, but had to be commanded by a U.S. Navy officer and had to mount at least two small guns in order to "establish identity as U.S. men-of-war." The ships were to be stationed at widely separated points. The message stated that the order was given directly by the president. (The mission was called off when the war began on December 7.)

Why had the president himself ordered such a curious operation? The revisionists say that Roosevelt hoped that one or more of the ships would be attacked by the Japanese, furnishing the act of war he needed.

The defenders of FDR say that the purpose was exactly as the order indicated, to report on where Japanese warships were headed. The business about making sure the ships could be identified as American, they say, was perhaps to guarantee that the crew members would be treated as prisoners of war and not as spies if they were captured. The defenders doubt that the loss of the ships would be considered an act of war, since much larger American ships had been sunk by Nazi U-boats in the Atlantic without precipitating a conflict. Finally, say his champions, Roosevelt often had small-scale, pet projects that he pressed on the navy, and this was simply one of them.

WERE THE BRITISH INVOLVED?

The revisionists believe that President Roosevelt made a secret commitment with the British to intervene in the war. This commitment, they charge, was agreed to by Roosevelt at his August 1941 meeting with Prime Minister Winston Churchill in Argentia Bay, Newfoundland. The revisionists also claim that in 1941 the Americans signed secret agreements with the British and the Dutch—variously called the ABC, A-2, ABD, or ABCD agreements—to the effect that if Japan invaded any of the territories of these nations or otherwise tried to expand its conquests in the Far East, the three powers would jointly go to war.

As proof, the revisionists cite telegrams sent independently on the eve of Pearl Harbor by American military attachés in Australia and Singapore that seem to indicate that the British expected the United States to honor their commitment to join in action against the Japanese.

FDR's defenders deny that there was any such secret agreement at Argentia Bay or elsewhere that committed the United States to war against Japan. They agree that American army and navy personnel worked out joint war plans with the Dutch and the British to be implemented in the event that the three nations went to war against the Japanese, but that these documents were not considered binding commitments that would force the United States to go to war when required by its allies.

Another charge in the revisionist argument appeared in 1991. In their book *Betrayal at Pearl Harbor,* James Rusbridger and Eric Nave claimed that British intelligence had learned from decoded Japanese naval messages that a Japanese task force would launch an attack on December 7. Rusbridger and Nave said that

British intelligence guessed it would fall at Pearl Harbor, and so informed Prime Minister Churchill. Churchill, they said, withheld this information from Roosevelt.

The opponents of the revisionist view dismiss this charge as completely unproved and highly unlikely, and they present counter evidence that Pearl Harbor caught British intelligence as much by surprise as it did the Americans.

Weighing the Evidence

Pearl Harbor was not an unmitigated disaster. The attack rallied the people of the United States behind the war effort. The ships were sunk in the shallow water of the harbor rather than at sea, which meant that most of them could later be salvaged and repaired. The major loss was to the navy's battleships, and not the aircraft carriers that happened to be away from Pearl Harbor on December 7; the subsequent course of the war proved that the slow battleships were essentially obsolete and that carriers were the key to victory in the Pacific. The navy's invaluable oil reserve and repair shops on the base were not damaged.

But these mitigating factors appeared mostly in hindsight. As viewed at the time, the Pearl Harbor attack was about as bad as it could possibly be. The United States was caught completely off guard, and the backbone of the navy was destroyed. It was a crushing setback to American confidence and a powerful boost to the morale of the Japanese enemy.

As we have seen, the revisionists are bitterly critical of the actions of the United States government prior to Pearl Harbor, and they accuse Roosevelt of deliberately orchestrating the attack. But it is quite possible to be critical of American foreign policy prior to Pearl Harbor without seeing it as a conspiracy. A case in point was the argument of University of Illinois historian Paul W. Schroeder, who believed that America erred in insisting that the Japanese surrender their conquests in China. By being less fixated on China and more conciliatory to the Japanese, he believed, the United States could have accomplished the more important goals of separating Japan from the Axis powers and limiting further Japanese advances while possibly avoiding war. Schroeder made many of the same criticisms that the hard-core revisionists do. He believed, for example, that Roosevelt should not have rejected Japan's modus vivendi proposal but instead should have continued to work toward a compromise. The failure to do so, he said, demonstrated blindness to reality. Schroeder believed that America made mistakes in its dealings with Japan, but he explicitly denied that this made Roosevelt guilty of treason. Schroeder can be termed a "soft" revisionist, in contrast to the "hard" revisionists, who accuse Roosevelt of treachery.

Even the defenders of Roosevelt see much to criticize in the actions of the United States toward Japan. They concede, for example, that American government and military officials erred in the belief that the attack would fall in the western Pacific, and that those officials failed to realize that the Japanese were capable of launching a secret attack on Hawaii, two thousand miles away from their home base. Further, they admit that American commanders dawdled inexcusably on the morning of December 7 when clear signs of an attack were received, and that those same commanders should have realized that defenses at Pearl Harbor were inadequate.

Roosevelt's defenders are willing to concede that FDR believed war against Germany and Japan was necessary and hoped for the enemy to strike the first blow. But again, where the revisionists and the anti-revisionists part company is whether there was a conspiracy, directed by Roosevelt, to bring America into the war. Those who oppose the revisionist position say that the Pearl Harbor disaster was due to simple blunders and shortsightedness on the part of the Americans, along with bold planning and good luck on the part of the Japanese.

Which interpretation is more plausible? Consider the episode of General Marshall's horseback ride on the morning of December 7. The revisionist Harry Elmer Barnes says that the only way to explain the fact that the chief of staff had gone off to take a horseback ride on the morning of December 7 was that he had been given secret orders by the president of the United States to be out of his office so that any warning sent to Pearl Harbor would be delayed. But is that indeed the only plausible explanation? Is it not infinitely more plausible that after weeks of being bound to his desk as the nation coped with a diplomatic crisis, Marshall stole some time on a Sunday morning to take a refreshing ride in the country? It is much more likely to assume it was an error of judgment and not part of a deliberate conspiracy.

Consider again the intercepted messages. The revisionists believe that American commanders clandestinely suppressed the information that the Japanese were interested in the defenses of Pearl Harbor. The anti-revisionists place the blame on the volume of background "noise" and the rush of events that made it impossible to sort the genuine from the spurious.

Perhaps the best evidence the revisionists present is the incident of the "three little ships." It is not beyond the realm of possibility that Roosevelt hoped that the ships would be attacked by the Japanese. But ironically, if this interpretation is correct, it would suggest that the president had no prior knowledge that the Japanese were about to attack Pearl Harbor.

The problem the revisionists face is that the central part of their argument—that there was a conspiracy within the American government—cannot be proved. In the absence of such proof, the most likely explanation is that the only conspiracy in the Pearl Harbor attack was the one undertaken by the Japanese when they secretly dispatched a task force to smash the American Pacific fleet on Oahu.

15

=⟐=

WAS ALGER HISS A COMMUNIST SPY?

The prothonotary warbler is an extremely rare bird, sightings of which are much prized by bird-watchers. It is about five and a half inches long and lives in wooded swamps. The coloring is yellow, with blue-gray wings. Its song is described as "zeet zeet zeet zeet zeet zeet," sung in a monotone. One other interesting fact about the prothonotary warbler: it played a small but dramatic role in the most spectacular American spy case of the cold war.

In 1948, Whittaker Chambers was trying to convince a committee of the United States House of Representatives that he and Alger Hiss had once associated together as Communists. To prove his point, he recounted details of Hiss's life, such as the car Hiss drove, the places Hiss lived, the china pattern in Hiss's home, and the pet names Hiss and his wife called each other. Chambers testified that Hiss was an amateur ornithologist who was proud of once having sighted a prothonotary warbler along the Potomac River.

Hiss appeared before the committee nine days later, without having heard Chambers's testimony. He firmly denied under oath that he had ever been a Communist or that he had ever met Whittaker Chambers. When one of the congressmen present at the hearing asked Hiss if he had any hobbies, Hiss mentioned tennis and bird-watching. "Did you ever see a prothonotary warbler?" the congressman asked innocently.

"I have right here on the Potomac," Hiss enthusiastically replied. "They come back and nest in those swamps. Beautiful yellow head, a gorgeous bird." Unknowingly, Hiss had confirmed a small portion of Chambers's testimony. The story of the warbler contributed to the identification of Alger Hiss as a Communist spy and to the destruction of his career.

Until the prothonotary warbler and other evidence led to his downfall, Alger Hiss (b. 1904) was one of the nation's outstanding young men. A graduate of Johns Hopkins and Harvard Law School, Hiss had served successively as a clerk for a Supreme Court justice, a member of a New York law firm, and a government lawyer on the fast track in Franklin Roosevelt's New Deal. The highlight of his career in government came in 1945 when, as an assistant secretary of state, he was a key figure in the establishment of the United Nations. He went on from the State Department to become the president of the prestigious Carnegie Endowment for World Peace.

His accuser, Whittaker Chambers (1901–1961), had also achieved a respectable position as a well-paid senior editor at *Time* magazine. But his passage through life had been far more turbulent than Hiss's. As a rebellious college student at Columbia in the 1920s, Chambers joined the Communist Party. He dropped out of college and became a writer for radical periodicals. He said that early in the 1930s he was recruited into the party's underground, where his assignment was to run secret Communist networks within the United States government and to obtain classified documents.

Chambers eventually became disillusioned with Communism, and he defected from the party. He emerged a fervid anti-Communist, and he recounted the story of his years in the underground to government officials. In 1948, Chambers testified before the House Un-American Activities Committee (HUAC), naming men he had secretly associated with during his years in the party, the most prominent of whom was Alger Hiss. It was this accusation that Hiss vehemently denied.

In the end it was Chambers who triumphed. A freshman congressman from California on HUAC, Richard Nixon, believed Chambers's testimony, and he pressed the committee to pursue the investigation of Hiss. Eventually the case was picked up by the Justice Department, and Hiss was indicted for perjury. The jury at Hiss's first trial could not reach a verdict. But on January 21, 1950, the jury in a second trial found him guilty.

Hiss served forty-four months in prison, lost his job, and spent the rest of his working life as a salesman for a stationery company. But he continued to maintain his innocence and to seek redress from the courts.

The case was a cause célèbre of the cold war. Like the Sacco-Vanzetti affair, it separated liberals, who believed that Hiss had been framed, from conservatives, who were convinced of his guilt. Even today, a half century after HUAC heard testimony about the prothonotary warbler, liberals and conservatives clash over who was lying—Alger Hiss or Whittaker Chambers.

CHAMBERS VS. HISS

Chambers said that he met Hiss for the first time in Washington in 1934. Chambers, according to his own testimony, was then in the Communist underground, using the alias "Carl." He said he had been assigned by his Communist superiors to work as a courier with a secret cell of Communists, known as the "Ware group," in the federal government. Chambers described Hiss as the group's most prominent member.

Chambers said that he and his wife, Esther, became close friends with Alger Hiss and Hiss's wife, Priscilla, a friendship that lasted for several years. The following were the most important particulars used by Chambers to prove that he had a close relationship with Hiss.

➤ *The apartment.* Chambers said that in 1935 he and his wife were looking for a place in Washington to live so that he could pursue his assignment as a Communist agent. Alger Hiss offered him the use of an apartment on Twenty-eighth Street. The Hiss family had recently moved out of the apartment to a rented house on P Street, and still had two months on the lease. As a fellow Communist, said Chambers, Hiss provided the apartment rent free and let Chambers use the furniture that had been left behind. For a few days before Chambers could move into the apartment, he and his family stayed with Hiss in the P Street house.

➤ *The Ford.* Chambers said that Hiss had a 1929 Ford automobile, which he frequently let Chambers use. In 1935,

Hiss purchased a new Plymouth, and, according to Chambers, he announced that he wanted to donate the Ford to the Communist Party to be used by an organizer. Chambers initially did not want to do it because the transaction would leave an incriminating paper trail, but he finally agreed. Documents produced by investigators showed that Hiss signed the title document turning the car over to a Washington auto dealership, which then transferred the ownership to one William Rosen, who later took the Fifth Amendment when asked if he had ever been a Communist. The accusers of Hiss believe that a Communist working for the dealership arranged the transfer of the car to Rosen.

➤ *The Loan.* Chambers said that Hiss gave him a $400 loan to buy a car. Investigators found that on November 19, 1937, Priscilla Hiss withdrew $400 from the couple's bank account. Four days later, Chambers purchased a car with a payment of $486.75.

➤ *The rug.* Chambers said that one of his Communist superiors decided that the leading men in the Washington underground should be given a reward for their work on behalf of the Soviet Union. Chambers accordingly arranged for the purchase of four Bokhara rugs and presented one of them to Hiss in 1937 as a gift from the Russian people.

Hiss presented a different version of his relationship with Chambers to explain the apartment, the Ford, the loan, and the rug. When first called before HUAC, Hiss said he had never known Whittaker Chambers or a man named Carl. Then, after searching his memory, he said that he had in fact known Chambers, but that the man had called himself "George Crosley." Hiss testified that he first met Crosley in late 1934 or early 1935. Hiss at that time was counsel to a United States Senate committee conducting an investigation into the influence of the munitions industry on American foreign policy. Hiss said that Crosley presented himself as a freelance journalist who wanted to write an article about the committee's work.

Hiss said that answering questions from journalists was an expected part of his job, so that he dutifully talked to Crosley from time to time, occasionally going to lunch with him. He came to regard Crosley as an interesting character, and when Crosley mentioned that he needed a place to stay in Washington with his wife and child while he was finishing his article, Hiss agreed to sublet the apartment he was vacating on Twenty-eighth Street for the two months that remained on the lease, along with the furniture. But according to Hiss, this was not a gift: he fully expected to be paid by Crosley once the writer sold his article. Because of a mix-up with a moving van, he let Crosley and his family move in with the Hisses for a few days at P Street.

As to the Ford, Hiss said that he decided to get rid of it by giving it to Crosley at the time he sublet the apartment. It was an old, practically worthless vehicle that Hiss no longer needed because he had purchased a new car. He carelessly gave Crosley the title certificate without bothering to sign it over. When confronted with the document that turned the car over to the Washington dealership, Hiss said he could not remember the circumstances under which he had signed it.

Hiss denied giving Crosley a four hundred dollar loan. He said that Priscilla had withdrawn that amount from the bank, but that the purpose had been to buy furniture. Hiss and his defenders theorize that a decade later Chambers, with the help of government investigators, found out from Hiss's bank records about the four hundred dollar withdrawal and concocted the loan story.

Hiss said he did in fact receive a rug from Crosley in 1935 (not 1937 as Chambers claimed) but regarded it as a belated form of payment for the use of the apartment. By this time, Hiss testified, he had become thoroughly disenchanted with Crosley, whom he had come to regard as a deadbeat and a sponger. Hiss said that except for an occasional encounter, his relationship with Crosley ended by mid-1936 (not 1938 as Chambers testified).

Thus, said Hiss, he was utterly astonished when, in 1948, the man he knew as George Crosley turned out to be Whittaker Chambers, and that Chambers had inflated and twisted their innocent relationship into a tale of Communist underground activities.

COMMUNISTS AND EX-COMMUNISTS

Those who believe Alger Hiss was guilty cite the word of others who operated in the half-lit world of Communists and leftists in prewar Washington. One such person was Hede Massing, a refugee from Nazi Germany who, like Chambers, was a self-confessed Soviet agent who subsequently defected from the party. She testified in court that she had known Hiss as a fellow Communist. She recounted that she first met Hiss at a dinner party in Washington in 1935, where they bantered about a State Department employee, Noel Field, whom Hiss and Massing were separately trying to recruit into espionage:

> I said to Mr. Hiss, "I understand that you are trying to get Noel Field away from my organization into yours," and he said, "So you are the famous girl that is trying to get Noel Field away from me," and I said, "Yes." And he said as far as I remember, "Well, we will see who is going to win," at which point I said, "Well, Mr. Hiss, you realize that you are competing with a woman," at which either he or I said, the gist of the sentence was, "Whoever is going to win we are working for the same boss."

Noel Field himself identified Hiss as a spy. In 1949, Field, who had fled behind the Iron Curtain to avoid being prosecuted as a Communist in the United States, was imprisoned in Hungary on suspicion of being an American agent. To prove he was a loyal Communist, he told his interrogators about his activities as an espionage agent for the Soviets. The transcripts of his interrogation, found by a Hungarian historian in 1992 in the files of the Hungarian secret police, show that Field named Hiss as one of the Communists he had known in the American underground. Another ex-Communist who fingered Hiss was Nathaniel Weyl, who told the FBI in 1950 that he had known Hiss as a member of the Communist Ware group in Washington in the 1930s.

Hiss's defenders criticize the testimony of Massing, Field, and Weyl as unreliable. A defense witness testified that he had heard the story of the dinner party from Hede Massing, but that she had been much more vague about the details and about how she knew Hiss was a Communist. As to Field, Hiss's champions point out that he was tortured while in prison in Hungary, and that it was to his benefit to invent tales of American Communists he had worked with in order to vindicate his own reputation as a good Party member. In regard to Weyl, Hiss's defenders say that although he may have testified that Hiss was a Communist to the FBI, his 1950 book, *Treason,* exonerated Hiss.

Those who believe Hiss was innocent cite others who explicitly denied that Hiss was a Communist. Henry Julian Wadleigh, a self-confessed member of Chambers's spy ring, reportedly characterized Hiss as "a very moderate New Dealer with strongly conservative instincts." Lee Pressman, who admitted being a member of the Ware group, denied that Hiss had been involved.

THE PUMPKIN PAPERS

To prove that Alger Hiss had been a Communist spy, Whittaker Chambers produced a collection of State Department documents, most of which he said had been passed along to him by Hiss. The collection consisted of four handwritten sheets of paper, sixty-five typewritten pages, and fifty-eight pages of documents on microfilm. The largest share of the items were dispatches sent to the State Department from American diplomats overseas and internal memos, most concerning international trade and United States foreign policy. The documents bore dates from January to April 1938.

Chambers said that these papers represented only a small portion of the documents smuggled out of the State Department by Hiss. Chambers explained that he would visit the Hiss home in Washington once a week to pick up the documents, which he would take away to be microfilmed. He would hurriedly return the documents to Hiss the same evening so that Hiss could bring them back to his office the next morning.

Chambers's assignment had been to turn the documents over to his superiors in the Communist intelligence network, but these papers he kept behind. Why? Chambers said that when he made the decision to break with the Communist Party, he realized that these documents constituted "life preservers" that would protect him from being assassinated. After he fled the Party he let it be known that if he was killed the incriminating papers would be released, and he entrusted the documents to a relative, who hid them in a dumbwaiter shaft in a New York home. Chambers said he retrieved them from the dumbwaiter shaft in 1948, where they had remained hidden for a decade.

The papers caused a sensation and helped to bring about Hiss's indictment by a grand jury and his conviction for perjury. The entire collection came to be known as the "pumpkin papers," because at one point in 1948 Chambers temporarily hid some of them in a hollowed-out pumpkin on his Maryland farm before handing them over to government investigators. The term is inaccurate, since only a small portion of the documents were ever in the pumpkin, but the name has stuck.

Alger Hiss, his team of defense lawyers, and his defenders ever since have attacked the pumpkin papers as part of a fraud. They concede that the documents are genuine, and that the handwritten notes are in Hiss's own hand. The State Department documents bear date stamps from the office in which Hiss worked at the time, and some have Hiss's initials indicating he received them. But Hiss's defenders believe that someone other than Hiss spirited the papers from the State Department. Security at the State Department in 1938 was lax, they say; in offices like Hiss's piles of documents lay unguarded on desks and were casually carted from office to office and to the burn room to be destroyed. Notes were carelessly tossed into wastebaskets.

Hiss and his defenders say that a Communist sympathizer who worked in or visited the State Department, even a file clerk or a janitor, could have easily pilfered documents and office notes like those in the pumpkin papers without being detected. Who could it have been? Perhaps it was Chambers himself. In 1938, Chambers was employed as an editor with a federal agency, a job he had obtained through his Party connections. Hiss's defenders say that Chambers could have used his government identification to visit the State Department in order to furtively sneak out documents.

Another suspect identified by Hiss's defenders is Henry Julian Wadleigh, the admitted spy. Wadleigh was a State Department economist who confessed that he had taken documents and passed them to Chambers. Hiss's defenders say that Wadleigh could have been the source of the documents attributed to Hiss.

Yet another theory offered by Hiss's defenders is that the pumpkin papers were actually culled from State Department files long after 1938. The fact that Chambers so abruptly and unexpectedly produced the pumpkin papers, they argue, shows that they could have been put together in 1948 as part of a sophisticated frame-up.

Hiss's defenders point to aspects of the pumpkin papers that, they say, support the argument that they were not stolen by Hiss. The documents were marked with date stamps from many different State Department offices besides Hiss's, and they could have been pilfered from any one of these. Many of the documents had been stapled together, each with its assortment of date stamps. Someone seeking to frame Hiss, say his defenders, could have shuffled the documents to put one with Hiss's office date stamp on the top of the stack in order to make it appear that they had been stolen by him. Many of the documents dealt with obscure matters that must have been of little concern to the Soviets, or contained information that could have been routinely obtained elsewhere.

As to the handwritten notes, Hiss's defenders say that these were simply summaries of incoming dispatches that Hiss wrote and used for his own reference during discussions with his boss at the time, Assistant Secretary of State Francis B. Sayre, and that they must have been taken from Hiss's wastebasket. No competent spy, say the defenders, would ever provide documents in his own handwriting.

The physical condition of the documents that were allegedly stored for ten years in the dumbwaiter shaft is another contested point. Hiss's defenders say that the documents do not all appear to have been of the same age, that they could not all have fit in the envelope in which they were supposed to be stored, and that the envelope itself showed signs of tampering.

The proof that there was something fishy about the pumpkin papers, say Hiss's defenders, is the fact that Chambers changed his story so dramatically. At first he testified that Hiss, although a Communist, had not been a spy and had not committed espionage. But by saying that the pumpkin papers had been supplied to him by Hiss, he contradicted his earlier testimony. And Chambers was caught in a lie once again in regard to his testimony about the date of his defection from the Communist Party. In his early testimony he repeatedly said that he left the Party in 1937. But after he produced the pumpkin papers that he supposedly collected from Hiss in 1938, he added a year to the date of his defection.

Hiss's accusers respond to these charges by saying that

Chambers originally denied that Hiss had committed espionage because he still had a lingering regard for his old friend and wanted to shield him from the grave charge of spying. But when Hiss threatened to sue for libel, Chambers reluctantly brought forward the hard evidence from the dumbwaiter shaft. The business about the date of his defection from the Communist Party was simply an error on Chambers's part. The abandonment of his former loyalties was a long, tortuous process, and he had been wrong about when the final break took place.

In regard to the handwritten notes, Hiss's accusers say they were not crumpled as they might have been if they had been stolen from Hiss's wastebasket. And they cite the testimony of Hiss's supervisor in the State Department, Francis B. Sayre, that he had never seen Hiss use or refer to these notes in their day-to-day office conversations.

THE TYPEWRITER

We now come to one of the most vexing and tangled parts of the entire mystery—the case of the Hiss family typewriter. There are three main pieces to the puzzle:

➤ *Woodstock N230099.* During the 1930s the Hiss family owned a Woodstock manual typewriter, serial number N230099. It had been given to the Hisses by Priscilla's father. At some point in the 1930s, the Hisses gave it to the family of Claudia Catlett, a Black woman who had worked for them as a maid. The Woodstock then passed through the hands of a number of friends and relatives of the Catletts. When the pumpkin papers emerged, the Hiss defense team and the FBI separately searched for the typewriter. The Hiss team found it first, in the possession of a Washington trucker named Ira Lockey, and turned it over to the court as evidence.

➤ *Copies of government documents.* These sixty-five typewritten pages were among the cache of documents that Chambers allegedly retrieved from the dumbwaiter shaft.

➤ *The Hiss standards.* Priscilla Hiss had typed assorted personal letters on the Woodstock, such as a letter to her son's school and an application for college admission.

These letters were introduced into evidence at the trials in order to be compared with the typewritten copies of government documents.

The accusers of Alger Hiss say that by examining the Woodstock, the Hiss standards, and the typewritten copies, it is indisputable that all but one of the copies of the State Department documents were typed on the Hiss family Woodstock. This was the testimony of Ramos C. Feehan, an FBI documents expert who appeared at the perjury trials as a witness for the prosecution.

Chambers described the following scenario: Alger Hiss would remove documents from his office and bring them home. He had to return the documents to his office the next day, so on those evenings when Chambers was not scheduled to arrive for a pickup, Priscilla would type copies of the pilfered documents that Alger brought home. These typed copies would be saved for Chambers's arrival.*

Hiss's defenders seek to poke holes in this scenario. No rational spy, they say, would risk exposure by using his own typewriter. And besides, they say, the Hisses gave away the Woodstock to the Catletts around December 1937, which means that Priscilla could not have been the typist, since the pilfered documents dated from 1938. The defenders of Hiss produce their own experts who dispute Feehan's testimony by claiming that the typed copies could have been done by a typist other than Priscilla Hiss on a machine other than the Hiss Woodstock.

One scenario advanced by Hiss's defenders is that Chambers may have gained access to the Woodstock while it was in the possession of the Catletts and typed the documents on it. An alternative theory is that the typewriting was done on a different Woodstock, which Chambers could have obtained from a dealer in used typewriters. A much more complex argument used by Hiss's defenders is that some person or persons with expertise—probably the FBI or HUAC—actually put together a

---

*Some who believe Hiss guilty speculate that Priscilla may have been the real culprit; that it was at her insistence that Alger brought the documents home from the State Department to be turned over to Chambers.

fake Woodstock N230099 whose output matched the Hiss standards. According to this argument, after the incriminating typewritten copies were produced on this machine, the conspirators planted the fake N230099 in the hands of Lockey. The Hiss defense team thought it had discovered the real typewriter, but it had been cleverly fooled.

Supporting evidence for the charge of "forgery by typewriter" is a curious paragraph by Richard Nixon in his 1962 book, *Six Crises*. In the book, Nixon stated that the Woodstock had been found by the FBI in December 1948. But how could this be, if the typewriter was supposedly found by the Hiss defense team in April 1949? Nixon said that the discrepancy was a "researcher's error," and he corrected it in later editions of the book. Hiss's defenders say that it was a slip of the pen that revealed the tip of a conspiracy.

Hiss's accusers dismiss the story of a counterfeit Woodstock as a fantasy. They also deride the idea that Chambers somehow snuck into the Catlett home to type incriminating documents on the Woodstock that could years later be used to frame Alger Hiss. The accusers say that contrary to the testimony of the Hisses, Alger and Priscilla still had Woodstock N230099 in their house in 1938, and that Priscilla did indeed type the stolen State Department documents on it.

MOTIVE FOR A FRAME-UP

If Alger Hiss was falsely accused by Whittaker Chambers, what was the latter's motive for bringing ruin to an innocent man who had once befriended him?

Hiss's defenders believe that the answer lies in Chambers's psychological makeup. They point out that he came from a difficult family situation: his beloved older brother committed suicide, his parents frequently fought, and his father was often absent. Hiss's defenders say that Chambers had engaged in homosexual sex (a damaging charge in that era), had blasphemed religion, and that he lived a life of lies and aliases. A psychologist, Dr. Carl Binger, testified for the defense at Hiss's second trial that Chambers had a "psychopathic personality" that was characterized by "a tendency to make false accusations." Said Binger:

These unfortunate people have a conviction of the truth and validity of their own imaginations, of their own fantasies without respect to outer reality; so that they play a part in life, play a role. They may be a hero at one moment and a gangster at the next. They act as if a situation were true which, in fact, is true only in their imaginations; and on the basis of such imaginations they will claim friendships where none exist, just as they will make accusations which have no basis in fact, because they have a constant need to make their imaginations come true by behaving as if the outer world were actually in accord with their own imagination.

Sex also enters into the explanations. It has been suggested that Chambers may have made advances or may have had an affair with Alger Hiss, Priscilla, or even the Hiss's son, and that when the advances were spurned or the affair broken off, Chambers decided to destroy Hiss's career in retaliation.

Hiss's champions say there was another motive behind the case against Hiss, a motive that went beyond Whittaker Chambers to infect Richard Nixon's HUAC and J. Edgar Hoover's FBI. By painting Hiss as a Communist, say Hiss's defenders, these right-wing forces sought to discredit the liberal Democratic tradition of Franklin Roosevelt and Harry Truman. It was thus no accident that Chambers made his explosive charges in the presidential election year of 1948. It was for this ideological reason, say Hiss's defenders, that the FBI and/or HUAC helped to corroborate Chambers's story by putting together a fake Woodstock and assembling a collection of purloined State Department documents that was falsely tied to Hiss.

Hiss's accusers say that the psychological analysis is a smoke screen. If Chambers had an unstable childhood, so did Hiss, whose father and sister committed suicide and whose brother died young. And if Chambers had done some disreputable things in his life, he had also done some reputable ones. He was a devoutly religious man with a wife and two children. As for the anti-Communist motive, the accusers of Hiss concede that in the heat of the cold war, some men and women may have been unjustly accused of being Communist subversives. But the charges against Hiss, they say, were nonetheless accurate.

In short, Hiss's accusers believe that even if Chambers was

mentally unbalanced and even if anti-Communists were motivated by political considerations, the charges against Hiss
were true.

Weighing the Evidence

Unlike the other controversies in this book, the mystery of Alger
Hiss may someday be resolved beyond a reasonable doubt.
With the collapse of Communism and the breakup of the Soviet
Union, the records of intelligence services once behind the Iron
Curtain are gradually being unearthed. In 1992, a Russian general, Dimitri Volkogonov, said that he had examined Soviet files
and concluded that Hiss was innocent. There was a flurry in
the American press at the news. But two months later Volkogonov said it had all been a mistake. He had made only a cursory
examination of the files at the request of an American supporter
of Hiss, and could not establish Hiss's guilt or innocence.
Though this first perusal of Soviet documents produced only a
false alarm, perhaps somewhere in the former Soviet Union or
one of its satellites the evidence that will settle the case once
and for all will be found.

But even if such a smoking gun is never found, the weight
of the evidence that already exists tips the balance against Alger
Hiss. The apartment, the Ford, the loan, the rug, the testimony
of other ex-Communists besides Chambers—all of this exposes
Hiss's tortured story about his aloof relationship with a deadbeat journalist as a lie. The pumpkin papers—some of which
were typed on Hiss's typewriter and some written in Hiss's
handwriting—appear to be genuine. At the perjury trials, the
federal prosecutor, Thomas Murphy, referred to the documents
and the typewriter as "immutable witnesses" to Hiss's guilt.
The defenders of Hiss have heaped scorn on that phrase. But
to believe Hiss innocent, one would have to imagine one of
two possibilities. The first is that back in the 1930s, Whittaker
Chambers decided to frame Alger Hiss, and that he purloined
State Department documents and surreptitiously used a Woodstock typewriter (either the actual Hiss machine or a close copy)
to create a body of evidence that he then put aside for a decade.
The second possibility is that in 1948, a team of conspirators

created a fake typewriter and ginned together old State Department documents to create the same body of evidence. Both scenarios are improbable.

Indeed, one of the chief mysteries of the Hiss case is why the faith of Hiss's defenders has remained unshaken for so long in the face of so much evidence to the contrary. One suspects that even if a smoking gun proving Hiss's guilt is one day found in the files of Soviet intelligence, that faith will continue. For some liberals, Hiss's innocence is a matter of dogma, just as much as his guilt has become dogma for conservatives.

Sam Tanenhous, a conservative writer, put it this way:

[Hiss's liberal champions] cannot afford to concede the presence of a single Communist in high office. To do so means to admit the inadmissible—that the Right was by no means "hysterical" when it insisted that there was a threat of Communist subversion at home even as the Soviet Union posed a threat of expansionism abroad. And so for nearly half a century an unassailably guilty man has been recast as a spotless innocent—and as a martyr. To his supporters, Alger Hiss is not a man but a symbol, and they have invested so much in his innocence that they may remain forever incapable of owning up to the truth.

16

⬅➡

WAS MARILYN MONROE MURDERED?

Marilyn Monroe was born Norma Jeane Mortenson in 1926. Her childhood was difficult. Her father deserted the family; her mother was institutionalized with mental illness. Monroe grew up in foster homes and orphanages. But she had two assets: uncommon beauty and driving ambition. By her mid-twenties she had risen from being a nude pinup model to being a successful film star. She appeared in hit movies like *All About Eve, Gentlemen Prefer Blondes, The Seven Year Itch, Bus Stop,* and *Some Like It Hot.* She was envied, lusted after, and fantasized about by millions around the world.

But on the night of August 4, 1962, she was found dead in her home in Los Angeles. She was thirty-six years old.

The civil servants who saw her dead body were struck with philosophic thoughts about the fragility of beauty and fame. The deputy medical examiner who performed the autopsy said that when he first pulled back the sheet and looked at the face of the famous film star, he thought to himself:

Here, before me, was a person so incredibly fortunate in every way—from the endowment of an astonishing beauty to the talent, and drive, that had transported her from the ranks of factory workers to a woman who walked with presidents. All gone, so young.

A deputy district attorney who was present at the autopsy recalled that he and the medical examiner had seen many dead bodies, "but we were both very touched. We had a sense of real sadness, and the feeling that this young, young woman could stand up and get off the table any minute." A policeman who saw photographs taken at the death scene thought that without makeup and lighting the famous actress looked quite ordinary, and he noted how "the ravages of drugs and alcohol had unmercifully taken their toll."

The official verdict in the case of Marilyn Monroe, delivered two weeks after her death by the chief medical examiner of Los Angeles, Theodore J. Curphey, was that Monroe died of "a self-administered overdose of sedative drugs and that the mode of death is probable suicide." This verdict was reaffirmed twenty years later when, in response to demands that the case be reopened, Los Angeles district attorney John Van de Kamp issued a report declaring that the original determination was justified by the evidence.

Opposing this view has been a flood of books, articles, and television shows that allege that Monroe did not die by her own hand but was instead murdered as the result of a conspiracy. Many possible culprits are identified as being part of this conspiracy, including the CIA, the FBI, the Mafia, but at the center is the attorney general of the United States, Robert Kennedy, who was alleged to have had an affair with the star.

Another interpretation is that Monroe died not by suicide or murder but by an overdose of sedatives negligently administered by those who were supposed to care for her.

So did Marilyn Monroe die by her own hand, or by the malice or carelessness of others?

THE OFFICIAL VERDICT

The official verdict of probable suicide was based largely on the results of the autopsy performed by the medical examiner's office. The autopsy showed that Monroe had high levels of chloral hydrate and pentobarbital in her system—well over the dosage needed to bring about death. The chloral hydrate measured 8 percent in her blood (meaning eight milligrams of chloral hydrate per 100 milliliters of blood.) The pentobarbital (the main ingredient in Nembutal capsules) measured 13 percent in her

liver. A large quantity of pills and pill containers were found
in her bedroom and elsewhere in the house, including a partly
empty bottle of chloral hydrate and an empty bottle of
Nembutal.

The critics of the official verdict agree that the cause of death
was probably an overdose of drugs, but they do not believe
that the drugs entered Monroe's system because she swallowed
them. They point to a curious passage in the autopsy report:

> No residue of the pills is noted. A smear made from the
> gastric contents and examined under the polarized micro-
> scope shows no refractile crystals. . . . The contents of the
> duodenum is also examined under polarized microscope
> and shows no refractile crystals.

More than any aspect of the case, this finding has led the
critics to claim that Monroe was murdered. If she had killed
herself by swallowing a lethal dose of sedatives, charge the
critics, the remains of capsules and tablets would have been
found in her digestive system. Moreover, the critics say that
yellow dye from the Nembutal capsules would have been found
in the lining of her throat, esophagus, and stomach, and that
she would have vomited. In the absence of yellow dye, vomit,
or remains of pills, the critics contend that she did not swallow
the fatal overdose; that instead the drugs were introduced into
her body either by diffusion (a drug-laced suppository or enema
inserted in the anus) or by hypodermic injection—presumably
by some person whose purpose was to kill her.

The defenders of the official verdict—including Thomas Noguchi, who as deputy medical examiner in 1962 conducted the
autopsy on Monroe—reply that Monroe was a longtime, heavy
user of drugs, well accustomed to taking large quantities of
sedatives and sleeping pills. Her digestive system was thus able
to absorb drugs very quickly, leaving no residue in the stomach.
Moreover, there were signs of redness and rawness in the stomach, described by the autopsy report as "marked congestion
and submucosal petechial hemorrhage diffusely," which could
indicate that pills had entered her system by mouth. The fact
that more drugs were found in the liver than in the blood, say
the defenders, tends to confirm that the fatal dose had been
swallowed and that the normal process of digestion had taken
place. The defenders add that vomiting only occasionally occurs

in drug overdose cases. As to the claim about yellow dye, the defenders say that the dye used in Nembutal capsules does not produce a stain.

In regard to the possibility of a fatal "hot shot" injection, Noguchi said that he minutely examined the body and could find no needle marks. The critics ask why Noguchi did not find traces of an injection that her doctor had given her two days before her death. The defenders of the official verdict answer that in a living body, the puncture from an injection heals quickly. An injection given shortly before death would remain as a noticeable bruise, especially if the hypodermic contained a quantity of drugs massive enough to cause death. Further, such a massive injection would have left a higher level of toxic material in the blood and less in the liver than was found in the autopsy.

The possibility of a fatal enema is more problematical. Noguchi's autopsy report stated that there was a "marked congestion and purplish discoloration" in the colon, which could indeed be an indication that drugs were administered rectally, although the report does not say in what part of the colon the congestion and discoloration appeared. Had the stomach and intestines been subjected to a toxicological study, this question might have been answered. But unfortunately, only the blood and liver were so tested. Noguchi described this as a mistake on the part of the toxicology examiner, Raymond J. Abernathy. Once the blood and liver were found to have a high level of drugs, said Noguchi, the toxicology examiner thought it unnecessary to test the other organs and had them destroyed. But Noguchi concluded nonetheless that "on the basis of my involvement in the case, beginning with the autopsy, I would call Monroe's suicide 'very probable.' "

Another aspect of the autopsy cited by critics is Noguchi's finding that there was a fresh bruise on the left side of Monroe's lower back and hip. The critics believe this is proof that Monroe was attacked by whoever administered the fatal dose. But Noguchi said that given the location of the bruise, it probably resulted from bumping into a table or some other innocent cause, particularly since there were no bruises on the throat or skull, which might be expected from the use of force against her.

Besides the physical evidence, the supporters of the official verdict use Monroe's psychological condition as proof of suicide. Not long before her death, Monroe had been dismissed from a 20th Century Fox movie production, *Something's Got to Give*. On the morning of her death, she reportedly asked her housekeeper, "Mrs. Murray, do we have any oxygen?"—a revealing question, since oxygen is used to resuscitate seriously ill patients. In the afternoon she quarreled with an old friend. In the evening, she spoke to actor Peter Lawford by telephone; according to Lawford, she sounded drugged and depressed. In the course of the conversation with Lawford, who was President Kennedy's brother-in-law, she said, "Say goodbye to Jack [President Kennedy], and say good-bye to yourself, because you're a nice guy." This melancholy line has been taken as the equivalent of a suicide note.

A "Suicide Investigative Team" convened by the Los Angeles chief medical examiner issued a report on Monroe's psychological state that supported the verdict of suicide. The members of the team found that Monroe had long suffered mental illness and had been subject to depression and rapid, unpredictable mood swings. She had been taking sedatives for many years, and knew well that an overdose could kill her:

> In our investigation, we have learned that Miss Monroe had often expressed wishes to give up, to withdraw, and even to die. On more than one occasion in the past, when disappointed and depressed, she had made a suicide attempt using sedative drugs. On these occasions, she had called for help and been rescued.
>
> From the information collected about the events of the evening of August 4th, it is our opinion that the same pattern was repeated except for the rescue. It has been our practice with similar information collected in other cases in the past to recommend a certification for such deaths as probable suicide.

The critics reject this psychological evidence. They believe that the Suicide Investigative Team did a superficial job. They say that in those last days, Monroe was in fairly good spirits. Negotiations were underway to reinstate her in the *Something's Got to Give* production, and she and ex-husband Joe DiMaggio were, according to one account, talking of remarriage. On the evening of her death, she had a conversation with Joe DiMaggio,

Jr., the son of the baseball player, which the young DiMaggio described as alert and friendly.

But, say the conspiracy advocates, one element in her life had gone wrong: her connection with Robert Kennedy.

THE KENNEDY CONSPIRACY

The conspiracy advocates believe that Marilyn Monroe had an affair with President John Kennedy and subsequently with the president's brother-in-law, Attorney General Robert Kennedy. They say that the relationship with Robert led directly to her death. They believe Monroe met the attorney general at a party thrown by Peter Lawford in 1961 or 1962, and that Robert Kennedy and Monroe meet frequently thereafter.

Conspiracy advocates allege that Robert Kennedy eventually called off their affair for fear of political scandal. The angry Monroe threatened to expose her relationship with John and Robert, and to reveal government secrets that she had learned from them—such as the plan of the CIA to murder Cuban leader Fidel Castro. According to conspiracy advocates, Monroe had actually scheduled a press conference for this purpose. They say that Robert Kennedy secretly came to see Monroe on the night of her death to persuade her not to reveal what she knew, and that they quarreled.

Those who believe in a conspiracy disagree over what happened next. One version has it that Monroe was so disconsolate after Robert Kennedy left her home that night that she killed herself with an overdose of drugs. Another is that Robert Kennedy murdered her himself, perhaps by smothering her with a pillow, perhaps with an injection of sedatives administered by a doctor Kennedy brought with him.

Other theories attribute the murder to outside forces, brought into the Monroe home as a result of her affair with Kennedy. One scenario is that the FBI or the CIA, acting with or without Kennedy's knowledge and approval, committed the murder in order to make sure that Monroe never revealed her liaison with Robert or John Kennedy and to stop her from revealing secrets about clandestine government operations.

Yet another group believes that Monroe was killed by the Mafia. This theory hinges on the fact that as attorney general, Robert Kennedy was a firm opponent of organized crime and had become a target for Mafia revenge. Chicago Mafia boss Sam Giancana thus orchestrated Monroe's murder in order to blackmail Kennedy or to otherwise destroy his political career through scandal. According to a 1992 biography of Giancana, *Double Cross: The Explosive Inside Story of the Mobster who Controlled America*, the mob dispatched a team of hit men to Los Angeles. Using electronic bugs planted in Monroe's home, the hit men overheard the star quarreling heatedly with Robert Kennedy. They then heard Kennedy order someone with him, presumably a doctor, to inject Monroe with sedatives to quiet her. Once Kennedy left, the mobsters (one named Needles Gianola and another Mugsy Tortorella) made their move:

> The killers waited for the cover of darkness and, sometime before midnight, entered Marilyn's home. She struggled at first, it was said, but already drugged by the injected sedative, thanks to Bobby's doctor friend, their rubber-gloved hands easily forced her nude body to the bed. Calmly, and with all the efficiency of a team of surgeons, they taped her mouth shut and proceeded to insert a specially "doctored" Nembutal suppository into her anus.

The suppository was the perfect murder weapon, runs this interpretation, because it would leave no needle marks or other signs of force.

There are many variants of the conspiracy thesis. In some, other underworld figures are involved, such as Jimmy Hoffa, president of the Teamsters Union, or John Rosselli, a West Coast mobster. Frank Sinatra and Peter Lawford are mentioned as links to the criminals, and they are supposed to have accompanied Monroe to a mobster-dominated resort hotel at Lake Tahoe a week before she died, where she had sex with Sam Giancana. Yet another variant is that Monroe was killed by Communists who were out to protect their agent, Robert Kennedy, from being ruined by scandal.

The entire scenario of Kennedy, the Mafia, the CIA, and/or the Communist Party is rejected by those who believe Monroe committed suicide. They believe that Monroe never had an affair with Robert Kennedy. Arthur M. Schlesinger, Jr., the author of a biography of Robert Kennedy, said that although the attorney general and the actress were friendly, there was no sexual relationship. He quoted Marilyn's remark to a close friend about the rumors of her liaison with Kennedy: "It's not true, I like him but not physically."

Donald Spoto, in *Marilyn Monroe: The Biography* also dismissed the Bobby-Marilyn affair as a myth. He said that Monroe did have sex with Robert Kennedy's brother, John, but that she had simply a "socially polite relationship" with Robert over a ten-month period that consisted of several telephone calls and four chaste meetings. Spoto claimed to have used the attorney general's travel logs and testimony of his associates to establish the fact that clandestine trysts alleged by the conspiracy advocates never took place.

What about the crucial date of Saturday, August 4, 1962, when Kennedy is supposed to have come to Monroe's home for a final confrontation? That day Kennedy was with his wife and children at the ranch of a friend in Gilroy, California. Kennedy was staying there in preparation for a speech he was scheduled to give before the American Bar Association convention in San Francisco on Monday. The conspiracy theorists say that Kennedy snuck away to visit Monroe. But according to Spoto, who claimed to have interviewed those who were at the ranch at that time, Kennedy remained for the entire weekend and could not have left for a clandestine trip to Los Angeles, 350 miles away. The L.A. district attorney's office found that witness accounts of the arrival of Kennedy at Monroe's home were second- and even third-hand reports told to the witnesses by others, and that those sources were often vague and uncertain.

Opponents of the conspiracy theorists also attack the talk of FBI, CIA, Mafia, and Communist involvement as completely unsupported by any hard evidence.

MANSLAUGHTER?

Donald Spoto offered a different theory—one that dispenses with Robert Kennedy, gangsters, the FBI, and other powerful forces, but which also rejects the verdict that Monroe committed suicide. He believed the star's death was caused by the negligence of her psychoanalyst Ralph Greenson and her housekeeper Eunice Murray.

Ralph Greenson was a Los Angeles psychoanalyst whom Monroe began seeing in 1960. He prescribed medicine for her, including Nembutal to help her cope with her insomnia. Greenson persuaded Monroe to hire Eunice Murray, age sixty, as a housekeeper and companion. Spoto theorized that on August 4, when Greenson paid a visit to Monroe's home, he found the actress deeply upset and unable to sleep. To calm her down, Greenson prepared an enema containing chloral hydrate, and he instructed Mrs. Murray to administer it. Greenson failed to realize that Monroe had already consumed a large amount of Nembutal, which had been prescribed by another doctor. According to Spoto, the chloral hydrate together with the Nembutal killed Monroe. Spoto speculated that the enema was administered sometime between roughly 7:15 P.M., when Joe DiMaggio, Jr. telephoned and found Monroe alert and happy, and roughly 7:45, when Lawford heard her slurred "say goodbye to yourself" over the phone.

Spoto said that when they discovered what had happened, Greenson and Murray covered up the traces of the accident. The first policeman to arrive on the scene later claimed that he observed Murray doing a load of laundry. Spoto suggested that the enema caused a bowel movement that soiled the sheets, and Murray was laundering them to hide that fact. To support his argument, Spoto said that it was Monroe's custom to take enemas as a weight-control device.

COVER-UPS

Those who believe that Monroe was killed because of her connection with Robert Kennedy believe that after she died, law enforcement authorities covered up the real circumstances of her death. They believe that the Los Angeles Police Department, the L.A. district attorney, the coroner, the FBI, and other law enforcement agencies and offices conspired together to withhold the truth from the public.

A case in point is the "little red book." The conspiracy advocates say that Monroe kept a diary in which she recorded the details of her assignations with John and Robert Kennedy, and what they had told her about world events and organized crime. The existence of the diary was testified to by a friend of Monroe's named Jean Carmen. An employee of the coroner's office, Lionel Grandison, claimed that the diary came to the coroner after Monroe's death and was locked in a safe, but that it mysteriously disappeared.

Another frequently cited element of the cover-up is the electronic eavesdropping on Monroe. According to the conspiracy advocates, one or more underworld figures (Sam Giancana and Jimmy Hoffa are usually mentioned) hired a surveillance expert named Bernard Spindel to collect damaging information on Robert Kennedy. The conspiracy advocates say that Spindel placed hidden microphones in Monroe's home and recorded her many meetings with Kennedy. One of these tapes contains Kennedy's final, angry confrontation with Monroe on August 4, in which he can be heard demanding that she hand over the incriminating diary. What happened to these tapes? In 1966 Spindel was under investigation for illegal wiretapping activities, and his home in New York was raided by the Manhattan district attorney. The conspiracy theorists believe that the Monroe-Kennedy tapes were among those seized in the raid, and that they were destroyed as part of the cover-up.

The defenders of the official version say that the "little red book" and the tapes never existed—that they were the invention of conspiracy buffs. The defenders cite the fact that Grandison, who supposedly saw the diary, was an unreliable character who was dismissed from his job in the coroner's office for stealing property from corpses and was, on another occasion, convicted of forgery. Jean Carmen, say the defenders, never knew Monroe and so could not have known about any diary, or any of the other aspects of Monroe's life she claims to have seen, including the star's love affair with Robert Kennedy. According to Donald Spoto, "Carmen's name is nowhere to be found in Marilyn's address books, nor did anyone who knew Marilyn ever hear of or see (much less meet or know) her."

In regard to the tapes, the 1982 investigation by the L.A. district attorney's office reported that investigators from the Manhattan D.A.'s office had listened to the tapes seized from Spindel and heard nothing concerning Marilyn Monroe.

Another loose end is the manner and timing in which Monroe's death was reported. The call that Monroe was dead came into the police department at about 4:25 A.M. on August 5. When the police arrived at Monroe's home, they found Ralph Greenson, Eunice Murray, and Monroe's physician, Hyman Engelberg, present. The story the witnesses told was that at about 3:30 A.M., Murray had discovered that the light was on in

Monroe's bedroom and the bedroom door was locked. Murray quickly telephoned Greenson, who advised her to look into the bedroom through the outside window. She did so, and saw the actress lying motionless on the bed. Murray then summoned Greenson from his home. Greenson broke a pane of glass in the window so he could let himself into the bedroom. He then placed a call to summon Engelberg, who came to the house and determined that Monroe was dead. It was then that the police were called.

The critics of the suicide verdict cast doubt on this account. They claim that a new rug with a thick pile had been installed in Monroe's bedroom, which would have prevented Murray from seeing a light under the door, and that the windows were blocked with thick blackout fabric, so Murray could not have peeked through (Monroe used the fabric because any trace of light prevented her from sleeping). They also say that Monroe never locked her bedroom door, so that Murray could not have found it barred. Murray, in fact, later changed her story, saying it was the telephone cord running into the room, rather than light coming from under the door, that aroused her suspicion.

Another problem exists with the time Monroe was found dead. Several people have come forward to say that they learned of Monroe's death well before 3:30 A.M., when the actress's body was supposedly found by Mrs. Murray. Monroe's lawyer, Milton Rudin, said he received a telephone call from Greenson sometime before midnight telling him that Monroe was dead, and that he drove over to the house. Natalie Jacobs, the widow of Monroe's public relations agent Arthur Jacobs, said that Arthur received a phone call at about 10:30 P.M., perhaps from Rudin, telling him of his client's death. Peter Lawford said he received a call around midnight telling him the same thing.

THE JOHN MINER OPINION

John Miner was an assistant district attorney at the time of Monroe's death; he participated in the investigation and represented the D.A.'s office at the autopsy. Shortly after Monroe's death, Miner talked at length to Dr. Greenson and listened to tapes made by Monroe and given to Greenson as part of her therapy. Miner promised Greenson that he would not reveal the details of what he had learned. But Miner did report to his supervisor, and has said since then, that he doubted Monroe committed suicide.

Miner's disagreement with the official verdict has been used by the conspiracy advocates to support their claim that Monroe was murdered, and by Spoto to support his claim that Monroe died from Greenson's negligence.

The 1982 reinvestigation of the death by the L.A. district attorney suggested that what Miner learned from Greenson and from the tapes was that Monroe seemed to be making genuine progress in her psychiatric therapy, and that suicide was therefore unlikely:

> Mr. Miner was specifically asked by our investigators if he thought this was a murder and if so, why. He said he did not and never had alleged murder, but instead reiterated his position that the psychological profile of Miss Monroe was inconsistent with an intentional act of self-destruction, as proffered by the Suicide Investigation Team.

Does Miner therefore believe that Monroe accidentally gave herself an overdose? He isn't talking. But he did tell the present author that he absolutely disagreed with the murder and manslaughter claims of Spoto and the conspiracy buffs, and he expressed anger that his position was being distorted by them.

Weighing the Evidence

Those who believe Marilyn Monroe did not die from a self-administered overdose present two competing theories. The first is the Kennedy-Mafia hypothesis of the conspiracy theorists; the second is the Greenson-Murray manslaughter theory presented by Donald Spoto.

The hypothesis that Marilyn Monroe was murdered as a consequence of an affair with Robert Kennedy is hard to accept. It is simply improbable that Monroe possessed such earth-shattering secrets that the attorney general, the Mafia, the CIA, or other powerful forces would have risked exposure to silence her. If it were true, then Kennedy must have spent so much

time discussing secret government information that the couple
would have had little time for sex. The idea of Robert Kennedy,
the Mafia, and the FBI racing in and out of Monroe's home on
the night of August 4, 1962, seems more like a scene from a
Marx Brothers movie than real life. It is also improbable that
once the murder was committed, a nationwide conspiracy
would swing into place, involving the Los Angeles coroner's
office, the Los Angeles Police Department, the CIA, and the
White House. It is improbable that the "little red book" and
the tapes ever existed, since they have not turned up after three
decades. If Sam Giancana, Jimmy Hoffa, or some other enemy
of Robert Kennedy went to the trouble of bugging Monroe's
home and making incriminating tapes—tapes that were allegedly not confiscated from Spindel until four years after Monroe's death—why were they not used against the attorney
general? President John Kennedy had other bed mates, reput-
edly including actresses Angie Dickinson and underworld call
girl Judith Campbell; why were they not rubbed out or exposed
by the Mafia?

The writings of the conspiracy advocates smack of sheer sen-
sationalism and a willingness to accept anything, no matter how
bizarre. In these books and articles one can find accounts,
among other things, of Monroe and a friend (Jean Carmen)
going out naked under their fur coats and exposing themselves,
of Monroe's having an illegitimate child and giving it up for
adoption, of Robert Kennedy in false beard frolicking with Monroe on a nude beach, and of Monroe acting as a spy for the CIA.
Recently, a group of spiritualists published a book claiming that
they been in communication with the dead Monroe through
means of a Ouija board. Her spirit, they claim, had revealed
that she was killed on orders of the Kennedys and that she was
pregnant at the time with Robert's baby. At the fringe, conspiracy theories about Monroe come closer to the writings about
UFOs, reincarnation, and the Bermuda Triangle than to solid
investigation.

And in fact, the reliability of the conspiracy advocates themselves is questionable. These authors repeatedly distort the evidence. For example, they claim that no drinking glass was
found in Monroe's bedroom, and that Monroe therefore could
not have been able to swallow pills. But in fact photographs of
the room show what appears to be a water glass by the bed
and another vessel on her night table. The conspiracy advocates

frequently cite the autopsy finding of a bruise on Monroe's lower back as evidence of murder, without quoting Noguchi's conclusion that it probably came from an innocent household accident. As we have seen, Spoto discredited conspiracy advocates such as Jean Carmen and Lionel Grandison. But he reserved his greatest scorn for Robert Slatzer, the principal author of the Kennedy-Mafia conspiracy hypothesis, and the source of endless information about Monroe's affair with Kennedy, her contact with the underworld, and so on. Slatzer has claimed that he actually married Monroe in Tijuana, Mexico, on October 4, 1952, and that although the marriage was soon annulled, he remained Monroe's close friend and confidant.

In his biography of Monroe, Spoto attacked Slatzer as a complete fraud who invented his marriage to the movie star. Spoto claimed that Monroe's close friends never heard of Slatzer nor did her address books list his name; Spoto used both as proof that Slatzer was never part of Monroe's circle. Spoto charged further that Slatzer invented the myth that Robert Kennedy had been involved in Monroe's death, a myth that Slatzer spread to the media for his own profit. In short, said Spoto, Slatzer created a "long-running, grotesque literary charade that matches any other for brazen audacity."

There is, however, one place where the conspiracy advocates do seem to have a valid case—the mystery about how and at what time the corpse was discovered. It does appear from the testimony of reliable witnesses that some people close to Monroe learned of her death before midnight on August 4, although the police were not notified until after 4:00 A.M. on August 5. But this does not prove that Monroe was killed by some hand other than her own; only that the people who made a living from caring for her—including her doctor, her lawyer, and her housekeeper—negligently delayed summoning the police.

What about Spoto's theory that Monroe was accidentally killed by Greenson and Murray? This explanation is more plausible than the Kennedy-Mafia-CIA conspiracy theory. But many problems remain. Why would Greenson give Monroe sedatives via an enema when he had routinely done this in the past through injections? There is no evidence presented anywhere that Greenson had ever before used enemas as a way of administering sedatives. Physicians and other medical personnel consulted by the present author say that while enemas are sometimes used to administer medication, the technique is reserved for cases in which a seriously ill patient is so nauseated or in such pain that pills and injections cannot be employed. There would be no reason to use this technique for the healthy thirty-six-year-old actress. Spoto takes the crucial testimony that Monroe's housekeeper was doing a laundry from police officer Jack Clemmons, but elsewhere Spoto accuses Clemmons of being an unreliable witness.

So in the last analysis, the best explanation is the simplest and most in accord with what we know of Marilyn Monroe's life. She had previously attempted suicide, she had access to large quantities of drugs, and she had reason for being despondent. There were 20,207 suicides in the United States in 1962, and there is no reason to suspect that Monroe did not number among those victims just because she happened to be famous.

There is, of course, the possibility that she did not intend to kill herself when she took the overdose; that she miscalculated the dosage. As the L.A. district attorney put it, "she may have been in such a state of emotional confusion that she, herself, lacked a clearly formed purpose."

But whether it was suicide, accident, or something in between, the weight of the evidence indicates that the most likely person responsible for the death of Marilyn Monroe was Norma Jeane Mortenson.

17

WHO KILLED MARTIN
LUTHER KING, JR.?

On the evening of April 4, 1968, the Reverend Martin Luther King, Jr. stepped out onto the balcony of the Lorraine Motel in Memphis, Tennessee.

King was one of the most controversial men in America. As the leading figure in the civil rights movement, he had campaigned for racial equality through nonviolent means. He had won the Nobel Prize and international fame for his efforts, but he had also earned the hatred of White racists and the resentment of some militant Blacks. Now he was in Memphis in support of a strike of sanitation workers. The strike had been bitter; a march through Memphis a week before had turned violent, and King was having a difficult time establishing his leadership.

But this evening he had taken a moment to relax. He and his aides were going to go to a soul food dinner at the home of a local minister. King stepped out on the balcony for some air, leaning over to chat with friends and supporters in the courtyard below. It was 6:01 P.M.

From across the street came a gunshot; a bullet struck King in the jaw and smashed into his spine. He fell backward onto the balcony, bleeding. He was taken to a local Memphis hospital, where he was pronounced dead at 7:05 P.M. Two months later, the alleged assassin, a White man named James Earl Ray, was arrested in England. Ray was brought back to Memphis, where he pleaded guilty to King's murder and was sentenced to a prison term of ninety-nine years. He is still serving that sentence.

Who was James Earl Ray and did he actually kill Martin Luther King, Jr.? The official version of the assassination proceeds along the following lines. Ray, born to a poor family in 1928, grew up as a small-time criminal with a long record of arrests for vagrancy and robbery. On April 23, 1967, he escaped from Missouri State Prison. He lived on the lam, using different aliases and traveling around the country and into Canada and Mexico. At some point during this period he decided to kill Martin Luther King, Jr., and he began to stalk the civil rights leader.

On March 29, 1968, Ray purchased a high-powered hunting rifle in Birmingham, Alabama. He then traveled to Memphis, where, on April 4, he took a room in a boarding house at 422½ South Main Street, a building whose back directly faced the Lorraine Motel, where King was staying. From the bathroom on the second floor, Ray fired the shot that killed King. Ray then ran from the rooming house and made his escape out of Memphis in his car, a white Mustang. He traveled to Toronto, where he obtained a passport that enabled him to get to England. The arrest came on June 8 at Heathrow airport outside London, where Ray had gone to take a plane for the Continent.

Many who have investigated the King assassination believe that Ray could not have accomplished all this without outside help. Indeed, some of the conspiracy theorists say that Ray may not have even pulled the trigger; they believe he was set up as a fall guy for the real killers.

Reverend Jesse Jackson, a follower of Dr. King who was present in Memphis, expressed the doubts felt by many about whether a lone assassin had committed the crime:

No thoughtful person, after reviewing the evidence, can believe that this one man, James Earl Ray—who had bungled virtually everything he had ever tried, including criminal activity—acting alone, killed Martin Luther King, escaped during the evening traffic rush in Memphis on April 4, 1968, traveled to Canada and England with international passports, avoided an international network in search of him, and was only caught sometime later. Such a scenario strains the imagination, not to mention the reasoning process.

RAOUL AND THE CONSPIRACY

If Ray was part of a conspiracy, who were the other conspirators? Ray himself said that, while in Canada nine months before the assassination, he encountered a man named "Raoul," who enticed him into assorted illegal smuggling ventures. Ray said that he subsequently met with Raoul in Mexico, New Orleans, Birmingham, and Memphis, and that under Raoul's direction he brought contraband into the United States across the Canadian and Mexican borders. One of Raoul's schemes, according to Ray, was a plan to run guns to Latin America; Raoul instructed Ray to purchase a hunting rifle and a pair of binoculars and to rent the room at the Memphis boarding house where, Raoul told Ray, he planned to meet with clients. Ray said it was Raoul who actually did the shooting and that he, Ray, was not even in the boarding house at the time.

Those who believe that King was killed as part of a conspiracy say that Raoul was using Ray as a dupe in the assassination plot. Raoul's purpose was to make Ray appear to be the lone assassin, thus shifting blame away from the real plotters. Who was Raoul working for? The international Communist movement? The Ku Klux Klan? The Mafia? All have been mentioned at one time or another as powers behind Ray. But the most frequently mentioned culprits are the Federal Bureau of Investigation and the Central Intelligence Agency. Only these organizations, it is argued, could have had the power to manipulate events behind the scene, such as Ray's escape from Missouri State Prison and his flight from Memphis after the assassination.

The argument is that these organizations saw King as a threat to national security because of his opposition to the war in Vietnam, his supposed Communist influence, his agitation for economic equality, and his stature in the Black community. It is, in fact, indisputable that J. Edgar Hoover, director of the FBI, fiercely hated King and suspected him of Communist connections. Under Hoover's orders the FBI bugged King's hotel rooms and placed wiretaps on his telephone conversations. An FBI arm known as COINTELPRO (for "Counter-Intelligence Program") attempted to discredit and embarrass King.

The critics of the conspiracy theory say that despite hostility to King in the FBI, there was no high-level assassination plot, and that Raoul was the invention of James Earl Ray, who was in fact the lone assassin. As proof, they point to the fact that no reliable witness ever came forward to identify Raoul, and that Ray's account of Raoul is confused and contradictory. Ray changed his description of Raoul, referring to him once as a "red-haired French Canadian" and another time as a "sandy-haired Latin." Ray's version of events on the day of the assassination also changed.

Why, ask the critics of the conspiracy theory, would the FBI, the Communist party, or anybody else need James Earl Ray, a petty criminal utterly inexperienced in assassination?

But some skeptics of the conspiracy theory are willing to accept the idea that Ray may have had some outside help and encouragement. He had two brothers, John and Jerry, who, like him, had criminal records. John and Jerry could have provided assistance to James while he was on the run after his escape from prison, and they may have known of his plan to kill King. One bit of evidence of this relationship comes from James Earl Ray's purchase of the rifle from a Birmingham store. He first bought a .243-caliber Winchester, but he later called the store and asked if he could exchange the rifle for a more powerful .30-06-caliber Remington. According to the store clerk, Ray said he had decided to make this exchange on the advice of his brother. In his version of this incident, Ray said it was not his brother but Raoul who advised him to exchange the weapon.

The House Select Committee on Assassinations, a congressional panel that in 1978 investigated the murder of King, found evidence that in the mid-1960s, two well-to-do, arch-segregationist St. Louis residents, John Sutherland, a lawyer, and John Kauffman, a businessman, put out an offer through the underworld grapevine that they would pay up to fifty-thousand dollars for the assassination of King. The HSCA theorized that James Earl Ray learned of this offer while in Missouri State Prison, or perhaps later through his brother John Ray, who owned a tavern in St. Louis that was known as a hangout for local white supremacists.

In brief, we can divide the writings about the King assassination into two groups. One is the theory that King was killed by a conspiracy that operated at the highest levels of government and worked behind the scenes at every stage of the operation.

In this interpretation, whether or not Ray pulled the trigger, he was only part of a vast web.

The second theory is that although Ray may have received some aid and comfort from his brothers and from White racists, he planned and carried out the assassination on his own.

Which interpretation is supported by the evidence?

THE FATAL SHOT

Those who believe in Raoul and the high-level conspiracy say that the events of April 4 in Memphis constitute damning proof. Without the assistance of well-placed individuals, they ask, how could Ray have found the motel where King was staying, and then a boarding house located conveniently across the street with a room that faced the motel balcony? And how could he have known that King would conveniently walk out onto that balcony at 6:00 P.M. and provide a target?

The critics of the conspiracy theory say that the events are not all that difficult to understand. Ray had been stalking King for some time, and he had come to Memphis for the purpose of killing him. The April 4 issue of the Memphis *Commercial Appeal* (a copy of which was later found among the possessions left behind by Ray) informed its readers that King was staying at the Lorraine Motel; a news photograph showed King entering room 306. Simply by driving in the vicinity of the motel, Ray was able to find the rooming house across the street. He entered the rooming house, owned by a Mrs. Bessie Brewer, and asked her for a room; he rejected the first one she showed him because it did not face the motel. The second one did afford a view, and he took it. He then went out and purchased a pair of binoculars, which he took back to the rooming house so that he could keep up surveillance of the motel. The bathroom on the second floor of the rooming house offered the best vantage of the motel, and it was from there, say the critics of the conspiracy theory, that Ray shot King. The critics say that Ray would have shot the civil rights leader at whatever time King emerged from his room onto the balcony.

But nobody saw James Earl Ray pull the trigger. The official version is that Ray was alone in the bathroom when he fired the shot. An occupant of the boarding house, Charles Stephens, came out of his room when he heard the gunshot, and saw a man running toward the stairs carrying a long bundle. He later identified the man as James Earl Ray. The conspiracy buffs attack the veracity of Stephens. They say that he was an alcoholic, who had been drinking heavily that day. A taxi driver, James McGraw, claimed that he had come to Stephens's room before the assassination and found him lying drunk on his bed, too intoxicated to move. Then there is the case of Grace Walden Stephens, Charles's common-law wife. According to the conspiracy theorists, Mrs. Stephens disagreed with her husband's identification of Ray, and as a result was forcibly confined to a mental institution by the authorities.

The testimony of two other witnesses casts doubt on the official version. Harold "Cornbread" Carter was drinking wine in the bushes below the boarding house. He claimed he saw a man in the bushes fire a rifle and then run away. Solomon Jones, Jr., the chauffeur of Dr. King who was in the Lorraine parking lot, also said he saw a man running from the bushes.

The anti-conspiracy writers believe that Charles Stephens was correct in his testimony, and that Carter and Jones were wrong, perhaps because they were misled by the rush of spectators and police after the assassination. As for Mrs. Stephens, they say that she was an unstable personality whose statements were confused. She was placed in an institution, they say, because she was genuinely mentally ill, and not as part of a plot to silence her.

Another debate concerns the fact that in the moments after the assassination, a bundle wrapped in a bedspread was dropped in front of a store a few feet away from the rooming house. The bundle contained a rifle in a box, a radio, a zipper bag, a pair of binoculars, assorted toiletries, some tools, underwear, two cans of beer, and other odds and ends. Many of those objects were eventually traced to Ray: he had purchased the rifle and the binoculars before the assassination; the radio had his prison number scratched on it; and the underwear bore laundry marks that were from a dry cleaning establishment he had used. (Some of the objects may also have contained Ray's fingerprints and palmprints, although there is debate about this.) How did the bundle get there? The official version is that Ray dropped it during his escape. But those who believe in a conspiracy say it was unlikely that an assassin would toss such incriminating evidence on the sidewalk where it could be found by police. Mark Lane, a supporter of the conspiracy theory, put it this way in his 1977 book, *Code Name Zorro*:

> If Ray acted alone, used the weapon that he purchased in Birmingham, and then was motivated to flee quickly from the scene, why did he take the time to pack the weapon in a cardboard box and then place his bulky belongings in a bedspread? Indeed, why had he not left the articles not required to kill Dr. King in the trunk of the Mustang before he fired the shot? If he was going to carry the rifle, binoculars, radio, clothing, and other articles from the bathroom, taking precious time to wrap them up, why did he leave them on the sidewalk? Why did he not just throw them in the Mustang parked a few feet away? The gratuitous placement by Ray of evidence that would, without doubt, lead to him, is inexplicable.

The skeptics of the conspiracy theory offer a different explanation. They argue that right after Ray shot King from the bathroom window, he ran to his room and hurriedly wrapped his possessions in a blanket in order to leave nothing behind that could be traced to him. Holding the bundle, he then ran out of the rooming house toward his Mustang, which was parked nearby. His intention was to take the bundle with him, but as he neared the Mustang he saw police cruisers on the street. He quickly dropped the bundle and proceeded to his car.

THE MEMPHIS POLICE

To support the argument that some force high in the law enforcement community deliberately wanted King to die and Ray to escape, those who believe in a conspiracy point to suspicious actions on the part of the Memphis police. As one example, the conspiracy buffs describe the case of Edward Redditt, a Black Memphis police officer who, they say, was assigned to a security detail to protect King. On the day of the assassination, Redditt was stationed in a firehouse across the street from the Lorraine Motel. In the afternoon, word came from police headquarters that a death threat against Redditt had been received. He was taken off his assignment and driven home by a superior officer, so he was not at his post when King was assassinated.

As a result, a Black policeman who might have been zealous in protecting King and apprehending his killer was removed from the scene, and his superiors, who should have been concerned with the presence of King in the city, were instead preoccupied with a spurious threat to Redditt.

Those who are skeptical of a conspiracy reply that the threat against Redditt was genuine and came as the result of his role as a policeman in the sanitation strike. They say the police acted reasonably in taking him off his assignment in order to shield him. Moreover, they believe that Redditt himself was responsible for inflating the episode. He originally claimed that he had been part of a security detail assigned to protect King, but he later admitted that his assignment had been surveillance, not security.

Another issue concerns Ray's escape from Memphis. There were dozens of police officers in the vicinity of the Lorraine Motel at the time of the assassination. Yet Ray was able to elude police and escape in his distinctive white Mustang. The police failed to issue to neighboring states an all-points bulletin for the Mustang and failed to establish roadblocks on the routes out of Memphis. All of this is used by conspiracy theorists as evidence that the Memphis police wanted Ray (or the real assassin) to avoid capture.

Those who deny the existence of a conspiracy interpret the role of the police differently. The House Select Committee criticized the Memphis Police Department for failing to come up with a contingency plan to seal off the Lorraine Motel area in the event of an emergency, for not issuing an all-points bulletin, and for not blocking off the roads. But the committee concluded that there had been no plot:

> The committee found no evidence that the substandard performance of the Memphis police in the aftermath of the assassination was part of a conspiracy to facilitate the assassination of Dr. King or the escape from Memphis of James Earl Ray. The committee found, instead, that these defects resulted from inadequate supervision, lack of foresight and individual negligence. They did not constitute complicity in the assassination.

Another puzzle connected with Ray's escape from Memphis is the fact that there were reports of several speeding white

Mustangs in different locations in and around Memphis immediately after the assassination. The conspiracy theorists say this may have been part of a plot to confuse pursuers. The skeptics reply that, according to estimates by Ford dealers, there were perhaps four hundred white Mustangs owned in the Memphis vicinity, and that when the bulletin went out on the radio that police were seeking one such car, the owners of white Mustangs drove furiously to get home.

The so-called phantom broadcast is yet another controversy. A half hour after the assassination, a broadcast was heard on citizens band radio describing a high-speed police chase of a Mustang in north Memphis. The broadcast was a hoax; there was no such chase, and Ray actually made his escape out of south Memphis. Was this broadcast a deliberate ruse by the plotters to throw the authorities off Ray's track? Those who believe it was a conspiracy say yes; those in the opposite camp say no, that it was simply a prank by a CB enthusiast.

The Canadian Aliases

During the fourteen-month period between his April 1967 escape from the Missouri penitentiary and his June 1968 capture in England, James Earl Ray traveled extensively under several different names. His favorite was Eric S. Galt or Eric Starvo Galt, a name he used frequently up to the time of the assassination. He called himself John Lowmyer when he purchased the high-powered rifle, and John Willard when he checked into the boarding house on the day of the assassination. After the assassination he traveled to Canada, where he used the names Paul Bridgeman and Raymond George Sneyd. It was as Sneyd that he obtained the Canadian passport that enabled him to travel to England.

Those who believe that Ray was part of a conspiracy are struck by the fact that there were real people who lived in the vicinity of Toronto named Eric Galt, John Willard, Paul Bridgeman, and Raymond George Sneyd. What makes this all the more remarkable is that these Canadians were adult White men with about the same height, weight, and dark hair as Ray. Published photographs of Galt, Bridgeman, and Sneyd show a reasonably close facial resemblance to Ray. Galt even had scars on his face and palm, as did James Earl Ray.

Could it have been a coincidence? Those who believe in a conspiracy say no; only with sophisticated outside aid could Ray have obtained the names of men who looked so much like him.

But the opponents of the conspiracy thesis offer explanations of how Ray could have selected the Canadian names. The real Eric S. Galt (the S stood for St. Vincent) was a sportsman and writer. In some publications his picture appeared with his signature. In the signature, the real Galt used the abbreviation "St. V." for his middle name, with elaborate circles instead of periods. The anti-conspiracy theorists believe that while in prison or at some other time, Ray had seen the photo and the signature in a magazine, and misinterpreted the "St. V." middle name for "Starvo." He filed the name away in his head for later use.

In regard to the Sneyd and Bridgeman aliases, the anti-conspiracy theorists offer the following explanation: When he was in Canada, Ray selected the names Sneyd and Bridgeman by going into the public library in Toronto and looking up in microfilm newspaper files the names of males born thirty-six years before in Toronto. (Ray was actually forty years old; the anti-conspiracy theorists say he selected younger men because he looked younger than his forty years.) From these sources he could obtain the birth dates, places of birth, and parents' names of thirty-six-year-old men—information he needed to obtain birth certificates. He then looked these men up in the telephone book and called them, posing as a passport official, and asked each man if he had a passport. (The real Bridgeman and Sneyd remembered receiving these telephone calls.) When he found that Sneyd had never applied for a passport, Ray used the Sneyd birth certificate to obtain one from the Canadian government.

As for the resemblance, the skeptics of conspiracy say that in any randomly selected group of Anglo-Saxon males of roughly the same age, most would meet the general description of Ray— medium build, medium height, dark hair. Moreover, it may be that Ray actually went to Sneyd's and Bridgeman's neighborhood to observe the two men in order to confirm that they looked somewhat like him.

FINANCES

Ray needed money during the fourteen-month period between his escape and his arrest. During this period he traveled extensively in the United States, Canada, and Mexico, and across the Atlantic to England, with a side trip to Portugal. He made many purchases during this time, including clothing, a used car, camera equipment, a rifle, and binoculars. He paid for dancing lessons, bartending lessons, locksmithing lessons, airplane tickets, and bus fare, and for the company of prostitutes. He rented rooms in boarding houses and motels. With the exception of six weeks of work as a dishwasher in a restaurant, Ray was not employed. The House Select Committee estimated that Ray spent roughly $9,000 during this period, of which only $664.34—his dishwashing wages—can be accounted for.

All of this has been used as evidence that Ray was not a lone assassin—that he was directed by a conspiracy that provided him with money. Ray himself said he received payoffs amounting to $7,750 from Raoul. One of Ray's Canadian landladies told police that a heavyset man came to call on Ray one day and handed him an envelope, shortly after which Ray purchased his airplane ticket for London.

But the anti-conspiracy writers argue that it is not necessary to believe in a conspiracy to account for Ray's finances. They believe that Ray obtained cash through robberies of gas stations and supermarkets, using a pistol he bought after his prison escape. Ray himself admitted that he stole $1,700 in a robbery in Canada. The HSCA speculates that Ray may have participated in a robbery of a bank in Alton, Illinois, in July 1967, and later made some money smuggling marijuana from Mexico to the United States.

The anti-conspiracy writers also stress that Ray lived frugally, staying in inexpensive motels and rooming houses, buying the cheapest airline tickets, eating hamburgers, pizza, and other cheap food, and wearing patched underwear; when he was arrested he had only $125 in his possession.

What of the heavyset man (known in the assassination literature as the "Fat Man") from whom Ray received an envelope? The anti-conspiracy group says that the Fat Man was located by the Canadian authorities and turned out to be a good Samaritan who found an envelope addressed to Ray (under the alias George Sneyd) and returned it to him.

WEAKNESS IN THE EVIDENCE

James Earl Ray never went through a trial for the murder of
Martin Luther King, Jr. There was no courtroom clash between
prosecution and defense; no witnesses cross-examined by opposing lawyers. Instead, Ray pleaded guilty to the charge of
first-degree murder and signed a confession. After a brief pro-
ceeding in a Memphis courtroom, Judge W. Preston Battle, Jr.
instructed the jury to return a verdict of guilty. The jury did
so, and as agreed to in advance by Ray and his lawyer, Ray
was sentenced to a prison term of ninety-nine years.

Those who believe in a conspiracy say that Ray was railroaded. They believe that his defense lawyer persuaded Ray
that pleading guilty was the only way to escape the electric
chair. They believe that the real motive of the State and the
defense was actually to avoid a trial at all costs in order to
prevent any evidence of the conspiracy from leaking out. The
conspiracy theorists find it suspicious that the judge who sentenced Ray died of a heart attack shortly after the proceedings,
at a time when he was considering an appeal by Ray for a
new trial.

The conspiracy advocates believe that if a trial had actually
taken place, weaknesses in the case against Ray would have
been revealed. One such weakness, they argue, was Charles
Stephens's testimony that he saw the assassin coming out of the
bathroom—testimony that was put in doubt by the allegations of
Stephens's drunkenness and the testimony of Harold Carter and
Solomon Jones that they had seen a gunman in the bushes.

A second weakness is the lack of scientific proof of the path
of the bullet, caused by the fact that the precise position King
was standing in when he was shot could not be determined.
The ballistic evidence is also poor. The official explanation is
that the bullet that killed King became distorted and broke into
fragments, making it impossible to compare with a bullet from
a test firing. The conspiracy theorists say that the authorities
deliberately failed to pursue other tests that might have established that the bullet that killed King did not come from Ray's
rifle. The main physical evidence that the shot was fired from
the bathroom is a small depression in the wooden windowsill
that corresponds to a rifle barrel.

The fingerprints are another source of confusion. Those who
believe in a conspiracy and those who do not differ about

whether identifiable fingerprints of James Earl Ray were found at the crime scene. Presumably this would have been debated by expert witnesses had a trial taken place.

"Nobody Can Reason with Jimmy"

If James Earl Ray assassinated Martin Luther King, Jr., why did he do it? Those who believe he acted alone attribute his action to the fact that he was an obsessive racist with an unbridled desire for notoriety. In his 1968 book, *He Slew the Dreamer*, writer William Bradford Huie described Ray's background:

> This, then, is what his record shows James Earl Ray to be: a man with a deprived childhood who developed into a habitual criminal who should never be paroled from prison, an antisocial man capable of murder and incapable of considering the rights of any other human being.

As to Ray's racism, it is said that he was a fervent supporter of George Wallace, the Alabama segregationist who ran for president in 1968. Biographer Huie quoted Ray's brothers Jerry and John on the subject of their brother James:

> All his life, Jimmy's been wild on two subjects. He's been wild against niggers, and he's wild for politics. He's wild against any politician who's for niggers, and he's wild for any politician who's against niggers. Nobody can reason with Jimmy on the two subjects of niggers and politics.

As to his delusions, Ray is reported to have longed to achieve enough notoriety to be placed on the Ten Most Wanted list. He reportedly told his guards that he expected that he would obtain a pardon when George Wallace became president.

Those who believe that Ray was part of a conspiracy paint a different picture. They believe that Ray had no special animosity toward Blacks. They point out that when he went to work as a dishwasher in a restaurant after his escape from prison, many of his fellow employees were Black, and that he seemed to have gotten along well with them. They also find him reasonably intelligent and well balanced. And although he had a long criminal record, murder was not part of it. There is nothing in his history to indicate that he ever fired a gun to kill another human being. So if he was not driven by hatred of Blacks or by delusions, then it becomes more likely that he was simply a dupe of Raoul and was suckered into playing a role in a high-level conspiracy.

Weighing the Evidence

In the end, it all comes down to Raoul. If one believes that Raoul actually existed, then the existence of a high-level conspiracy is credible. But if there was no Raoul, then it is likely that Ray acted alone to kill Martin Luther King, Jr. with, at most, encouragement of White racists and occasional help from the Ray brothers.

So how credible is Raoul? At bottom, his existence rests on the testimony of James Earl Ray. And Ray equivocated about Raoul, to say the least. Over the years he has given three different versions of what happened in Memphis. The first version was contained in the confession that he signed as part of the plea bargain agreement that resulted in his ninety-nine-year sentence. In that confession Ray stated simply that he shot King; there was no mention of Raoul.

The second version was what Ray told the lawyer Arthur Hanes, Sr. and the writer William Bradford Huie. Ray said that he was parked outside the boarding house at the time of the shooting while Raoul was inside the building:

> I was sitting in the Mustang when I heard a shot. In a minute or so Raoul came running down the stairs carrying my zipper bag and the rifle which was in the box and wrapped up in a bedspread I had brought from California. Just before he got in the car Raoul turned around and threw the rifle and my zipper bag down on the sidewalk. Then he jumped in the backseat, and covered up with a sheet, and I took off.

The third version is the one Ray told the House Select Committee on Assassination in 1978 and repeated in his 1992 book *Who Killed Martin Luther King*. Once again Raoul is inside the rooming house and Ray outside. But this time Ray is returning in his car from a gas station, where he went to get a flat spare tire repaired. As he approaches the rooming house he sees that the police have blocked the street where the rooming house is located and he hears on the radio that King has been shot and that police are looking for a White man in a white Mustang, so he drives away and never sees Raoul again.

Why did Ray change his story? He says that he invented the story of Raoul covering himself with a white sheet as a joking reference to the Ku Klux Klan. He says he signed the plea bargain version because his attorney pressured him to do so. Ray now defends the gas station version as the truth, but his critics say he has latched onto it because of a dubious account that appeared some years after the fact that Ray was seen at a Memphis gas station at the time of the shooting.

When his interrogators at the 1978 House investigation asked Ray why he withheld the gas station story from his attorney Arthur Hanes, Sr. at the time of the Memphis court proceedings, Ray blithely replied that he intended to tell about the gas station once he was put on the witness stand. "You were going to spring this on your attorney at the trial?" asked an astonished congressman. "Yes, that's correct," Ray replied. The HSCA final report pointed out how improbable this was:

> The committee was unable to understand why Ray, who planned to go to trial and take the stand, would have decided to withhold a valid alibi from his own attorney, especially since Ray faced the possibility of capital punishment. If the gas station story were true and Hanes had been told of it, he could have found witnesses to corroborate it and support Ray's testimony. By withholding his story, Ray guaranteed that his testimony, which was subject to impeachment because of his prior criminal record, would stand alone without independent corroboration.

The weight of the evidence is that there never was a Raoul as described by Ray—a shadowy figure who duped the escaped convict into assassination. On the contrary, the one fact that emerges from Ray's changing versions of the story is that Raoul was an invention, made up by Ray as it suited his fancy. Without Raoul, the argument for a high-level conspiracy collapses. What about a lower-level conspiracy? That Ray confided in and took some assistance from his brothers is likely. That he was lured into the act in the first place by the Sutherland-Kauffman reward offer remains a possibility, but an unproved one.

In the end, it is evident that Ray planned and carried out the murder on his own, and, blinded by racism and delusions of his own self-importance, cut down the best hope for racial equality in America.

18

WAS ANITA HILL LYING?

Newspaper reporter Tmothy M. Phelps recalled what it was like when the witness testified before the Judiciary Committee of the United States Senate on Friday, October 11, 1991.

> Members of the audience, including normally blasé reporters, could not believe what they were hearing. A month before we had all been in this same room listening to talk about legal concepts such as natural law and the right of privacy. Now, we were listening to a discussion of the size of a Supreme Court nominee's penis.

The witness was Anita Hill, a professor of law at the University of Oklahoma. She had come to Washington to testify against Clarence Thomas, an appeals court judge who had been nominated by President George Bush to a seat on the Supreme Court. Both Thomas (b. 1948) and Hill (b. 1956) were African Americans, both had been born to poor Southern families, both were graduates of Yale Law School.

As a national television audience looked on, Anita Hill told the Senate Judiciary Committee that in 1981 she had gone to work as an aide to Thomas, who was then the assistant secretary for civil rights at the Department of Education. She said that after three months, Thomas began to ask her out on dates. She declined, but he continued to press her and to make sexual comments.

She said that the harassment had ceased for a time, and she was hopeful it had ended. When Thomas obtained a new job as chair of the Equal Employment Opportunity Commission, she followed him there to serve as an assistant. In the fall and winter of 1982, the harassment began again. She said he would talk about the large size of his penis, about oral sex, and about pornography, including movies featuring "Long Dong Silver." One of the oddest episodes, she said, concerned a can of Coca-Cola that Thomas was drinking in his office: "He got up from the table at which we were working, went over to his desk to get the Coke, looked at the can and asked, 'Who has put pubic hair on my Coke?' "

Hill said that the stress of this situation was so great that she was hospitalized for five days because of acute stomach pain. She finally left to take a teaching position at Oral Roberts University in Oklahoma. On her last day at the EEOC, Thomas talked to her privately: "He said that if I ever told anyone of his behavior that it would ruin his career."

When he testified before the Senate committee, Thomas vigorously and angrily denied the allegations. He said he had never spoken improperly to Hill:

> I would like to start by saying unequivocally, uncategorically, that I deny each and every single allegation against me today that suggested in any way that I had conversations of a sexual nature or about pornographic material with Anita Hill, that I ever attempted to date her, that I ever had any personal sexual interest in her, or that I in any way ever harassed her.

Thomas went on to say that the charges against him were politically motivated because, as a conservative Black, he was bucking the liberal establishment:

> This is a circus. It's a national disgrace. And from my standpoint as a Black American, as far as I'm concerned, it is a high-tech lynching for uppity Blacks who in any way deign to think for themselves, to do for themselves, to have different ideas, and it is a message that unless you kowtow to an old order, this is what will happen to you. You will be lynched, destroyed, caricatured by a commit-

tee of the United States Senate rather than hung from a tree.

And so it continued on national television. Both Hill and Thomas were questioned by the members of the Judiciary Committee. Witnesses for both appeared before the committee, and were in turn grilled by the senators. In the end, Thomas was confirmed by the full Senate in a remarkably close 52 to 48 vote.

Who was telling the truth? It was a question that obsessed the nation at the time of the hearings and remains unanswered today.

HILL'S CORROBORATING WITNESSES

Anita Hill went public with her charge of sexual harassment against Clarence Thomas a decade after the events supposedly took place. At the Judiciary Committee hearings, four witnesses testified that years before the charges became public, Hill had spoken about being harassed. The four were Susan Hoerchner, Ellen Wells, John Carr, and Joel Paul.

Hill met Susan Hoerchner when they were students at Yale Law School, and they remained friendly after both landed jobs in Washington. They lost contact after Hoerchner moved to California, where she eventually became a workman's compensation judge. In her testimony to the Senate Judiciary Committee, Hoerchner said that in the early 1980s she and Hill had a telephone conversation in which Hill complained that she was being harassed on her job by her boss. If true this provides important corroboration of Hill's allegations.

When did the call take place? During the initial investigations by the FBI and Senate staff, Hoerchner stated her belief that the call occurred in Washington in the spring of 1981.

The critics argue that Hill did not begin working for Thomas until July 1981, and that her own testimony establishes that the harassment by Thomas could not have begun until November or December of 1981. Thus, Hill could not have complained to Hoerchner about Thomas if the call actually took place in the spring.

Hill's critics say that Hoerchner suffered a curious attack of amnesia when confronted with this discrepancy. She told Senate staffers that she could not remember the date, and later testified before the Judiciary Committee that the call must have taken place after Hill began working for Thomas because Hill referred to the boss who was harassing her as "Clarence."

Hill's defenders say that Hoerchner had never really been precise about the date of the call; that when she mentioned a spring 1981 date to the FBI and to Senate staff, she was simply making a guess, and that this guess was blown out of proportion by the supporters of Thomas.

Another witness who corroborated Hill's testimony was her friend John Carr, an African-American lawyer. Carr testified that in the fall of 1982 Hill had a tearful conversation with him on the telephone, during which she said that "her boss was making sexual advances toward her." Carr testified, "In this telephone conversation, it was immediately clear to me that she was referring to Judge Thomas."

Joel Paul, a professor of law at American University, met Hill when she was a visiting professor in the summer of 1987. At lunch one day, Paul asked Hill why she had left the EEOC. Paul testified: "Professor Hill responded, reluctantly and with obvious emotion and embarrassment, that she had been sexually harassed by her supervisor at the EEOC." Paul said that he had recounted the story to another faculty member, Susan Dunham, who confirmed this conversation with Paul.

Ellen Wells, an African-American friend from Hill's Washington days, testified that in the fall of 1982, Hill had told her, without providing detailed information, that Thomas had exhibited "inappropriate" behavior that Wells interpreted to be sexual harassment.

Hill's critics argue that these corroborating witnesses were ideologically opposed to Thomas's nomination to the Supreme Court, and that much of what the four said was invented to support Hill's allegations. Why, ask the critics, did Carr, Paul, and Wells not come forward until after Hill's charges were made public? And why was it that when she was first asked who she had told about harassment, Hill could name only Susan Hoerchner? Further, the critics point out, Wells could not say with certainty that Hill had spoken of sexual harassment, and Carr, Paul, and Wells could not recall whether Hill had mentioned Thomas by name when she talked of her supervisor.

A few years after the Senate Judiciary Committee hearing, another witness appeared. Bradley Mims, an African-American government employee, told the authors of a 1994 book on the case, *Strange Justice,* that he had befriended Hill in the early 1980s. According to Mims, Hill told him that Thomas was saying "crazy stuff" and "talking wild" to her, which Mims took to mean sexual harassment. The authors say that Mims did not come forward with this information at the time of the Senate hearings because he was reluctant to jeopardize his government career.

WHY DIDN'T SHE AVOID HIM?

The critics of Anita Hill say that if she was the object of sexual harassment by Clarence Thomas at the Department of Education, why did she not avoid him from then on, as one might expect in such a case? They say that far from distancing herself, she followed him to his new job as chairman of the EEOC. After she left the EEOC to begin her teaching career, she continued to remain on good terms with her former boss. One example of this continued contact was the fact that from 1983 to 1991, ten telephone messages recorded by Thomas's secretary on the office phone log contained friendly words from Hill to Thomas, among them the following:

➤ "Just called to say hello. Sorry she didn't get to see you last week."

➤ "Needs your advice on getting research grants."

➤ "Pls call."

➤ "In town 'til 8/15. Wanted to congratulate on marriage."

Charles Kothe, a dean at Oral Roberts Law School when Hill taught there, stated that on one occasion in 1987, Thomas came to Tulsa to give a speech and stayed the night at Kothe's home. Hill joined Thomas for breakfast there the next morning, where, said Kothe, the conversation between Hill and Thomas was relaxed and friendly. Kothe said that after breakfast Hill voluntarily drove Thomas to the airport for his return flight. The critics of Hill charge that a victim of sexual harassment would never have associated herself with her attacker in this manner.

In answer to these accusations, Hill said that she had followed Thomas to the EEOC because his harassment seemed to have ended. "I began both to believe and hope that our working relationship could be a proper, cordial, and professional one." She said that by taking a new job at EEOC she would be able to pursue her professional interest in the area of civil rights. She was also concerned that her job at the Department of Education might cease after Thomas left and a new, unknown boss took over. Adding to her decision to leave the Department of Education was the announced intention of President Reagan to abolish the department entirely.

Hill said that after she left the EEOC for a teaching career her contact with Thomas became minimal. As to the phone messages, she said that she called Thomas's office from time to time to talk to Diane Holt, Thomas's secretary, and on those occasions she would pass along a casual greeting to Thomas. Hill also said she contacted Thomas to help friends who wanted to get the EEOC chairman to come to Oklahoma as a conference speaker. In regard to the trip to the airport, she said that she had been asked to drive her former boss there.

Hill's critics attack her statement that she believed her job at the Department of Education would end. She was a career civil service employee rather than a political appointee, and could not have been fired. Hill's former coworkers at the Department of Education said that Hill was made aware of her protected position. Thomas's successor at Education, Harry Singleton, contradicted Hill's statement that she did not know who would replace Thomas. Singleton said he had met with Hill before Thomas left and asked her to stay on in her position. In regard to the telephone calls, Thomas's secretary, Diane Holt, said that Hill had not been calling her, but instead was calling directly for Thomas, and that in fact there had actually been more calls from Hill to Thomas than those on the log.

THE POLYGRAPH TEST

To support her testimony, Anita Hill took a polygraph test in a Washington lawyer's office. She answered no to questions such as the following:

➤ "Have you deliberately lied to me about Clarence Thomas?"

➤ "Are you fabricating the allegation that Clarence Thomas discussed pornographic material with you?"

➤ "Are you lying to me about the various topics that Clarence Thomas mentioned to you regarding specific sexual acts?"

➤ "Are you lying to me about Clarence Thomas making reference to you about the size of his penis?"

The polygraph operator, Paul K. Minor, concluded that "there was no indication of deception to any relevant question."

The critics of Anita Hill attack this evidence on the grounds that polygraphy is an inexact science, and evidence from the polygraph is not admissible in a court of law. It has been shown that it is possible to trick the machine, and a person suffering from mental delusion can say falsehoods that appear as the truth. The critics also charge that the polygraph operator in this case had made errors in previous cases.

Hill's defenders respond that although polygraph tests are not foolproof, the fact that Hill voluntarily submitted to such a test is an argument in her favor. Hill's defenders say that Minor was an experienced polygraph expert who had previously worked as the director of polygraph operations for the FBI.

QUESTIONS ABOUT HILL'S CHARACTER AND BELIEFS

Hill's critics paint an unflattering portrait of her. They depict her as a liberal feminist whose attack on Thomas was motivated by a desire to keep a conservative voice off the Supreme Court. They charge that she was also obsessed with sex and subject to fantasies of erotic relationships with men. Witnesses who worked with Hill and Thomas at the EEOC charged that Hill seemed to have what amounted to a crush on Thomas; that she constantly tried to be with him and was resentful when others came between them.

At the Senate hearing, a Black attorney named John Doggett III testified that he had known Hill slightly in Washington in the early 1980s. Doggett said that from her remarks to him at various times, he intuited that she thought he was sexually interested in her.

The critics charge that Hill exhibited an obsession with sex after she left Washington for the teaching profession. David Brock, a leading critic of Hill, charged that she had a fascination for pornography and kinky sex. Brock quoted an unnamed man who knew Hill at the University of Oklahoma Law School who said that she and her friends would frequently discuss pornographic topics: "Anita would describe the size of men's penises, and talk about firm butts. She was obsessed with oral sex." The critics of Hill cite a former student at Oral Roberts University, Lawrence Shiles, who claimed that on one occasion he and two of his male classmates found pubic hairs placed in their written assignments that had been graded and returned to the students by Hill.

Hill's defenders refute this portrait. They describe her as a prim, even prudish academic who was deeply shocked by the harassment she received at the hands of Thomas. They describe her politics as either apolitical or mildly conservative, and claim that she had even supported the nomination of the conservative Robert Bork to the Supreme Court. Hill's defenders dismiss the accounts of the pubic hair as a joke created by hostile students and spread by supporters of Thomas.

The Brock Hypothesis

The critics of Hill, and particularly David Brock in his 1993 book, *The Real Anita Hill*, build a hypothesis of how she came to make her charges against Thomas.

Hill, say her critics, was not a particularly good lawyer. When she graduated from Yale, she went to work as a junior associate for the Washington law firm Wald, Harkrader & Ross. The firm found her to be inadequate, and told her to find another job— the genteel way of being fired. This allegation was confirmed in an affidavit by a former partner of the law firm, John Burke, who said he had told Hill to leave. Hill could not accept her own failings, and used the excuse of sexual harassment to justify her problems with the firm. One of those she used this excuse with was Susan Hoerchner.

Hill was rescued from her difficult situation at Wald, Harkrader & Ross by Clarence Thomas, who was persuaded by a friend at the firm to hire Hill at the Department of Education, where Thomas was a new assistant secretary. Hill thus owed a great deal to Thomas, and she was drawn to him as an African American who had risen from poverty to a respected position in national affairs. Thomas, in return, genuinely liked his young assistant.

But Thomas gradually discovered that she was not as able as he had originally thought, and he came to rely less and less on her. At the EEOC he promoted another Black woman over Hill. For her part, Hill became disenchanted with Thomas. She was distressed by his growing conservative political philosophy, which clashed with her own liberal beliefs, particularly in regard to affirmative action. Added to Hill's poor job performance and divergent political opinion was her fantasy of a romantic attachment to Thomas and his rejection of her. Once again she needed to escape from a difficult position; this time it was to a teaching career.

In July of 1991, when Susan Hoerchner saw on television that Clarence Thomas had been nominated to the Supreme Court, she called her former friend Anita Hill. According to Brock's hypothesis, Hoerchner mistakenly thought that Thomas was the harasser that Hill had complained to her about a decade before, when in reality Hill had been speaking about her situation at the law firm. Said Brock:

> When Hoerchner called out of the blue ten years later and suggested that the conservative Black who had just been nominated to the Supreme Court that day was the "pig" Hill had been talking about ten years before, Hill would have been caught off balance. In the split second in which she had to respond, she may have chosen to go along with Hoerchner's misimpression rather than explain that it had been at the law firm where she had been harassed, in which case she would have had to come up with another name from the distant past, and embellish an old story so that it remained convincing.

Brock believed that Hoerchner was thus guilty of planting the whole allegation against Thomas in Hill's head.

Brock argued that when word of Hill's charges against Thomas reached Washington, liberals who had been attempting to block the Thomas nomination seized on these charges and got in touch with Hill. These liberals—a combination of feminists, Senate staffers, reporters, and other Washington insiders Brock calls the "Shadow Senate"—led Hill to believe that she could make her charges against Thomas without going public, and that this would be enough to bring down the nomination. But events moved too swiftly. Her name was leaked to the press, and she was forced to tell her story before the Senate Judiciary Committee and the television audience. With the coaching of the Shadow Senate, she spun her story of sexual harassment, adding lurid details to increase the dramatic effect.

To support this scenario, Brock and other critics charge that Hill and her supporters derived some of her allegations against Thomas from other sources, particularly a 1988 Kansas legal case, *Carter v. Sedgwick County*, in which the female plaintiff charged that her male harasser showed her a picture of Long Dong Silver, and also placed a plastic penis on a can of soda. Another possible source cited by Hill's critics is the best-selling book *The Exorcist*, in which a character finds a pubic hair floating in his drink. As proof that Hill's story was deliberately embellished, her critics point to her testimony to the Federal Bureau of Investigation. When her allegations against Thomas first surfaced, the FBI, at the request of the Senate, dispatched two agents to interview her, and she described to them the harassment she claimed to have received. But when she later testified before the Senate, Hill provided many details—such as the pubic hair on the Coke—that she never mentioned to the FBI.

Hill's supporters reject the Brock hypothesis. They say that Hill was not under the gun at the law firm. Other members of the firm stated that Burke would not have made such a decision or handled such a matter, and that Hill was in no danger of being let go.

As to the allegation that the Shadow Senate embellished the harassment charge, Hill's supporters say that thirteen days prior to the FBI interview, Hill spoke at great length on the telephone to a Democratic Senate staffer, James Brudney, and that Brudney's notes of the conversation contain the Coke story and other details that Hill subsequently gave in her Senate testimony.

PORTRAITS OF THOMAS

At the hearings, Clarence Thomas refused to discuss matters involving his personal life. But his friends and former employees testified to his moral character. Twelve women who had worked for Thomas testified to the Judiciary Committee that he behaved with scrupulous correctness toward females in the office; that he never made sexual advances, never discussed pornography, never sought dates with them. Phyllis Berry-Myers, an African American who served as special assistant to Thomas at the EEOC, put it this way:

> Clarence Thomas's behavior toward Anita Hill was no more, no less than his behavior toward the rest of his staff. He was respectful, demand[ing] of excellence in our work, cordial, professional, interested in our lives and our career ambitions.

J. C. Alvarez, another woman who worked as an assistant to Thomas at the EEOC, said:

> Clarence was meticulous about being sure that he retained a very serious and professional atmosphere within his office, without the slightest hint of impropriety, and everyone knew it.

A male employee, Armstrong Williams, said that when he purchased a copy of *Playboy* magazine, he was severely criticized by Thomas.

Three Black women who served on Thomas's staff at the EEOC disagreed with this portrait. Angela Wright, who had been the director of the press office after Hill had left the agency, said that Thomas had made leering comments about her anatomy and had asked her out on dates. A friend of Wright's from the EEOC, Rose Jourdain, said that Wright had complained to her at the time of Thomas's improper behavior. Sukari Hardnett, a special assistant, said that although she had not been harassed by Thomas, he would frequently talk to her about his relationship with women. Moreover, Hardnett felt sexual tension in Thomas's presence: "If you were young, Black, female, and reasonably attractive, you knew you were being inspected and auditioned as a female."

Hill's defenders claim that Thomas was a habitué of pornographic media. They say that while a student at Yale he regularly attended and enthusiastically discussed X-rated movies such as *Deep Throat* and *The Devil in Miss Jones* and that later, while the chairman of the EEOC, he rented hard-core pornographic videos. Kaye Savage, an EEOC employee, said she once visited Thomas in his bachelor apartment and saw an extensive collection of *Playboy* magazines and nude pinups.

Hill's critics charge that Wright, Jourdain, and Hardnett had been fired by Thomas and so may have held grudges against him that came to the surface when Hill's charges were made public. (Hardnett claims she was not fired but quit voluntarily.) In particular, the critics describe Angela Wright as a loose cannon; an unstable woman who had been dismissed from many jobs and had frequently acted in an erratic, eccentric manner. And as to Thomas's supposed interest in pornography, they say that watching X-rated movies at Yale was a harmless pastime shared by many students, that there is no evidence that he rented porn videos while at the EEOC, and that the statements of Kaye Savage are contradicted by others who visited Thomas's apartment and saw no pinups and no *Playboy* magazines.

PSYCHOLOGY AND SOCIOLOGY

Some observers of the Hill-Thomas affair say that it is an over-simplification to say that one party was consciously lying and the other telling the truth. Instead, they offer interpretations that allow for unconscious motivation.

In a *New York Times* op-ed piece published at the time of the judiciary hearings, the Harvard sociologist Orlando Patterson speculated about the world of Clarence Thomas. According to Patterson, sexual banter between men and women was common in the working-class, Black, Southern background from which Thomas sprang. Patterson stated that such behavior was in fact well understood by working-class Whites and by most African Americans. Thomas had achieved success in a different environment: the White, upper-middle-class world in which raunchy talk between male bosses and female employees was taboo. But Patterson believed that Thomas may have let his "mainstream, cultural guard down" when he encountered Anita Hill, an admiring young woman from the same background he came from.

Patterson contended that when, ten years later, Hill broadcast her charges, Thomas was shocked. In his mind his words to her were mostly harmless—"a verbal style that carries only minor sanction in one subcultural context." But now Hill had exposed those words before the "overheated cultural arena of mainstream, neo-Puritan America," where it threatened to utterly destroy Thomas's hard-won career—a punishment that in Patterson's judgment far outweighed the seriousness of Thomas's offense. Patterson thus believed that at some level, Thomas's sense of outrage and his angry denial were genuine.

Another theory offered at the time of the hearings was that Hill was lying, but that the lie was not a deliberate, conscious falsehood but rather the result of a psychiatric condition known as "erotomania," a disorder usually affecting young, single women in which the subject falsely believes that she is having a romantic relationship, often with a powerful male. When the male refuses to reciprocate the affection, the victim becomes bitter and revengeful.

According to one psychologist, Paul Ekman, Hill was utterly convinced of the truth of her remarks: "The more often you tell a lie and the longer the period of which you tell the lie, the greater the likelihood is that you will no longer remember it's a lie and believe it's the truth." Other psychologists and psychiatrists dissented from the erotomania diagnosis.

Weighing the Evidence

Much of the evidence in the Anita Hill-Clarence Thomas case is inconclusive. For example, there is the question of Hill's character and motivation. Her supporters picture her as an earnest woman who, with much to lose and nothing to gain, told the world of her shameful treatment by Clarence Thomas. This is counterbalanced by her opponents' depiction of her either as a liberal feminist with a political agenda or an erotomaniac obsessed by fantasies of revenge against the man who spurned her. The lie detector test is equally inconclusive; although it speaks well for her that she volunteered to take it, the validity of the evidence is questionable. Her hospitalization, too, could be due to many different causes besides the stress of being harassed.

Also inconclusive are the inconsistencies that Brock and other critics find in the testimony against Thomas, such as the contrast between Hill's testimony to the FBI and her later testimony to the Senate, and Hoerchner's confusion about the date of her telephone conversation with Hill. These might be evidence of a lie, or equally likely, they may be nothing but evidence that Hill was reluctant to reveal all the details at first and that Hoerchner was struggling to recollect events of a decade before.

Another category of evidence works against Hill. It is certainly damaging to her credibility that she exhibited no outward signs of animosity toward Thomas in the decade between the time the alleged harassment began and the time she made her charges public. The telephone messages and the ride to the airport are signs of an amicable relationship between Hill and Thomas, as is the fact that she followed him to the EEOC even though as a permanent employee she could have remained at the Department of Education.

It is also telling against Hill that reputable women who worked with Thomas at EEOC appeared as character witnesses on his behalf and seemed genuinely sincere in their belief that he never would have behaved in the grotesque manner described by Hill.

But there is a category of evidence that tips the balance in her favor: the testimony of the corroborating witnesses. Four people—Susan Hoerchner, Ellen Wells, John Carr, and Joel Paul—said that years before the Supreme Court nomination, Anita Hill had told them she had been harassed by Clarence Thomas.

There was a revealing moment when these four witnesses appeared as a panel before the Senate Judiciary Committee. One of the senators who had remained largely silent during the preceding days of testimony, Herbert Kohl, Democrat of Wisconsin, asked what he termed "just one quick question."

SENATOR KOHL: Yesterday Judge Thomas said that there was a plot afoot in this country to derail his nomination to the Supreme Court. As I hear your comments today, it is obvious to me that if there was a plot afoot, it must have originated ten years ago. So, do you think that Anita Hill plotted for as long as ten years ago to derail Judge Thomas's nomination to the Supreme Court?

JUDGE HOERCHNER:	I think that would have been impossible.
MS. WELLS:	The same, Senator, that would have been impossible and unthinkable.
MR. PAUL:	No, Senator, she would be not only deserving of an Academy Award, but she would be a prophet.
SENATOR KOHL:	But he yesterday said, as you know, if you followed his testimony, he made a very, very big point of stating that what was happening here was that there was a huge plot among Anita Hill and others to see to it that he never achieved his nomination. Are you saying that you regard that sort of analysis on his part to be almost out of the question?
MS. WELLS:	Senator, I would like to point out that the members of this panel met when they walked into this room, so in order for us to have been part of a conspiracy or plot, we needed to have met one another at some point to get our facts straight and whatever, and we did not have that opportunity.
MR. PAUL:	That's correct, Senator.
JUDGE HOERCHNER:	That is correct.
MR. CARR:	I agree with that.
MR. PAUL:	That's correct, Senator, we don't know each other.

It strains credulity to believe that all four of these witnesses were wrong—that they had either misinterpreted what Hill had told them or were simply lying in order to sink the nomination. It strains credulity even more to believe that there was what Senator Kohl referred to as the ten-year-old plot—that Anita Hill planted the account of her harassment among her friends in anticipation that she would one day use the story to bring down Thomas.

Perhaps elements of Hill's story were exaggerated, and certainly her testimony played into the hands of the ideological opponents of Clarence Thomas. But the probability remains that the story of harassment that Anita Hill told Hoerchner, Wells, Carr, and Paul—and then to the United States Senate and the nationwide television audience—was substantially true.

SELECTED BIBLIOGRAPHY

What Happened to the Lost Colony?

Betts, Robert E. "The Lost Colony," *The Cornhill Magazine* 158 (July 1938), 50–67. Argues that the lost colonists may have been killed by the Spanish.

Durant, David N. *Ralegh's Lost Colony.* New York: Atheneum, 1981. A lively history.

Kupperman, Karen Ordahl. *Roanoke: The Abandoned Colony.* Totowa, N.J.: Rowman & Allenheld, 1984. A good history of the Roanoke colony that touches on larger themes about Indian-White relations and Elizabethan society.

Quinn, David Beers. *England and the Discovery of America, 1481–1620.* New York: Knopf, 1973. Includes an excellent chapter, "The Lost Colony in Myth and Reality, 1586–1625."

————. *Set Fair for Roanoke: Voyages and Colonies, 1584–1606.* Chapel Hill: University of North Carolina Press for the America's Four Hundredth Anniversary Committee, 1985. Written for the general reader; includes a chapter on the lost colony.

———— (ed.). *The Roanoke Voyages, 1584–1590.* 2 vols. London: The Hakluyt Society, 1955; reprint, New York: Dover, 1991. A collection of original sources, with extensive commentary by Quinn.

Sams, Conway Wittle. *The Conquest of Virginia: The First Attempt.* Norfolk, Va: Keyser-Doherty, 1924. Sams believes the colonists were attacked by Indians on Roanoke Island.

Sparkes, Boyden. "Writ on Rocke: Has American's First Murder Mystery Been Solved?," *Saturday Evening Post* April 26, 1941. The exposé of the Dare Stones hoax.

Stick, David. *Roanoke Island: The Beginnings of English America.* Chapel Hill: University of North Carolina Press for the America's Four Hundredth Anniversary Committee, 1983. A good survey of the history of Roanoke and the controversy that followed, flawed by the lack of a bibliography.

Weeks, Stephen B. "The Lost Colony of Roanoke: Its Fate and Survival," *Papers of the American Historical Association* 5 (1891), 441–480. Advances the theory that the Lumbee Indians are the descendants of the lost colonists.

Was General Charles Lee a Coward?

Alden, John Richard. *General Charles Lee: Traitor or Patriot?* Baton Rouge: Louisiana State University Press, 1951. The strongest and best-argued defense of Lee.

Bill, Alfred Hoyt. *New Jersey and the Revolutionary War.* New Brunswick, N.J.: Rutgers University Press, 1964. Criticizes Lee for cowardice at Monmouth.

Fiske, John. *The American Revolution.* 2 vols. New York: Houghton Mifflin, 1891. A history of the war that includes a slashing attack on Lee.

Flexner, James Thomas. *George Washington in the American Revolution.* Boston: Little, Brown, 1967. An attempt to arrive at a balanced view of the controversy.

Freeman, Douglas Southall. *George Washington: A Biography.* 5 vols. New York: Charles Scribner's Sons, 1948–1952. Generally critical of Lee.

Moore, George H. *The Treason of Charles Lee.* New York: Charles Scribner, 1860. The exposé of "Mr. Lee's Plan," and a bitter condemnation of Lee as a traitor.

Murrin, Mary R., and Richard Waldron (eds.) *Conflict at Monmouth Court House: Proceedings of a Symposium Commemorating the Two-Hundredth Anniversary of the Battle of Monmouth.* Trenton: New Jersey Historical Commission, 1983. A collection of papers about the battle and Lee's role.

Proceedings of a General Court Martial, Held at Brunswick, in the State of New-Jersey, by Order of His Excellency Gen. Washington, Commander-in-Chief of the Army of the United States of America, for the Trial of Major-General Lee. July 4th 1778. New York: Privately printed, 1864. The trial transcript.

Thayer, Theodore. *The Making of a Scapegoat: Washington and Lee at Monmouth.* Port Washington, N.Y.: Kennikat Press, 1976. A concise, well-reasoned defense of Lee.

Did Thomas Jefferson Have a Slave Mistress?

Brodie, Fawn. *Thomas Jefferson: An Intimate History.* New York: W. W. Norton, 1974. The centerpiece of the Hemings controversy. Brodie uses psychological evidence to argue that Hemings and Jefferson were lovers.

Dabney, Virginius. *The Jefferson Scandals: A Rebuttal.* New York: Dodd, Mead, 1981; reprint, Lanham, Md.: Madison Books, 1991. A concise attack on the Hemings legend.

Egan, Clifford. "How Not to Write a Biography: A Critical Look at Fawn Brodie's *Jefferson.*" *Social Science Journal* 14, no. 2 (April 1977), 129–136. Egan blasts Brodie's biography of Jefferson as unsound.

Jordan, Winthrop D. *White Over Black: American Attitudes Toward the Negro, 1550–1812.* Chapel Hill: University of North Carolina Press, 1968. Discusses the Hemings story in the context of White-Black relations and concludes that Jefferson did father Heming's children.

Malone, Dumas. *Jefferson the President: First Term, 1801–1805.* Boston: Little Brown, 1970. A defense of Jefferson's reputation from the Hemings accusation.

Miller, John Chester. *The Wolf by the Ears: Thomas Jefferson and Slavery.* New York: Macmillan, 1977. An account of Jefferson's attitude toward slavery. Miller is critical of the Hemings legend.

Peterson, Merrill D. *Thomas Jefferson and the New Nation: A Biography.* New York: Oxford University Press, 1970. A defense of Jefferson.

Wills, Gary. "Uncle Tom's Cabin," *New York Review of Books* April 18, 1974, 26–28. A stinging review of Brodie's book.

Was Aaron Burr a Traitor?

Abernethy, Thomas Perkins. *The Burr Conspiracy.* New York: Oxford University Press, 1954. Abernethy argues that Burr was guilty of treason.

Adams, Henry. *History of the United States of America During the Administrations of Thomas Jefferson*. New York: Library of America, 1986. Originally published in 1889–90, an early and influential work in the anti-Burr school.

Kline, Mary-Jo, and Joanne Wood Ryan (eds.). *Political Correspondence and Public Papers of Aaron Burr*, vol. 2. Princeton: Princeton University Press, 1983. Contains a lengthy analysis of the Cipher Letter, and concludes that Burr did not write it.

Lomask, Milton. *Aaron Burr: The Conspiracy and Years of Exile, 1805–1836*. New York: Farrar, Straus, Giroux, 1982. An excellent modern account of the conspiracy that argues for Burr's innocence.

McCaleb, Walter F. *The Aaron Burr Conspiracy*. New York: Dodd, Mead, 1903. The first scholarly work to argue that Burr was not guilty of treason.

Robertson, David (ed.). *Reports of the Trials of Colonel Aaron Burr*. 2 vols. Philadelphia: Hopkins and Earle, 1808; reprint, New York: DaCapo Press, 1969. A transcript of the trial that contains the full testimony of the witnesses and the arguments by the lawyers on both sides, along with Justice Marshall's rulings.

Schachner, Nathan. *Aaron Burr: A Biography*. New York: Frederick A. Stokes Co., 1937; reprint, New York: A. S. Barnes, 1961. A colorful, popularized biography that maintains Burr's innocence.

Vail, Philip. *The Great American Rascal: The Turbulent Life of Aaron Burr*. New York: Hawthorne Books, 1973. A colorful, popularized biography that says Burr was guilty as sin.

How Did Meriwether Lewis Die?

Bakeless, John. *Lewis & Clark: Partners in Discovery*. New York: William Morrow & Company, 1947. Straddles the fence on whether Lewis was murdered. Says Bakeless: "it is impossible to make a positive statement, either way."

Biddle, Nicholas, and Paul Allen. *History of the Expedition under the Command of Captains Lewis and Clark*. Philadelphia: Bradford and Inskeep, 1814. An early account of the Lewis and Clark expedition that contains Jefferson's memoir of Lewis in which he offers a psychological profile of Lewis and concludes that he committed suicide.

Chandler, David Leon. *The Jefferson Conspiracies: A President's*

Role in the Assassination of Meriwether Lewis. New York: William Morrow, 1994. A ridiculous book that claims, on the basis of no evidence whatsoever, that General Wilkinson had Lewis murdered and that Jefferson knew about it.

Coues, Elliott (ed.). *The History of the Lewis and Clark Expedition*. 4 vols. New York: Francis P. Harper, 1893; reprint, New York: Dover, n.d. A highly regarded edition of the history of the expedition. Coues surveys the evidence in an introductory essay, and concludes: "The mystery remains, and it is not probable that the truth will ever be known."

Fisher, Vardis. *Suicide or Murder: The Strange Death of Governor Meriwether Lewis*. Denver: Alan Swallow, 1962. The most exhaustive examination of the controversy, written by a popular novelist who turned to writing history. After presenting the evidence pro and con, Fisher confesses at the end that "if a gun at our head forced us to choose," (strange choice of words!) he would opt for murder rather than suicide as the solution to the mystery.

Moore, John H. "The Death of Meriwether Lewis." *American Historical Magazine* 9 (1904), 218–230. Presents evidence, via the ex-slave Malinda, that Lewis died by his own hand.

Phelps, Dawson A. "The Tragic Death of Meriwether Lewis," *William and Mary Quarterly*, Series 3, 13, no. 3 (July 1956), 304–318. A strong argument that Lewis committed suicide.

Ravenholt, Reimert Thorolf. "Triumph Then Despair: The Tragic Death of Meriwether Lewis," *Epidemiology* 5 (May 1994), 366–379. Advances the theory that Lewis's suicide was due to syphilis, which he contracted on his expedition to the West.

Wheeler, Olin D. *The Trail of Lewis and Clark*. New York: G. P. Putnam's Sons, 1904. 2 vols. A cautious vote for the murder hypothesis.

Did Abraham Lincoln Love Ann Rutledge?

Angle, Paul. "Lincoln's First Love," *Bulletin, Lincoln Centennial Association*, 1 (December 1927) 1–8. The first major attack on the Rutledge legend.

Barton, William E. *The Life of Abraham Lincoln*. 2 vols. Indianapolis: Bobbs Merrill Co., 1925. A reasonably balanced look at the legend by a Lincoln biographer.

Donald, David. *Lincoln's Herndon*. New York: Alfred A.

Knopf, 1948. A critical biography of Herndon, with a chapter that attacks the Rutledge story.

Fehrenbacher, Don E. "Lincoln's Lost Love Letters," *American Heritage*, 32, no. 2 (Feb./March 1981), 70–80. An account of the Minor forgery case.

Herndon, William. *Herndon's Lincoln: The Story of a Great Life*. Chicago: Belford, Clark, 1889; reprint, New York: Da Capo Press, 1983. A classic biography of Lincoln by his friend and law partner; contains Herndon's account of the Lincoln-Rutledge romance.

———. *Lincoln and Ann Rutledge and the Pioneers of New Salem*. Herrin, Illinois: Trovillion Private Press, 1945. A reprint of the 1866 lecture in which Herndon unveiled the Rutledge legend.

Randall, J. G. *Lincoln the President: Springfield to Gettysburg*. 2 vols. New York: Dodd, Mead & Company, 1945. Randall is the principal critic of the Rutledge story. His appendix to volume two, *Sifting the Ann Rutledge Evidence*, rips apart Herndon's claim that Lincoln loved Rutledge. Randall is credited with convincing historians, until recently, that the legend is false.

Simon, John Y. "Abraham Lincoln and Ann Rutledge," *Journal of the Abraham Lincoln Association* 2 (1990), 13–33. A recent rehabilitation of the Rutledge story.

Walsh, John Evangelist. *The Shadows Rise: Abraham Lincoln and the Ann Rutledge Legend*. Urbana: University of Illinois Press, 1993. The only full-length book on Rutledge and Lincoln. Walsh is one of the recent group of historians—Simon and Wilson are the others—to argue that the story is authentic.

Wilson, Douglas. "Abraham Lincoln and the Evidence of Herndon's Informants," *Civil War History* 36, no. 4 (December 1990) 301–324. An important work in the effort to rehabilitate Rutledge. Wilson reexamines the testimony of the New Salem witnesses in a favorable light.

Was Dr. Mudd an Accomplice to Lincoln's Assassination?

Carter, Samuel III. *The Riddle of Dr. Mudd*. New York: G. P. Putnam's Sons, 1974. A colorful book that argues for Mudd's innocence.

Chamlee, Roy Z., Jr. *Lincoln's Assassins: A Complete Account of Their Capture, Trial, and Punishment*. Jefferson, North Carolina: McFarland & Co., 1990. A careful reconstruction of the assassination, which paints Mudd as guilty.

Mudd, Nettie (ed.). *The Life of Dr. Samuel A. Mudd.* New York: Neale Publishing Co., 1906. A heartfelt defense of Mudd by his daughter.

Mudd, Richard D. *The Mudd Family of the United States.* 2 vols. Saginaw, Michigan: privately printed, 1951. A family geneology that contains a lengthy and passionate defense of Mudd by his grandson.

Oldroyd, Osborn H. *The Assassination of Abraham Lincoln.* Washington, D.C.: privately printed, 1901. An anti-Mudd interpretation.

Pitman, Benn. *The Assassination of President Lincoln and the Trial of the Conspirators.* Cincinnati: Moore, Wilstrach & Baldwin, 1865; reprint, Greenwood Press, 1974. A transcript of the trial.

Roscoe, Theodore. *The Web of Conspiracy: The Complete Story of the Men who Murdered Lincoln.* Englewood Cliffs: Prentice-Hall, 1959. An extreme example of the school that holds that Lincoln was killed as part of a high-level government conspiracy. Roscoe says that Mudd was an innocent victim of this conspiracy.

Tidwell, William A. with James O. Hall and David Winfred Gaddy. *Come Retribution: The Confederate Secret Service and the Assassination of Lincoln.* Jackson: University of Mississippi Press, 1988. Theorizes that Mudd was part of the secret Confederate "action team" that sought to kidnap Lincoln.

Weichmann, Louis J. *A True History of the Assassination of Abraham Lincoln and of the Conspiracy of 1865.* New York: Alfred A. Knopf, 1979. An account by the chief witness against Mudd and the other accused conspirators at the 1865 military trial.

Why Did Custer Lose?

Connell, Evan S. *Son of the Morning Star.* San Francisco: North Point Press, 1984; Harper Perennial, 1991. A wonderful, quirky book—perhaps the most entertaining ever written about Custer and the Little Bighorn.

Fox, Richard A. *Archeology, History, and Custer's Last Battle: the Little Big Horn Reexamined.* Norman: University of Oklahoma Press, 1993. An interesting interpretation of the battle in the light of archaeology.

Graham, W. A. *The Custer Myth: A Source Book of Custeriana.* Harrisburg, Pa.: Stackpole Co., 1953; reprint, 1986. A fascinating collection of material on the Last Stand.

————. *The Story of the Little Bighorn: Custer's Last Fight*. New York: Century Co., 1926; reprint, Lincoln: University of Nebraska Press, 1988. One of the most influential book-length studies of the battle. Graham absolves Reno and Benteen of blame, and accuses Custer of errors.

Gray, John S. *Centennial Campaign: The Sioux War of 1876*. Ft. Collins, Colo.: The Old Army Press, 1976. A sober and scholarly examination.

————. *Custer's Last Campaign: Mitch Boyer and the Little Bighorn Reconsidered*. Lincoln: University of Nebraska Press, 1991. Perhaps the best book ever written on the battle; includes a minute-by-minute analysis.

Stewart, Edgar S. *Custer's Luck*. Norman: University of Oklahoma Press, 1955. A balanced look at the battle.

Utley, Robert M. *Cavalier in Buckskin: George Armstrong Custer and the Western Military Frontier*. Norman: University of Oklahoma Press, 1988. An excellent biography of Custer with two chapters on the Little Bighorn.

————. *Custer and the Great Controversy: The Origins and Development of a Legend*. Pasadena, Ca: Westernlore Press, 1980. Explores the history of the debate over Little Bighorn.

Whittaker, Frederick. *A Complete Life of General George A. Custer*. Vol. 2: *From Appomattox to the Little Big Horn*. New York: Sheldon, 1876; reprint, Lincoln: University of Nebraska Press, 1993. The first book on the battle, it paints a dramatic portrait of the hero Custer.

Did Lizzie Borden Kill Her Parents?

Brown, Arnold R. *Lizzie Borden: The Legend, the Truth, the Final Chapter*. Nashville: Rutledge Hill Press, 1991. Based on slim evidence, this poorly researched book accuses a family relative, William Borden, of committing the crime.

Hunter, Evan. *Lizzie*. New York: Arbor House, 1984. Written as a novel, it presents the argument that Lizzie killed her parents when her lesbian affair with Bridget was discovered.

Kent, David. *Forty Whacks: New Evidence in the Life and Legend of Lizzie Borden*. Emmaus, Pennsylvania: Yankee Books, 1992. Takes the position that Lizzie was innocent.

Lincoln, Victoria. *A Private Disgrace: Lizzie Borden by Daylight*. New York: G. P. Putnam's Sons, 1967. Argues that Lizzie killed her parents in an epileptic frenzy.

Pearson, Edmund. *The Trial of Lizzie Borden*. New York: Doubleday Doran & Co., 1937. Lizzie did it.

Porter, Edwin H. *The Fall River Tragedy: A History of the Borden Murders*. Fall River: J. D. Munroe, 1893; reprint, Portland, Me.: King Philip Publishing Co., 1985. Written by a Fall River reporter, this was the first book published on the crime, and remains one of the best. Porter believes Lizzie was guilty as charged. It is said that Lizzie was so upset by this book that she purchased nearly the entire edition to keep it out of circulation.

Radin, Edward D. *Lizzie Borden: The Untold Story*. New York: Simon and Schuster, 1961. The maid did it.

Spiering, Frank. *Lizzie*. New York: Random House, 1984. Emma did it.

Sullivan, Robert. *Goodbye Lizzie Borden*. Vermont: Stephen Greene Press, 1974; New York: Penguin, 1989. An excellent, well-argued book by a Massachusetts judge who pins the blame on Lizzie.

Who Blew Up the USS Maine?

Blow, Michael. *A Ship to Remember: The Maine and the Spanish-American War*. New York: William Morrow & Co., 1992. A popularized description of the sinking of the *Maine* and of the search for causes.

Bucknill, John T. "The Destruction of the United States Battleship 'Maine,'" *Engineering: An Illustrated Weekly Journal* 65 (Jan–June 1898), 650–651, 687–691, 716–717, 752–754, 782–783. An early examination of the disaster by a British engineer who believed it was an accident.

Naisawald, L. VanLoan. "The Destruction of the *Maine*: Accident or Sabotage?" *U.S. Naval Institute Proceedings* 98 (Feb. 1972), 98–100. Supports the accident theory.

Rickover, Hyman G. *How the Battleship* Maine *was Destroyed*. Washington D.C.: Department of the Navy, 1976. The best argument that the *Maine* was destroyed as the result of an accidental, internal explosion.

Sigsbee, Charles D. *The "Maine." An Account of Her Destruction in Havana Harbor*. New York: Century, 1899. The captain's defense of his conduct.

U.S. Senate. *Message from the President of the United States Transmitting the Report of the Naval Court of Inquiry upon the Destruction of the United States Battle Ship Maine in Havana Har-*

bor, February 15, 1898; together with the testimony taken before the court. 55th Congress, 2d session, 1898, Document 207. The 1898 Court of Inquiry report.

U.S. Congress. *Report on the Wreck of the Maine.* 62d Congress, 2d session, Dec 14, 1911, Document 310. The 1911 Vreeland report.

U.S. Senate. *Report of the Committee on Foreign Relations, United States Senate, Relative to Affairs in Cuba.* 55th Congress, 2d session, April 13, 1898, Senate Report 885. Contains the official Spanish investigation into the *Maine* explosion.

Weems, John Edward. *The Fate of the Maine.* College Station: Texas A&M University Press, 1958; reprint, 1992. An even-handed treatment.

Did Shoeless Joe Throw the World Series?

Asinof, Eliot. *Eight Men Out: The Black Sox and the 1919 World Series.* New York: Holt, Rinehart and Winston, 1963. The best work on the scandal; Asinof believes Jackson was guilty.

Bennett, Jay. "Did Shoeless Joe Jackson Throw the 1919 World Series?" *The American Statistician* 47, no. 4 (November 1993), 241–250. A sophisticated statistical analysis that argues Jackson played his heart out.

Frommer, Harvey. *Shoeless Joe and Ragtime Baseball.* Dallas: Taylor Publishing Co., 1992. A sympathetic biography of Jackson that finds him innocent.

Gropman, Donald. *Say it Ain't So: True Story of Shoeless Joe Jackson.* Revised edition. New York: Citadel Press, 1992. The bible for those who believe in Jackson's innocence.

Lardner, John. "Remember the Black Sox?" *Saturday Evening Post,* April 30, 1938, 14ff. A colorful account that puts Jackson in the lineup with the other Black Sox.

Ward, Geoffrey C., and Ken Burns. *Baseball: An Illustrated History.* New York: Alfred A. Knopf, 1994. This book, and the popular television documentary series on which it is based, accepts Jackson's guilt.

Were Sacco and Vanzetti Guilty?

Avrich, Paul. *Sacco and Vanzetti: The Anarchist Background.* Princeton: Princeton University Press, 1991. Much information on the political views and activities of Sacco and Vanzetti, without making a judgment about their guilt or innocence.

Ehrmann, Herbert B. *The Case That Will Not Die: Commonwealth vs. Sacco and Vanzetti.* Boston: Little, Brown, 1969. Expands on Ehrmann's 1933 argument that Sacco and Vanzetti were innocent.

————. *The Untried Case.* New York: Vanguard, 1933. A landmark of the school that regards Sacco and Vanzetti as innocent victims of official intolerance.

Felix, David. *Protest: Sacco-Vanzetti and the Intellectuals.* Bloomington: Indiana University Press, 1965. Although mostly a study of intellectual history, Felix believes Sacco and Vanzetti were guilty.

Fraenkel, Osmond K. *The Sacco-Vanzetti Case.* New York: Knopf, 1931. An early, encyclopedic work that argues for the innocence of Sacco and Vanzetti.

Joughin, G. Louis, and Edmund M. Morgan. *The Legacy of Sacco and Vanzetti.* New York: Harcourt, Brace, 1948. The innocent school.

Montgomery, Robert H. *Sacco-Vanzetti: The Murder and the Myth.* New York: Devin-Adair, 1960. The first major work since the execution to maintain that Sacco and Vanzetti were guilty; this book began a reevaluation of the case.

Russell, Francis. *Sacco and Vanzetti: The Case Resolved.* New York: Harper & Row, 1986. Expands and supports the argument contained in Russell's 1962 book.

————. *Tragedy in Dedham: The Story of the Sacco-Vanzetti Case.* New York: McGraw-Hill, 1962. A dramatically written narrative of the case, this was the first major work to argue that Sacco was guilty, Vanzetti innocent.

Young, William, and David E. Kaiser. *Postmortem: New Evidence in the Case of Sacco and Vanzetti.* Amherst: University of Massachusetts Press, 1985. A recent defense of Sacco and Vanzetti that, contrary to the subtitle, contains no new evidence.

Who Kidnapped the Lindbergh Baby?

Ahlgren, Gregory, and Stephen Monier. *Crime of the Century: The Lindbergh Kidnapping Hoax.* Brookline Village, Mass.: Branden Books, 1993. Advances the theory that Lindbergh kidnapped his son as a joke on his wife, and that the child accidentally died.

Behn, Noel. *Lindbergh: The Crime*. New York: Atlantic Monthly Press, 1994. Another bizarre theory—this time that the baby was killed by Lindbergh's sister-in-law.

Fisher, Jim. *The Lindbergh Case*. New Brunswick: Rutgers University Press, 1987. The best book of the school that believes Hauptmann was guilty. Fisher explicitly attacks the arguments put forward by Hauptmann's defenders. The book has been criticized, however, for its use of invented dialogue.

Kennedy, Ludovic. *The Airman and the Carpenter: The Lindbergh Kidnapping and the Framing of Richard Hauptmann*. New York: Viking Penguin, 1985. The best book in the Hauptmann-was-innocent school.

Milton, Joyce. *Loss of Eden: A Biography of Charles and Anne Morrow Lindbergh*. New York: HarperCollins, 1993. Argues that the Lindbergh servants were involved in the kidnapping and that Hauptmann was simply an accomplice.

Scaduto, Anthony. *Scapegoat: The Lonesome Death of Bruno Richard Hauptmann*. New York: G. P. Putnam's Sons, 1976. Argues that Hauptmann was framed.

Waller, George. *Kidnap: The Story of the Lindbergh Case*. New York: Dial Press, 1961. Supports the prosecution case against Hauptmann without explicitly saying that Hauptmann was guilty.

Was There a Cover-up at Pearl Harbor?

Barnes, Harry Elmer. *Pearl Harbor After a Quarter of a Century*. New York: Arno Press, 1968. A good summary of the revisionist view by the master revisionist.

——— (ed.). *Perpetual War for Perpetual Peace: A Critical Examination of the Foreign Policy of Franklin Delano Roosevelt and its Aftermath*. Caldwell, Idaho: Caxton Printers, 1953; reprint, New York: Greenwood Press, 1969. A collection of revisionist essays.

Beard, Charles A. *President Roosevelt and the Coming of the War, 1941*. New Haven: Yale University Press, 1948. A revisionist work by one of America's leading historians.

Clausen, Henry C., and Bruce Lee. *Pearl Harbor: Final Judgement*. New York: Crown, 1992. Clausen, an anti-revisionist, conducted one of the first official investigations of Pearl Harbor.

Prange, Gordon W., with Donald M. Goldstein and Katherine V. Dillon. *Pearl Harbor: The Verdict of History*. New York:

McGraw Hill, 1986; New York: Viking Penguin, 1991. An encyclopedic presentation of the anti-revisionist argument.

Rusbridger, James, and Eric Nave. *Betrayal at Pearl Harbor: How Churchill Lured Roosevelt into World War II*. New York: Touchstone Books, 1991. A different twist on the revisionist interpretation. Rusbridger and Nave pin the blame on the British prime minister.

Schroeder, Paul W. *The Axis Alliance and Japanese-American Relations, 1941*. Ithaca: Cornell University Press, 1958. A critical view of American foreign relations, but one that rejects the extreme revisionist interpretation.

Tansill, Charles C. *Back Door to War*. Chicago: Henry Regnery Co., 1952. A revisionist work dealing with the failures of American diplomacy.

Toland, John D. *Infamy: Pearl Harbor and Its Aftermath*. Garden City: Doubleday & Co., 1982. A best-selling revisionist work by a popular author.

Trefousse, Hans L. *Pearl Harbor: The Continuing Controversy*. Malabar, Fla.: Krieger Publishing Co., 1982. A good survey of the debate between revisionists and anti-revisionists by one of the latter. Includes many primary documents.

Wohlstetter, Roberta. *Pearl Harbor: Warning and Decision*. Stanford: Stanford University Press, 1962. A look at intelligence gathering before Pearl Harbor by an anti-revisionist.

Was Alger Hiss a Communist Spy?

Chambers, Whittaker. *Witness*. New York: Random House, 1952. Chambers's own account of the Great Case. It is fascinating to read this together with Hiss's *In the Court of Public Opinion*.

Cook, Fred J. *The Unfinished Story of Alger Hiss*. New York: William Morrow Company, 1958. A summary of the case that supports Hiss.

Hiss, Alger. *In the Court of Public Opinion*. New York: Alfred A. Knopf, 1957. Hiss's own account.

Smith, John Chabot. *Alger Hiss: The True Story*. New York: Holt, Rinehart and Winston, 1976. The best interpretation of the case from the pro-Hiss perspective.

Tiger, Edith (ed.). *In Re Alger Hiss*. New York: Hill and Wang, 1979. This book contains the text and related exhibits that comprised a legal petition filed by Alger Hiss in 1978 to establish his innocence.

Weinstein, Allen. *Perjury: The Hiss-Chambers Case.* New York: Alfred A. Knopf, 1978; reprint, New York: Vintage Books, 1979. A massive examination of the Hiss case that argues strongly for Hiss's guilt. This book has been the subject of great controversy, and Hiss's defenders have attacked it. It is fair to say that Weinstein changed the prevailing opinion of the case away from Hiss's side.

Zeligs, Meyer A. *Friendship and Fratricide.* New York: Viking, 1967. A pro-Hiss psychological analysis.

Was Marilyn Monroe Murdered?

Brown, Peter Harry, and Patte B. Barham. *Marilyn: The Last Take.* London: Heinemann, 1992. Supports the view that Monroe was killed because of her involvement with Robert Kennedy.

Giancana, Sam, and Chuck Giancana. *Double Cross: The Explosive, Inside Story of the Mobster who Controlled America.* New York: Warner Books, 1992. Argues that Monroe was killed by the mob.

Noguchi, Thomas T., with Joseph DiMona. *Coroner.* New York: Simon and Schuster, 1983. The coroner at Monroe's autopsy defends his suicide verdict.

Schlesinger, Arthur M., Jr. *Robert Kennedy and His Times.* Boston: Houghton Mifflin, 1978. An associate of RFK denies the rumors of the attorney general's affair with Monroe.

Slatzer, Robert F. *The Life and Curious Death of Marilyn Monroe.* New York: Pinnacle, 1974. The most sensational work of the RFK conspiracy school.

————. *The Marilyn Files.* New York: S.P.I. Books, 1992. More of Slatzer's conspiracy theories. Contains photocopies of the autopsy report and other original documents.

Spoto, Donald. *Marilyn Monroe: The Biography.* New York: HarperCollins, 1993. Spoto utterly rejects the conspiracy interpretation, and presents in its place a different theory—that Monroe died from an accidental overdose.

Summers, Anthony. *Goddess: The Secret Lives of Marilyn Monroe.* New York: MacMillan, 1985; Onyx, 1986. Summers believes that Monroe died by a self-administered overdose, but at the same time he accepts the allegations of an affair with Robert Kennedy.

Who Killed Martin Luther King, Jr.?

Frank, Gerold. *An American Death: The True Story of the Assassination of Dr. Martin Luther King, Jr. and the Greatest Manhunt of our Time.* Garden City, New York: Doubleday, 1972. Argues that Ray was the lone gunman.

Garrow, David J. *The FBI and Martin Luther King: From "Solo" to Memphis.* New York: Norton, 1981. Although Garrow condemns the FBI for its harassment of King, he dismisses as baseless the suggestion that the bureau was behind the assassination.

Huie, William Bradford. *He Slew the Dreamer: My Search for the Truth about James Earl Ray and the Murder of Martin Luther King.* New York: Delacorte Press, 1968. One of the first books to argue that Ray was the lone gunman.

Lane, Mark, and Dick Gregory. *Murder in Memphis: The FBI and the Assassination of Martin Luther King.* New York: Thunder's Mountain Press, 1993. (Originally published in 1977 as *Code Name Zorro.*) A classic of the conspiracy school.

Melanson, Philip H. *The Murkin Conspiracy: An Investigation into the Assassination of Dr. Martin Luther King, Jr.* New York: Praeger, 1989. An argument that the CIA was behind the assassination.

Ray, James Earl. *Who Killed Martin Luther King? The True Story of the Alleged Assassin.* Washington, D.C.: National Press Books, 1992. Ray's own account; he says he was framed.

U.S. House of Representatives. *Final Report of the Select Committee on Assassinations.* Washington, D.C.: U.S. Government Printing Office, 1979. Concludes there was a low-level conspiracy.

Weisberg, Harold. *Frame-Up.* New York: Outerbridge & Dienstfrey, 1971. An extreme work of the conspiratorial school. Weisberg links the King assassination to the murder of JFK.

Was Anita Hill Lying?

Brock, David. "Jane and Jill and Anita Hill," *The American Spectator* (August 1993), 24–30. A defense of his book *The Real Anita Hill* against the critical *New Yorker* review by Jane Mayer and Jill Abramson.

———. *The Real Anita Hill: The Untold Story.* New York: The

Free Press, 1993. The most complete and comprehensive attack on Hill's credibility.

————. "Strange Lies," *The American Spectator* (January 1995), 30ff. An angry review of Mayer and Abramson's *Strange Justice*. The title of the review sums it up.

Danforth, John. *Resurrection: The Confirmation of Clarence Thomas*. New York: Viking, 1994. An emotional defense of Thomas by a friend in the U.S. Senate.

Mayer, Jane, and Jill Abramson. *Strange Justice: The Selling of Clarence Thomas*. Boston: Houghton Mifflin, 1994. A defense of Hill and an attack on Thomas; the polar opposite of Brock's *Real Anita Hill*.

————. "The Surreal Anita Hill," *The New Yorker* (May 24, 1993), 90–96. A slashing attack on David Brock's book.

Patterson, Orlando. "Race, Gender and Liberal Fallacies," *New York Times* October 20, 1991, section IV, p. 15. A sociological perspective on the case.

Phelps, Timothy M., and Helen Winternitz. *Capitol Games: Clarence Thomas, Anita Hill, and the Story of a Supreme Court Nomination*. New York: Hyperion, 1992. Phelps was one of the journalists who first broke the story of Hill's allegations. His history of the events supports Hill's side of the story.

Simon, Paul. *Advice and Consent: Clarence Thomas, Robert Bork and the Intriguing History of the Supreme Court's Nomination Battles*. Washington, D.C.: National Press Books, 1992. An account favorable to Hill by a Democratic member of the Judiciary Committee.

U.S. Senate Judiciary Committee. *Hearings Before the Committee on the Nomination of Judge Clarence Thomas to be Associate Justice of the Supreme Court of the United States*. 4 vols. Washington, D.C.: U.S. Government Printing Office, 1993. The main sourcebook on the controversy, with transcripts of the testimony by Hill, Thomas, and the other witnesses.

INDEX